A Technological Arcadia

EMILIO

A Technological Arcadia

AMBASZ

Fulvio Irace

with an essay
by Paolo Portoghesi

SKIRA

Coordination
Giovanni Brambilla

Layout
Italo Lupi and Marina Del Cinque

Iconographical Research
Alessandra Rossi

Editing
Marta Cattaneo

Translations
Paraculture Inc.

First published in Italy in 2004
by Skira Editore S.p.A.
Palazzo Casati Stampa
via Torino 61- 20123 Milano, Italy
www.skira.net

Printed and bound in Italy.

ISBN 88-8491-823-5

Distributed in North America by
Rizzoli International Publications,
Inc., 300 Park Avenue South,
New York, NY 10010.
Distributed elsewhere in the world
by Thames and Hudson Ltd.,
181a High Holborn, London
WC1V 7QX. United Kingdom.

.index

Fulvio Irace

The Argentine Aesop

[1] E. Ambasz, *I ask myself*, in *Emilio Ambasz: The Poetics of the Pragmatic. Architecture, exhibit, industrial and graphic design*, Rizzoli, New York 1988, p. 25.

[2] J.J. Rousseau, *Emile ou De l'éducation*, Amsterdam 1762.

[3] V.J. Propp, *Morfologia della fiaba* (1928), Italian translation, edited by Gian Luigi Bravo, Einaudi, Turin 1980.

[4] M. Estrada, *Los señores de la Nada*, cited in E. Ambasz, *Anthology for a spatial Buenos Aires*, 1966, also in *Emilio Ambasz, The Poetics of the Pragmatic...* cit., p. 33.

[5] M. Sorkin, *Arcadia versus Utopia*, in "Modo", 22, September 1979, p. 34.

Fascinated by the eternal narrative of foundation myths, Emilio Ambasz's architecture enters the panorama of the Seventies with the eccentric traces of poetic narration. Introduced by the aphoristic tone of the "Working Fables," the first works of this Argentine Aesop are in fact visual charts accompanying a pedagogy of design that exhorts to rethink of ethical motifs behind the act of construction, and to restore the broken passages between the transformation of the world and the changes of society: "I opted to be a fabulist rather than an ideologist because fables retain the ring of immutability long after ideologies have wilted. The invention of fables is central to my working methods; it is not just a literary accessory. Sometimes the fable is a project and the descriptive literary part is purely technical, and sometimes the imagery becomes the illustration. In any case, the subtext of a fable is a ritual, and it is to the support of rituals that most of my work is addressed itself"[1].

Expression of a utopia that bends technology to the attainment of its goal, the project "narrated" by "Emile"[2] Ambasz takes up, with irony, the didactic intonation of the *conte philosophique*. Like the accounts of voyagers, ethnologists, and explorers of the eighteenth century or the stories of the great moralists of the Enlightenment, the landscape of an idealized Arcadia – whether it be an open landscape or a built urban nature – supplies the setting for a human comedy that, in the micro-history of a given project, reproduces in miniature rites outside of time, conferring upon personalities and secondary cameos the archetypal role of recurring figures, along the model developed by V.J. Propp in his well-known studies on the "morphology of the fable"[3].

Among the values of preindustrial humanity and the logic of serial production, the ideal "inhabitant" of Ambasz's "fables" takes on the role of someone who is trying to push beyond the constraints established by the products and progresses of his own culture, while fully aware that he must use these inherited products and progresses in order to create a new culture.

The context is not History, but the absolute space described by Martinez Estrada, where man "stands alone as an abstract being who would have to recommence the history of the species – or to conclude it"[4].

The last historic subject, but also the founder of a new anthropology, this ideal "inhabitant" is thus obliged to resolve the ambivalence of his condition in the indemonstrability of myth or in the simplification of the fable: "in choosing to be a fabulist instead of an ideologue – Michael Sorkin has written[5] – he grasped something fundamental: that fables preserve a quality of immutability long after ideologies have wilted. For Ambasz, the most productive critical faculty is irony. He does not attempt to adduce the definitive, only to find a good answer".

Fable versus Ideology

A bridge between Europe and America, Ambasz's architecture then makes its silent debut in a climate characterized by the last flickering flames of the technological utopia and by the first signals of a reduction of the discipline to the decisive role of its archetypes and its "figures." All the same, the choice of metaphor as the venue for conceptual elaboration contrasts sharply with the ideological option that characterizes, in Italy for instance, the rebirth of the urban theories of Aldo Rossi or Carlo Aymonino and the progressive consolidation of a school devoted to the cult of the permanence of the type and its "indifferent" constancy in a territory. The reiteration of the "autonomy" of architecture – with its well known corollaries of independence from function, of the stability of primary elements as "monuments" and the value of collective memory attributed to them, etc. – returns to relevance the normative knowledge stratified in the tradition of treatises, codices, and theories. If on the one hand there is a rejection of that break with History that the Modern had utilised as the legitimisation of a writing beginning from the *tabula rasa* of the twentieth century,

Casa de Ritiro Espiritual, Siviglia, Spagna

[6] *Five Architects*, Wittenborn & Co, New York 1972.

[7] E. Ambasz, *Summary*, in *Italy: The New Domestic Landscape*, The Museum of Modern Art, New York, Centro Di, Florence, Florence 1972, p. 422.

[8] *Ibid.*, p. 422.

Center for Applied Computer Research, Mexico City, Mexico

on the other however there is also a repudiation of every effort to "cross" the code of architecture with the supposedly spurious codes of urban studies, sociology, or psychology. These paths were well known to the young Argentine, thanks to his interactions with the Italian milieu in view of the preparation of the renowned exhibition, "Italy: The New Domestic Landscape," which he organised at the Museum of Modern Art in New York in 1972 . The same year as the group consecration of the Five Architects of New York, at the hands of Arthur Drexler[6], with the resulting affirmation of a "poetics of nostalgia" that placed at the centre of its own linguistic experiments a sophisticated interpretation of the intellectual and formal heritage of the Modern movement.

Focusing his analysis of the Italian situation on the counterpoint between the "apocalyptics" and the "integrated" into the practice of industrial design, Ambasz emphasised, against a merely formal interpretation of Italian design, the emblematic and allusive value of his participation in the social debate. Accepting the notion of "negative utopia"[7] adopted by certain fringes of the radical avant-gardes as an instrument of analysis of the present, he still tempered it in the light of a more balanced relationship with the "functional" component of the elite professionalism, underscoring the necessity of considering politics and aesthetics as complementary parts of an organic project of disciplinary refoundation. A diagnosis, in the final analysis, very close to the projection of that "poetics of the pragmatic", whose personal characteristics rapidly emerged in the statements of his subsequent projects. "Thus, design ultimately transcends both object-making and conflict, to encompass all the processes whereby man gives meaning and order to his surroundings and his daily patterns of life. Without claiming to solve everything, design can nevertheless move toward an authentic realization of himself."[8] Built on the intersection between history, criticism, and design, the catalogue that accompanied the exhibition "Italy: The New Domestic Landscape" can, thus, be considered – if we exclude the youthful exploratory essays on Buenos Aires – Ambasz's first attempt to construct a figure of the architect as a storyteller shifting between "words" and "things".

Restoring to the image its evocative function of myths also implies restoring to design its theoretical and utopian dimension of instrument of transformation above and beyond the narrow limits of the object. It meant, in other words, placing with emphasis the theme of "invention" through the notion of "prototype". Forerunner of a possible future, this indicates the opening to new symbolic systems of representation, capable of reflecting the contradictions and aspirations of the contemporary world.

Attracted to Utopia, Ambasz's architecture does not feel obliged to travel the paths of visionary technologism, a route that appears to have been obligatory for the international avant-gardes which, under various headings and with a broad array of intonation, proposed fanciful versions thereof under the insignia of machinist idolatry, situationist anarchism, or cosmic futurology. To him, technology have not the salvation-giving value attributed to it by the avant-gardes, but simply the role of instrument bent to a design imagination: it is not an image in and of itself, but a structure that makes possible to create images with a high degree of emotional content. It is the arrangement of the carefully planned system of canals and drainage of water that makes possible the "floating" buildings of the Center for Applied Computer Research and underlays the ingenious system of recycling of the water used in the air conditioning system in order to create the liquid "carpet" that slowly and continuously pours down along the staircase of the Grand Rapids

[9] E. Ambasz, unpublished typescript, p. 3. But also: *Some notes on a mental correspondence I have maintained throughout the last twenty-five years with Delfina Williams about Amancio's work*, in *Emilio Ambasz. Inventions the reality of the ideal*, Rizzoli, New York 1992, pp. 65-69.

[10] E. Ambasz, *Una relazione sul mio lavoro*, in *Europa/America. Architetture urbane alternative suburbane*, edited by F. Raggi, Edizioni La Biennale di Venezia, Venice 1978, pp. 196-197.

[11] E. Ambasz, *The architecture of Luis Barragán*, The Museum of Modern Art, New York 1976.

Grand Rapids Art Museum, Grand Rapids, Michigan, USA

Art Museum in Michigan. It is, in other words, the homage to the eccentric and isolated lesson of Amancio Williams, to his anti-historicist aptitude for "creating and inventing master examples"[9] such as the bridge-house on the Mar del Plata and to his propensity to conceal the "poetic nucleus" of the programme beneath the blanket of the functional paraphernalia of the project. "An architecture in dynamic consonance with a nature made by man in a state of constant development – Ambasz has written, specifying the methodology of his inventive practise – entails specialised tasks. The first one, *empirical*, is to construct a cartography of the products and techniques of production that populate the man-made garden. The second one, *normative*, is to develop a programme of individual needs and desires in the context of an ample programme of social necessities, to guide the utilisation of the empirical cartography. The third one, *synthetic*, is to give Form to new structures that will allow man to reconcile his fears and his desires with the limits imposed by the empirical domain and the pressures of the normative field. [...] The operative context of the architect can be changed but the transcendent task remains the same, to endow the pragmatic with a poetic form."[10]

Circumscribed to the context of the "everyday", the Argentine's "domestic utopia" is a metaphor for a change that has to do with the anthropological structures of inhabiting more than the architectural prefiguring of the renovated habitat: if anything, it is configured as a poetics of the "archaic", whose "frugal vocabulary" harks back, more or less directly, to an appreciation of the architecture of Luis Barragán, subject of one of the first critical essays dedicated to the Mexican architect and of a wonderful exhibition curated by Ambasz for MoMA in New York[11].

Between Borges and Barragán

Amancio Williams, Luis Barragán, Borges: there is no doubt that, in the admittedly composite landscape of New York in the Seventies, Ambasz's personality stood out for his idiosyncratic references and educational paths. Close to the teachings of Peter Eisenman and one of the founders of the Institute of Architecture and Urban Studies – the American institution most open in those years to the demands of the European neo-avant-gardes – he nonetheless established his distance from the consequences of his hermetic elitism. A leading figure of that generation of Latin-American young people who emigrated to the East Coast, such as Rodolfo Machado and Jorge Silvetti or Diana Agrest and Mario Gandelsonas, he differentiated himself from them by his instinctive rejection of a critical intellectualism strongly steeped in the theoretical influences of the structuralist research into the function of language and its possible applications to the practices of the urban setting. Originally from Buenos Aires – the South American capital most closely attuned to the influences of international modernism in the years between the two wars – Ambasz studied at Princeton University (New Jersey, USA) where, in two years, he took a Bachelor's degree and a Master's degree in Architecture: but, in contrast with his American and Argentine colleagues, he seemed from the very outset uninterested in the practices of teaching and the milieu of research that he considered merely refined but abstract exercises in intellectual rigour. After a short period of teaching at Princeton, he chose in fact to become a curator at MoMA. Among his first significant projects, in 1975, the Casa de Retiro Espiritual in the countryside around Seville, effectively summarises the odd aspects of his position; the solution of a typological theme in those same years elevated to a new scale of interest by a number of future protagonists of the architectural renewal, such as Richard Meier, Peter Eisenman, John Hejduk, Michael Graves, etc.,

11

[12] V. Scully, in "Progressive Architecture", July 1974, quoted in L. Sacchi, *Il disegno dell'architettura americana*, Editori Laterza, Rome-Bari 1989, p. 121.

[13] P. Eisenman, *To Adolf Loos & Bertold Brecht*, in "Progressive Architecture", No. 5 1974, p. 92.

[14] M. Tafuri, *Les bijoux indiscrets*, in *Five Architects NY*, edited by C. Gubitosi and A. Izzo, Officina Edizioni, Rome 1976, p. 17.

in fact, allowed the construction of an almost didactic confrontation with the experiments of the design elite of the East Coast. Dating back to the second half of the Sixties, for instance, are the elegant exercises by Meier on the heritage of European modernism, culminating, in 1974, in the renowned Douglas House at Harbor Spring, Michigan. A refined exegesis of Le Corbusier's lessons in decomposition, Meier's ethereal domestic architecture offers a subtle connective line for the selective re-evaluation of the characteristics of European rationalism, a few years prior to the post-modernist deluge. Emphasising the calibrated repagination of the dialectic between volume and structure, Meier's work set itself to recreate the aura of the *ésprit machiniste*, even adopting from it that exclusive shade of white that in time became an unmistakable motif of his work. "Whites", by no coincidence, was the name in the Seventies of the group of architects – such as Eisenman, Gwathmey-Siegel, Seligman, etc. – who shared a diffuse interest in the linguistic exploration of the European rationalist tradition and a faith "in the capacity of forms and space to mediate between individual and environment, individual and society"[12].

In this way, as it has been observed, the significance of that "heroic" period slipped into the limbo of formal purification, sheltering the research from any and all anxious quests for identity that might not coincide with the exclusive but antiseptic quest of the linguistic workshop. In other words, a "test-tube" architecture, which while it revived the tone of the modern tradition beyond the banal consumption of the approach of developers, painstakingly avoided any questions about the anxious nature of the architectural object, impeccably sealed in the shell of its immaculate candour. For almost all of them, of course, this was only a transitory phase, destined to be, shortly thereafter, spectacularly rejected or drastically recalibrated in the most extreme directions of a radical critique of the theoretical postulates of modernity. Like Peter Eisenman, who sustained architecture as conceptual art, strongly focused on processes of abstraction and self-reflection aiming at a progressive undermining of the foundation of the entire theoretical structure of the traditional notion of design. A hermetic, refined author, the "early" Eisenman isolated the theme of the single-family house as the almost exclusive field of experimentation: through the decade-long series of "houses", from House I at Princeton (1967-1968) to House XI at Palo Alto (1978), Eisenman built the space of a reflection on the syntax of the project as a solipsistic form of self-representation. Making a special effort to cut the umbilical cord between form and function in rationalist theory, he analyses the notions of centrality and planarity, focusing the fields of relation among isolated elements and structural grid, destructuring the idea of space and its perception. Avoiding any implication of an anthropological nature, his idea of house is articulated upon the construction of a field of rules of formation and transformation that lead architecture onto the plane of the purely intellectual, warding off as improper or not very pertinent the significance of the human presence in relation to the form and use of space. In House III in Lakeville, for instance, "when the owner first enters "his house", he is an intruder; he must begin to regain possession – to occupy a foreign container. In the process of taking possession the owner begins to destroy, albeit in a positive sense, the initial unity and completeness of the architectural structure"[13].

Authentic "machines in the garden," the Miller House (House III) in Lakeville (1968-1971), much like the Douglas House (1971-1974) by Meier or the Benacerref House by Graves in Princeton (1969-1970) represent in different ways, as Tafuri had observed, the return to an idea of art as the "liberation from the eternal essence of the human being"[14], an evocation of suspended tonalities in which silence is synonymous with a programmatic elision of human noise.

[15] G. Pesce, *Italy: The New Domestic Landscape...* cit., pp. 212-222.

[16] E. Ambasz, *The Architecture of Luis Barragán...* cit., p. 12.

[17] *Ibid.*, p. 33.

[18] *Ibid.*, p. 12.

Casa de Retiro Espiritual

Split in two in the dialectic structure of the upper "mask" and the underground residence, the house in the countryside around Seville makes no mystery of the surreal vein that runs during those years through Emilio Ambasz's architecture: steeped in aura-based mysticism, it can nonetheless be considered a tacit manifesto in favour of the "elimination" of architecture through the exhumation of its relics. Metonymous "surrogate" of Architecture, the façade is at the same time a signal and a ruin: a warning that architecture is about to disappear or a residual trace of its accomplished destruction. In the 1972 exhibition at MoMA, Gaetano Pesce had imagined a habitat that was expression of an architecture of the era of "the great contaminations"[15]. The proposal configured the possibility of an existential space whose principal physical features referred back to the seclusion and isolation: a symbolism open to many horizons of meaning suggested the notion of the house as a ritual site or shelter from life, as an anxious domestic landscape or the symbol of eternal life. The indeterminacy of the allusions, in any case, corresponded to the clarity of the compositional structure, characterised by the use of the square and the rectangle as fundamental forms.

The impositional geometry of a rotated square became a generator of volumes articulated symmetrically beginning with the primitive sign of the cross arranged on the ground. If an echo of this may perhaps be captured in the design of the underground chapel in the project for Borrego Springs – even in the shifting of the iconography of the cross, closer in this case to an idea of natural religion – the reflection on the house as a refuge is evidently central in Ambasz's project for Seville. A square carved out on the floor specifies the geography of the intervention; a diagonal cut divides it into two triangles, corresponding to two sections of the house: one that is more intimate and on a domestic scale, the patio; the other – a staircase –, more monumental, linking to the representative order of the façade. On the one hand, then, the house as a volume in space, and on the other its concretisation as space for life: a contrast that refers to the differentiation between Baukunst and Architektur, introduced by Loos in his well-known 1910 essay, and recovered by Ambasz in an almost literal interpretation to illustrate his notion of house as a primordial shelter that justifies the project as a pact of reconciliation between man and the world. With respect to the recurring phenomenology of the "machine in the garden", the House of Seville does not place in the foreground the analysis of language, and it proves indifferent to all mathematical furore that assimilates the project to a theorem to be demonstrated. Is it perhaps mere chance that, at the base of its roots, it is possible to glimpse, instead, the "emotional architecture" of a master like Barragán, profoundly admired and investigated in an effort at research on the occasion of the exhibition at MoMA in New York? Unrivalled creator of a "stage architecture" that found precisely in the space of the house its *pièce de resistance*, the Mexican architect "emphasized living in patios, behind walls"[16]. Superb composition of "voids", behind the intentional modesty of a not especially memorable façade, his house at Tacubaya (1947) shows how "rudimentary elements" can be used to "achieve a subdued visual drama"[17].

Stripping itself of any historical relics, the Mexican tradition, then, was subjected to drastic reduction to its spatial foundations: the return trip to the uncontaminated purity of the archetype thus took on the cadences of a refoundation, conferring upon the new architecture "the aura of inexorability which classical myths once possessed"[18].

It is thus possible to interpret as "exterior walls" the two

[19] Ibid., p. 34

[20] Ibid., p. 11

[21] E. Ambasz, Anthology for a spatial Buenos Aires, (1966), now in Emilio Ambasz: The Poetics of the Pragmatic... cit., p. 37.

[22] E. Ambasz, I ask myself, in Ibid., p. 26.

[23] M. Estrada, Los Señores de la Nada, in Anthology for a spatial Buenos Aires... cit., p. 33: "pampa, Indio word for space, land where man stands out in isolation as an abstract being who must either originate the history of the species, or else terminate it".

[24] Mary Miss, Costruire luoghi, edited by C. Zapatka, Motta Architettura, Milan 1996, pp. 53-55.

[25] Ibid., p. 10.

walls that make up the corner façade of the house of spiritual retirement: minimalist and "out of scale", they reveal their function only when they are observed from the far end of the house. Two steep staircases design a triangle culminating in the very high "mirador", thus configuring the entire façade as an observatory looking out on the landscape; its base, in contrast, completes the quadrilateral of the patio, emphasising its role as the centripetal "void" of the entire composition. In that sense, it is possible to apply to its organisation the reading that Ambasz offers of the house of Tacubaya – "the garden is enclosed by high walls on three sides; the fourth side is defined by the rear façade of the house"[19] – and of the residential complex of El Pedregal, with the garden that serves as the "soul of the house" and the rooms as "simple retreats meant just for sleeping, the storage of belongings, and shelter from hostile weather"[20]. An authentic "programme of metaphysical imperatives", the Casa de Retiro Espiritual theatricalises with its architecture of landscapes the metaphysics of the everyday evoked in a poem by Borges: "patio, channel of sky. The patio is the window through which God watches souls. The patio is the slope down which the sky flows into the house"[21].

With respect to the eighteenth-century myth of the "primitive hut", it is no longer a matter of assimilating architecture to the rationality of Nature, but rather a question of rewriting, perhaps, the vocation of artificial "shelter", beginning with the most elementary gestures of adaptation to the environment. "I am interested in rituals and ceremonies for the twenty-four hours of the day. I am not interested in rituals and ceremonies for very long voyages, voyages that can take forty or fifty years. Those are Utopians. And what a tragedy to discover that for the sake of such long-term dreams we have sacrificed our daily lives. No, I am interested in daily rituals: the ritual of sitting in a courtyard, slightly protected from your neighbor's view and the strong wind, gazing up at the stars. [...] Dealing with these types of situations attracts me. The ritual is not the house; I don't make it. And, f yet the house provides a backdrop."[22]

The Universal Garden

In silent isolation on a lot that the first presentation renderings tried to portray as an idealised vision of the Argentine "pampa"[23], the house to the north of Seville is not, then, a "machine in the garden": rather than being inserted into the landscape, it constructs a landscape, in which the sublime and the picturesque merge in a surrealistic hendiadys that recalls the exploration of the very concept of landscape attempted by Mary Miss in one of her famous "works" from 1978, "Perimeters/Pavillions/Decoys"[24]. At the edges of a meadow, a tower standing about 6 metres tall simulates the scaffolding of a building; at the centre, to a depth of nearly 5 metres beneath the surface of the earth, a well bounded by a wooden structure suggests the idea of an ambulatory around an underground courtyard, in a poetic confirmation of the Heideggerian metaphor of the "protective Earth"[25].

As in the work of the American artist, the Casa de Retiro Espiritual also conceals, behind the allure of the image created, the meticulous reality of an artefact constructed as a simulation of a landscape: the empty centre of gravity is below ground level, the façade is a banner visible from afar. Rising in sharp-edged geometric emphasis, the Casa includes all the same an irregular organism, emerging at points from the artificial ground in the form of sinuous incisions along the surface of the grassy covering.

An astronomical observatory and at the same time a sundial that makes it possible to measure the geography of the earth, it corresponds to a vision of architecture as the "reflection of a need for cosmological models" and confirms an idea of

[26] E. Ambasz, unpublished typescript... cit., p. 13.

[27] "We should not forget that the garden, an extraordinary creation that has existed for millennia now, possessed in the East very profound and overlapping significances. The classical garden of the Persians created a sacred space that was meant to gather within its rectangle four sections that represented the four parts of the world, and which in their turn enclosed a space that was even more sacred than the others, similar to the umbilicus, the centre of the world: in the centre of the garden (it was there that the basin and the burbling jet of water were found); and all the vegetation had to be divided within this space, in this sort of microcosm [...]. The garden is the smallest particle of the world and it is also the totality of the world. The garden represents, from the earliest antiquity, a sort of happy and universalising heterotopy."
M. Foucault, *Des espaces autres*, lecture to the Cercle d'études architecturales, Tunis 14 March 1967, now in *Dits et écrits*, edited by D. Defert and F. Ewald, Gallimard, Paris 1994, vol. IV, pp. 752-762.

[28] Ch. Jencks, *The Language of Postmodern architecture*, Academy Editions, London 1977.

[29] R. Krauss, *Sculpure in the expanded field*, in *The originality of the Avant-Garde and Other Modernist Myths*, Cambridge (Mass.) 1984.

[30] Cfr. B. Diamonstein, (edited by), *Collaboration*, Whitney Library of Design, New York 1981.

Union Station, Kansas City, Missouri, USA

design as an aspiration to reflect the "desire to possess at least one attribute of the universe"[26].

An icon of the house, the interrupted backdrop is sufficiently abstract to be configured as an out-of-scale sculpture that marks the site: a landmark that proffers the landscape not as an entity to itself but as the result of a process of perception that presupposes dynamism and change. Only by walking around can you see that the edge of the façade is actually a simulacrum, and only by getting close to the edge of the patio do you begin to see the elements of iconography with enigmatic outlines: the undulations and fissuring of the soil, the skylights that allow natural light to penetrate to the far end of the house and the curved membranes that house the stairs. An asymmetrical centre of a rewriting of the landscape as a garden, it therefore offers a declension that is very close to that "happy and universalising heterotopy" described by Foucault as "the smallest particle of the world" as well as its "totality"[27]. When the first images of the Casa de Ritiro Espiritual began to circulate, Charles Jencks had already published his influential manifesto in favour of post-modernist historicism[28]: and yet, despite Ambasz's proclaimed attention to the primordial values crystallised in the evocative repertoire of recurring archetypes, his distance from the current theories amounted almost to a proud isolation. The points of references in his intellectual construction in fact are not located within the tradition of the disciplinary debate, but rather in that of the artistic research of the American avant-gardes of the Sixties, which Rosalind Krauss was relaunching in those very same years in her well-known essay, *Sculpture in the expanded field*[29].

In the process of Ambasz's design education, the area of "collaborations"[30] with artists is an important chapter, and not only because the image is the only gate that offers access to the deeper meanings of the myth. His admiration for artists such as Robert Smithson, Michael Heizer or Richard Serra corresponds in fact to the sharing of a project characterised by a common attention to the analysis and construction of sites:

to rethink the relationship with nature and the environment, thus reacting in a creative manner to the awareness of the ecological theme, set forth in an increasingly alarmed tone, beginning in 1970, by such publications as the *Report on the State of the Planet*.

By defining the patio as the central element of the residence and using the cuts in the ground as ventilation holes for the interior rooms, the Casa in Seville in fact is a forerunner of the present-day attention to the problems of environmental sustainability, offering, in a non-nostalgic way, the use of natural resources and a reliance on traditional typologies and construction techniques.

As in the contemporary experiments with minimalism by Donal Judd, Carl Andre, Robert Morris or Sol Lewitt, the quest for primary forms does not look to History, however, but combines the rarefaction of the geometry with the realism of the industrial catalogue: the Center for Applied Computer Research in Mexico City (1975) utilised the runoff water from the network of canals extending beneath the suburbs of the capital city as an artificial lagoon defined by the sculptural elements of large inclined solar panels. Interpreting in a literal manner the concepts of flexibility and growth, the rafts of the offices determine compositions of variable landscapes as a function of the demands and requirements of growth.

Water, earth, and air become from this moment onward recurring elements of Ambasz's landscape architecture, and, at first, as in the projects for the Grand Rapids Art Museum (1983) in Grand Rapids, Michigan and for Union Station (1986) in Kansas City, they almost take on the value of a revenge by nature on the human artefacts conveyed to the state of noble "ruins". It was, nonetheless, in the proposal for the Schlumberger research laboratories (1982) in Austin, Texas, that, for the first time, Ambasz's "natural" vocabulary was on display in all its most radical effects, protesting against the practise of concentrated construction through the metaphor of the "inhabited garden".

Schlumberger Research Laboratories, Austin, Texas, USA

[31] *Europa/America. Architetture urbane alternative suburbane*, edited by F. Raggi. Edizioni La Biennale di Venezia, Alfieri Edizioni d'Arte, Venice 1978. Catalogue of the exhibtion "Europa-America, Centro storico-suburbio", Venice 31 July-10 October 1976.

[32] E. Ambasz, *Una relazione sul mio lavoro*, in *Europa/America. Architetture...* cit., p. 106.

[33] R. Smithson, *A Sedimentation of the mind: earth projects*, in *The Writings of Robert Smithson*, edited by N. Holt, New York 1979, p. 35.

[34] E. Ambasz, unpublished typescript... cit. p. 20.

Texan Arcadia

Actually, this had already made its first appearance as early as 1976, with the project for a cooperative of Mexican-American grape growers that Ambasz had presented at the exhibition "Europa/America" at the Venice Biennale[31], accompanied by this explanation: "the eternal quest of Europe remains Utopia, the myth of the end. The recurring myth of America is Arcadia, the eternal beginning. While the traditional vision of Arcadia is that of a humanistic garden, the American Arcadia has been transformed into a man-made nature, a forest of artificial trees and shadows of the mind"[32]. The farmers of Borrego Springs – practically a metaphor for the "noble farmer" that Loos set against the uncertainty of the rootless city-dweller – staged the contrast between the eternity of needs and the variable landscape of the Artificial Garden: but more than symbols of a Romantic aptitude for the organic form of expression as the means whereby contrasts could be overcome, we may consider them so many hard-working Robinson Crusoe on a quest for a way out that is more in tune with the characteristics of new post-technological era. Analogously, executives and researchers at the Schlumberger complex live and work in a landscape that can be assimilated to the Anglo-Saxon culture of the informal garden, yet denatured of its historic iconography of the picturesque: aware of the necessity of an effective "ecological pact", as well as a new "social pact", they demonstrate the importance of building a less mechanical and consequential relationship with the results of the new technology and with the future scenarios of its impact on the environment. Likewise, the employees of the research centre in Mexico City come close to the utopia of an ideal community which, in its most profound aspirations, is perhaps more in continuity with the enlightenment symbolism of Ledoux than the contemporary technologism of Yona Friedmann.

The idea of an inhabited landscape overlays that of the anthropised environment, integrating in an original manner the rich visual patrimony offered by the experimentation of landscape art. The technological centre of Austin emphasises, first and foremost, the predominance of the totality over the individual interventions, leading to the emergence of the structure of a landscape that establishes the value of the "layers of the terrain" as a "limitless museum" and therefore relaunching on an unprecedented scale of function the intuition of Robert Smithson's "earth projects": "buried in the sediments there is a text that eludes rational order and the social structures that limit art"[33]. As for the artist, for the architect as well the language of the "rocks" subjected to an attentive analysis reveals a syntax of flaking and ruptures: and while Robert Heizer "designs" in the Nevada desert the colossal incision of the "Double Negative", moving and reshaping 240,000 metric tons of sandstone and hyalite, Ambasz carves the green plane of his gardens with the irregular "scratches" of serpentine paths that bring light and air to the underlying spaces. The practise of removal corresponds to that of elevation: geometric embankments collaborate in the integration of architecture with the ground, reducing energy costs and providing the working spaces with generous views.

Against the background of the relationship between man and nature, then, runs the history of an eternal domestic return, inspired nonetheless by the dream of a reconciliation on a rational basis between the words and the things of architecture: "I believe that in our pursuit to master Nature-as-found, we have created a second man-made-Nature, intricately related to the given Nature. We need to redefine architecture as one aspect of our man-made nature, but to do so we need first to redefine the contemporary meaning of Nature"[34].

[35] E. Ambasz, *Green towns*, typescript, February 24, 1995, pp. 4-5.

[36] M. Sorkin, *Et in Arcadia Emilio*, in *Emilio Ambasz: The Poetics of the Pragmatic...* cit., p. 17.

[37] E. Ambasz, *Manhattan, capitale del XX secolo*, in "Casabella", 397, January 1975, p. 4.

[38] J. Wines, *Green Architecture*, Taschen, Cologne 2000, p. 69.

[39] E. Ambasz, *Una relazione sul mio lavoro...* cit. p. 106.

Green over grey

"Making new towns by repeating old suburban models, and worse still, repeating old mistakes, is not what I have tried to do. What I would like to propose is that we create a new town which is a Green Town. We propose to go beyond the house in the garden to have the house and the garden. I have spent the last 25 years of my professional life making proposal to create buildings which give back to the community as much as green as possible [...] Year after year, I have worked on the idea, piece-by-piece-, over the last 20 years. My method of work has been to create first a catalog, a typological sampling, of the different types of buildings which would be needed to house the diverse need of such a new Green Town"[35].

The imaginative compiler of "catalogues of the ineffable"[36]. Ambasz worked, then, on the "materialisation of a recurring idyll, making and unmaking the map of his own private order of signs." Comparable to the surrealistic technique of collage, the strategy of the catalogue is however functional to the quest of the foundational principles of the act of building: in the "apologia," *Manhattan, capitale del XX secolo*[37], the creation of a Catalogue of Domestic Places combines the exercise of memory with the design of the future. On the one hand, then, the taxonomy of fragments of the past that have survived the disappearance of their context – Japanese terraces to watch the sunset, Roman baths, patios and courtyards, medieval window seats, etc. – and on the other hand, the exercise of the perspectival imagination to identify places with no historic antecedent, corresponding to such spatial concepts as flexibility, adaptability, territoriality, and privacy.

It is perhaps from this combinatory obsession with the composition of a well identified repertory of "signs" that there derives the singularity of a position that, as James Wines observed[38], never tired of proposing a vision of Arcadia in a professional universe dominated by the fetish of technology. An extraordinary consistency of objectives obliges us to perceive each of Ambasz's projects as an element of a "patient research," evaluating each piece of his architecture as a "figure" of a unitary compositional "grammar". The office complex in the La Venta region, at the far outskirts of Mexico City, can be considered exemplary from this point of view. Defining a method of intervention based on the idea of establishing in the area of an abandoned forest new buildings without losing even a bit of greenery, the project called for arrange the earth in stepped terraces, with the tall-trunk trees of the nurseries looming high above the space of the offices. The architecture does not fit into the landscape because, in fact, it resolves itself in the landscape: there emerges a great variety of solutions that extend in clusters along the stalk of a twisting access road. Each of this terracing arrangements, in fact, takes on a different form, composing an imaginary topography of square, triangular, trapezoidal, or amoeboid forms, that effectively synthesise Ambasz's propensity to conceive geometry as an instrument of "synthesis" in general morphology of great complexity. For this reason, each of his projects unleashes the impression of the primordial gesture of cutting the earth in a sort of ritual pact of refoundation. The Nuova Concordia Resort Housing Development at Castellaneta, in Italy, the Winnisook Lodge in the Catskill Mountains, in New York State, or the Worldbridge Trade Center in Baltimore, Maryland, are authentic "architectural geologies" that allude to a cosmological vision of the territory: carved like traces of ancient civilisations or laid out as grassy knolls, they set forth the signs of a ceremony of reconciliation with Nature, offering the commitment of a "mitigated" architecture, that is, in a state that is very close to a "ruin."

Twentieth-Century Paxton

To keep from "finding himself the gardener of a desert made by man"[39], an architect must in fact convert technology into the chart of "natural" elements: designed the same year as the Schlumberger laboratories, the Botanical Gardens of San Antonio help to define the terms of an environmental pact that resolves ecological values into aesthetic values, connoting in an optimistic and creative direction the much-lamented "death of the landscape".

Little more than a decade separates the Lucille Hansen Conservatory in Texas from the Nicholas Grimshaw's Eden Project in Cornwall and Norman Foster's Great Glasshouse in the National Botanic Garden of Wales: an extreme reproposal of the consolidated British technological tradition, Grimshaw's geodetic domes and Foster's sophisticated metal toroid update, rather than revolutionising, the image of the nineteenth-century greenhouse with the spectacle of Nature enclosed within light translucent "bubbles" set on features of the ground. Ambasz refuses to consider technology as a theme and reformulates the typology of the greenhouse, innovating its iconography and going so far as to overturn its functional presupposition. Traditionally, greenhouses were used to protect plants from the harshness of the climate by making the best possible use of sunlight; in San Antonio, in contrast, the need is to protect vegetation from the harshness of the sunlight and therefore the earth is the true site of the preservation of plants, for which the large glass skylights – with variable inclination depending on the angle of the sunlight – provide a simple covering.

More than alluding to the Future, this "techno-ecological" vision proposes an image of the entire botanical complex as an archaeological site: a suggestive panorama of open-air "ruins," where the vegetation become an integral part of the construction and indeed, almost a symbol of a revenge of the natural element over the pride of the human artefact.

The contrast with the "biological" interpretation of the environmental question is clear and marks, with its successive developments, the gap that divides the complex of his more recent work from the ecological design as an application of the more refined technological components with stereotypical typologies and conventional volumes.

The rehabilitation of the ecological point of view has produced scientific protocols and promoted environmental policies, but it has not yet succeeded to a similar degree in producing convincing applications in the field of architecture. Sustained by the consolidation of technical expertise and the diffusion of schools, it has written its catalogue of commitments in the priority of the national and super national agendas, linking up in the public opinion of the most diverse nations with the justified expectations of an improved quality of life and at the same time, the sophisticated demands of an opulent society that celebrates the body as the reflection of an almost religious conception of the environment. But the effects of its fallout on the typologies of building have only recently, and only sluggishly, undertaken the formulation of a different spatial modulation. Ambasz's merit was to have foreseen and sustained the visionary priority of the new pact of alliance between man and nature, avoiding at the same time any nostalgic misunderstanding as the reproposal of a world of lost forms.

Establishing in full right the principle of environmental redemption in the dominion of architectural prefiguring, Ambasz contributed in an original manner to the consolidation of a culture of the landscape which, from an elitist "art of gardens" circumscribed to limited, exemplary cases, affirmed itself as the preferred instrument of environmental requalification, to which many would not hesitate to actually attribute the role of new paradigm of design as modification. Viewed again from the variegated setting of the international contemporary experience, Ambasz's work anticipates with generosity many of the most diffuse characteristics of the so-called "green architecture". The exploration of the potential of subterranean space, the comprehension of the importance of land design as a horizon line within architecture, the typological declension of the "green façade", the intuition of the "garden" as an informal landscape for urban and territorial requalification: these are a few of the many themes that Ambasz has proposed in the relative isolation of a distracted critical opinion, winning for himself the appellation of "new Messiah of environmental architecture"[40].

In an architectural panorama that is increasingly characterised by a relentless quest for theories borrowed from philosophical thinking, Ambasz's architecture has taken a path of eccentric solitude, preferring the originality of a constant and obsessive research to the standardisation imposed by the system of criticism as a trademark of recognisability and belonging to an orientation. Repaid with the attitude that is reserved for the "irregulars" that don't fit in, he withstood the shifts in fashions, imposing a working method that over the course of a few years that succeeded in transferring to the practicability of the construction yard hypotheses that were apparently unrealistic: the house in Seville – with the house in Montana, the most emblematic of his "fabulae" in stone – the Lucille Hansell Conservatory in San Antonio, the series of his successful Japanese works, to which this last decade is adding the unhoped-for line of the very productive Italian design "tour", all testify to the singular visionary quality of a position whose success can also be measured by the enormous diffusion of his motifs. Those which might have seemed foreshadowing of an intimistic utopia that reduced to a poetic dimension the futurological anticipations of the avant-gardes of the Sixties, proved

San Antonio Botanical Center Lucille Halsell Conservatory, San Antonio, Texas, USA

Private Estate, Montana, USA

at the same time to be very brief experimental samplings of a more mature and self-aware interpretation of the mission of the design, opening an unexpected window on Adam's eternal dream of returning to his old "house in Paradise".

19

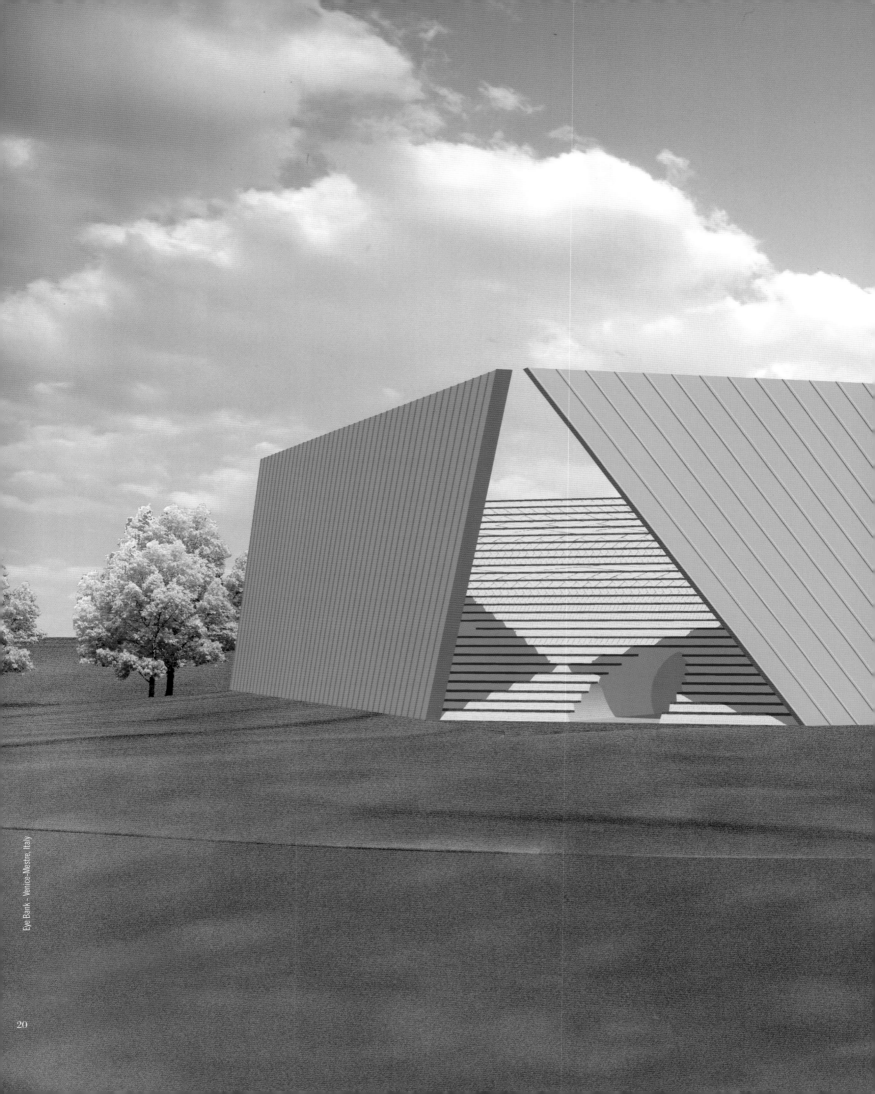

Eye Bank - Venice-Mestre, Italy

Visual A

phorism

"The garden of Alcinous disappeared and instead I beheld universal garden; why are we so distracted, we people of today?"

J.W. Goethe, *Viaggio in Italia*.

[1] M. Sorkin, *Et in Arcadia Emilio*, in *Emilio Ambasz: The Poetics of the Pragmatic...* cit., p. 22.

[2] *Ibid.*, p. 17.

"Instead of becoming an ideologue, I chose to become an author of fables, because there is an unchanging core in them, destined to survive the withering of ideologies."

"Working Fables", the design fables, are the instruments that Ambasz over a long period of time identified as central moments in a working method that rejects the unilateral approach of Theory in favour of the ambiguity of Metaphor. Based essentially on rational reflection, the former, in fact, is totalitarian and absolute; it constructs, around an organising principle, a process controlled by logical sequences. Comparable to the preparatory rites for the "long voyage" to Utopia, in the name of a perfect order, it overlooks the creative disorder of the short span of life, crystallising the present in the image of an abstract Future. The poetic expression of a condition that is not immediately rational, the metaphor expresses itself in visual thought and literary construction, restoring to the image a function evocative of myths: myths of refoundation that reinstall architecture into the heart of that social calling described by Vitruvius himself as the corollary of the discovery of fire by primitive man. A post-industrial revision of the enlightenment myth of the "primitive hut", the village of the grape growers of Borrego Springs illustrates the construction of a process animated by the "ethical ritual of growth and rebirth"[1]: but nature does not appear in it anymore as a point of reference for a rational order destined to be translated into the hardness of stone, but rather as a benign model of conciliation which, by including the ephemeral dimension of the passage of time, exercises a mitigating action upon the individualistic demands of the members of the community. Converting the eighteenth-century predilection for the aesthetics of the picturesque into the narrative pretext of the description of a private garden, the "island" of Emilio's "folly" offers a little theatre of memory in which the mechanism of memory and the complementary pause of amnesia in the construction of the design image is analysed. A figural manifesto and an allegory for the creator's idiosyncrasies, Emilio's Folly is also a catalogue of the recurring metaphors of his architecture: water and earth, the Mediterranean patio house, underground architecture, and the descent toward the depths; his personal "Aleph," as Sorkin suggests: "a summary offered with the full certification of the unconscious"[2]. The passage from the entrance baldachin to the misty cavern is a didactic description of an elaboration of memory through the "subterranean" strata of thought and at the same time the testimonial of a design hope that is not paralysed by the restriction of repetitious memory.

Cooperative of Mexican-American Grapegrowers, Borrego Springs, California

This project has been created at the request of a small cooperative of Mexican-American grape growers. The nine families that constitute the nucleus of this cooperative have, with the aid of federal and state grants and loans, been able to acquire land in a Southern California valley.

The climate there is warm and not ideal for grape growing. However, on the advice of viniculturists at the University of California, the farmers will employ a technique, used in Southern Europe, for growing grapes on an elevated grid of wires. The grid runs horizontally atop concrete or wooden columns ten foot high and 15 feet apart The grapevines grow up, close to each column, and then branch out horizontally, supported by the wire grid. The grape leaves create a dense roof that shades the grapes from the sun, and also leaves the shaded ground free for the cultivation of other crops, such as asparagus.

This project is designed for a four phase settlement process. In the first phase, the nine founding families will live directly under the vineyard, where they will move with the mobile homes they already own. The entrance to the vineyard will be defined by opening a passage at the corner of two walls of a long-abandoned adobe ranch. Out of respect for the settlers' cultural heritage, the nine families' square plots will be laid out in a formal pattern reminiscent of early Hispano-American town. Parallel walls of hedges, defining the access road that runs from the entrance gate to the housing settlement, are planted to express the first settlers' hopes that the cooperative will prosper and grow along this avenue.

A small open-air chapel will be excavated in a stepped section until the first water level is reached. The chapel's cross will emerge from the water, and be repositioned as the water level changes. Every Sunday, as the parishioners go to church, they will take a shovelful of excavated earth from one of the two mounds at the chapel's entrance and shovel it onto the second mound, until only one mound remains. Then the cycle will begin again.

Electricity will be provided by a generator connected to a large wooden paddle wheel at a pond. An earthen aqueduct will carry water from the pond to the animals' pen, which is sited so that the prevailing winds carry animal odors away from the settlement.

In the second phase, 16 new families will come and also bring their own trailers with them. But the organization of the hedge walls that form these families' private territories will be somewhat different. Two large residential squares, one for each group of eight families, will define a triangular plaza where dances will take place on Friday nights, and where an open-air market will be held each Saturday to sell the cooperative's products to the inhabitants of the neighboring towns. Each of these two squares will be divided into nine smaller squares. The central square will be a playground for small children, while the teenagers can meet for dates in the garden created at the pond's edge. Prism-like hedge formations, each about six feet square and 20 feet high, will form this garden; their arrangement in a gridded pattern provides the only urban order in the valley's vastness. A succession of small, private spaces hollowed out of the hedges offers secluded places where one can find privacy or two friends can meet.

One of the smaller squares facing the triangular plaza will be semi-public space, with a brick oven for cooking and large tables for communal noontime meals. These tables also serve as benches for the lessons on Mexican heritage that children will receive, in addition to their regular schooling.

By the time the second group of settlers arrives, the cooperative's production will have increased sufficiently to permit the building of a winery, which will be located near the entrance. Grapes will be stored in a conical silo, a structure traditionally used in Mexico for warehousing produce. The winery itself will be underground, in order to keep the wooden vats cool.

It is hoped that in the third phase, the internal hedge walls separating each family's private territory, will have been clipped away, and a more communal pattern of living will have developed.

The fourth phase stands as a metaphor for the eternal wish that all walls wither away, and that man will be able to live in peace under a vineyard's shade, and off of its generous grapes.

Emilio Ambasz

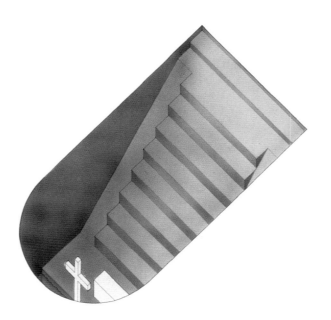

"A small open-air chapel will be excavated in a stepped section until the first water level is reached. The chapel's cross will emerge from the water, and be repositioned as the water level changes. Every Sunday, as the parishioners go to church, they will take a shovelful of excavated earth from one of the two mounds at the chapel's entrance and shovel it onto the second mound, until only one mound remains. Then the cycle will begin again."

"In the first phase, the nine founding families will live directly under the vineyard, where they will move with the mobile homes they already own. Out of respect for the settlers' cultural heritage, the nine families' square plots will be laid out in a formal pattern reminiscent of early Hispano-American town. Parallel walls of hedges, defining the access road that runs from the entrance gate to the housing settlement, are planted to express the first settlers' hopes that the cooperative will prosper and grow along this avenue."

"In the second phase, 16 new families will come and also bring their own trailers with them. But the organization of the hedge walls that form these families' private territories will be somewhat different. Two large residential squares, one for each group of eight families, will define a triangular plaza where dances will take place on Friday nights, and where an open-air market will be held each Saturday to sell the cooperative's products to the inhabitants of the neighboring towns."

"Prism-like hedge formations, each about six feet square and 20 feet high, will form this garden; their arrangement in a gridded pattern provides the only urban order in the valley's vastness. A succession of small, private spaces hollowed out of the hedges offers secluded places where one can find privacy or two friends can meet."

"The entrance to the vineyard will be defined by opening a passage at the corner of two walls of a long-abandoned adobe ranch."

Earthly

"Because, if I consider carefully, among all the works of man a nice garden is what what offers

Paradise

me the truest happiness. Paradise itself was a garden. I find this myth to be profound and significant."

E.R. Curtius, *Italienische Eindrücke*, in "Luxemburger Zeitung", 22.5.1924.

the green façade

It is not only "catalogues of the ineffable" that, with his architecture, Emilio Ambasz constantly tends to produce: seen retrospectively, in fact, the abacus of his design production has the regular cadence of a combinatory system in which recurring families of typologies or construction materials are, from time to time, reinterpreted and declined, in keeping with an experimental approach, in relation to specific programmes.

Appearing for the first time (1976) in the design for the *Chicano* grape growers cooperative as a metaphor for the idea of roofing, the "figure" of the metal netting is translated from pergola into a trellis wall in the labyrinth of the Hortus Conclusus at the Exposition Parcs et Jardins held by the Centre Pompidou (1989), to the point of taking on the role of "structural" sheathing principle in the New Town Center of Chiba (1989), which, for many reasons, Ambasz considered as the prototype of one of those "green towns" that are intended to characterise Japan's new urbanistic policy in consideration of the advanced degree of development of a society that is technologically in the avant-garde and at the same time keenly aware of an age-old tradition of attention to and respect for nature. Based on the principle of the integration between man and environment and designed with the awareness of the possibilities offered by electronics for remote work, Japan's "green towns" should house no more than 10,000-13,000 inhabitants and should be accessible to the new network of high-speed trains: thus the station becomes the very heart of the city, enriching its configuration in the form of a full-fledged town center that, as in the example of Chiba, presents itself as a multifunctional complex of public and private spaces, whose "green architecture" codifies a uniform design process for all the new façades of the surrounding urban context.

To mitigate the environmental impact of the new shopping centre of Chiba and to avoid that teetering sense of incompleteness that accompanies the long time spans of a demanding construction job, Ambasz thus entrusted to an open structural grid the role of structural element of the urban image: a three-dimensional metal netting – which Lauren Sedofsky[1] suggested could be traced back to the impressions of the cubic structures of Sol Lewitt –

[1] L. Sedofsky, *Peripheral Vision (Emilio Ambasz: Special Issue)*, in "Korean Architects", 131, luglio 1995, pp. 12-33.

allows the placement in each module of a plant in a vase, so as to offer at the same time a barrier against the arteries of train and car traffic and a visual continuity with the various parts of the complex to which it supplies a paradoxical element of permanence in the rapidly changing heart of the future civic centre.

Reelaborating the motif of the "vegetal" reticulation in the complete form of a full-fledged "vertical garden", Ambasz then anticipates certain explorations into "gridwork" façades, with noteworthy examples offered by Herzog & de Meuron (winery) and a forerunner of solutions like those adopted, for instance, by Gaetano Pesce in the Organic Building at Osaka (1994) or, more recently, by Jean Nouvel with the "vegetal" façades of the design for the French Embassy in Berlin (1997) and with the "green wall" for the intervention to recuperate the former Fiat Belfiore factory in Florence (2002). The western motif of the brise-soleil is transformed then into the continual façade of a vertical orangerie, where various types of trees compose the seasonal cycle of flowering, with a two-fold reference to the western culture of the orderly garden and the Japanese tradition of cultivated nature. The theme is echoed on a colossal scale in the Torii portal which, with its two office towers, already signals from the train the entrance to the city: the vegetation that grows around its façade conceals the curtain wall behind and refers to the covered verandas of Japanese houses.

A poetic gesture of redemption of nature, the conversion of the curtain wall into a vertical garden is also the reasonable re-elaboration in a bio-technological key of those concerns about energy that were so central to the agenda of contemporary architecture: it is no accident, then, that it became the figurative theme of the contemporary commercial building, as in the case of the "Grand Embrace" at the Koningin Julianplein in The Hague (2002), or of his radical "green" reconversion, as in the ENI Office Building in Rome's EUR, an exemplary testimonial to the success of the International Style in the design culture of Italy in the Fifties. If on the one hand Ambasz's proposal seems to incorporate the environmental point of view explored by Gabetti and Isola in the ENI-Snam building in Milan, on the other hand it

resolves in an original manner the iconography of the central headquarters of the national energy colossus, suggesting the image of a company that is respectful of the natural environment and sensitive to the problems of the ecological equilibrium. Wrapped in a double façade that makes use of the same system of stacked green tested in the Japanese complex of Chiba, the former glass building of ENI becomes a metaphor for the new industrial policy of "flowering energy" and a design indication of an improved relationship of the tall building with the surrounding environment. A vertical garden is found, also, in the interior of the nineteenth-century brick building of the former Tabacalera of Buenos Aires, the point of departure for the planned Museum of Modern Art and the Cinema (MAMBA, 1997). With a procedure that is reminiscent of the imaginative transformation of the Federal Building of Grand Rapids into a museum, Ambasz proposes the partial emptying of the monumental façade: adopted as an *objet trouvé*, the brick elevation become a structural grid punctuated by the order of the columns. As in the "subtractions" and the micro-demolitions with which Gordon Matta-Clark proposed the x-ray analysis of the more private sections of existing buildings, the project called for the removal of the window frames and several walls on the side bays, suggesting the opportunity of a façade that would reveal and at the same time conceal the buildings behind it. The gaps between the old façade and the new interior walls are thus filled with a "soft" sequence of trees, formalising a green façade emerging in a filigree from the dissolving of the brick façade. In the Grand Rapids Arts Museum, an inclined plane set between the two wings of the building served as a slide for the silent cascade of a light veil of water: in the same way that this translucent film resemanticised the federal architecture of the formerly public building, the vegetal façade of the future MAMBA contributed to a reformulation of the codes whereby the Tabacalera and the anonymous building in reinforced concrete were read, staging a sort of virtual, but not immaterial, architecture, which introduced a surreal aspect to the consolidated silhouette of the previously existing building, allowing artifice and nature, mineral and vegetable to interact.

Verdant access gate to the Hague, this "great embrace" develops the image of a vertical garden: a great green building rising on a meadow, welcoming inhabitants and visitors with open arms.

Underground, 10,000 sq. m. of parking space for offices and residents. A two-story socle becomes the foundation for a generous *hortus conclusus* that contains 7,500 sq. m. of stores and commercial spaces, creating a connection with the railroad station through the neighbouring Stitchage Building. A 27-metre tower, intended for offices and residences, extends into the air like a bridge so as not to block the views from the Stitchage Building: its greenish skin consists of a succession of multi-story terraces, glassed in like the greenhouses of so many private gardens.

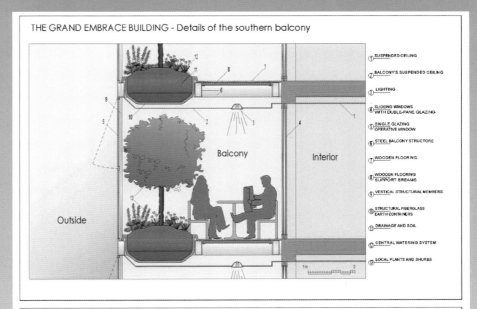

THE GRAND EMBRACE BUILDING - Details of the southern balcony

Balcony

Interior

Outside

① SUSPENDED CEILING
② BALCONY'S SUSPENDED CEILING
③ LIGHTING
④ SLIDEING WINDOWS WITH DOUBLE-PANE GLAZING
⑤ SINGLE GLAZING OPERATIVE WINDOW
⑥ STEEL BALCONY STRUCTURE
⑦ WOODEN FLOORING
⑧ WOODEN FLOORING SUPPORT BREAMS
⑨ VERTICAL STRUCTURAL MEMBERS
⑩ STRUCTURAL FIBERGLASS EARTH CONTAINERS
⑪ DRAINAGE AND SOIL
⑫ CENTRAL WATERING SYSTEM
⑬ LOCAL PLANTS AND SHRUBS

1m   0

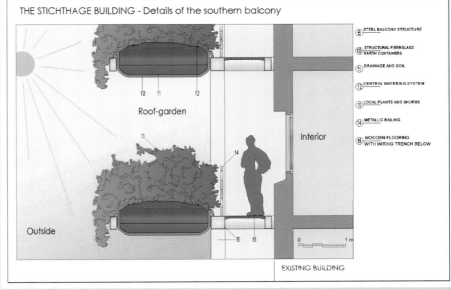

THE STICHTHAGE BUILDING - Details of the southern balcony

Roof-garden

Interior

Outside

⑥ STEEL BALCONY STRUCTURE
⑩ STRUCTURAL FIBERGLASS EARTH CONTAINERS
⑪ DRAINAGE AND SOIL
⑫ CENTRAL WATERING SYSTEM
⑬ LOCAL PLANTS AND SHRUBS
⑭ METALLIC RAILING
⑮ WOODEN FLOORING WITH WIRING TRENCH BELOW

0   1 m

EXISTING BUILDING

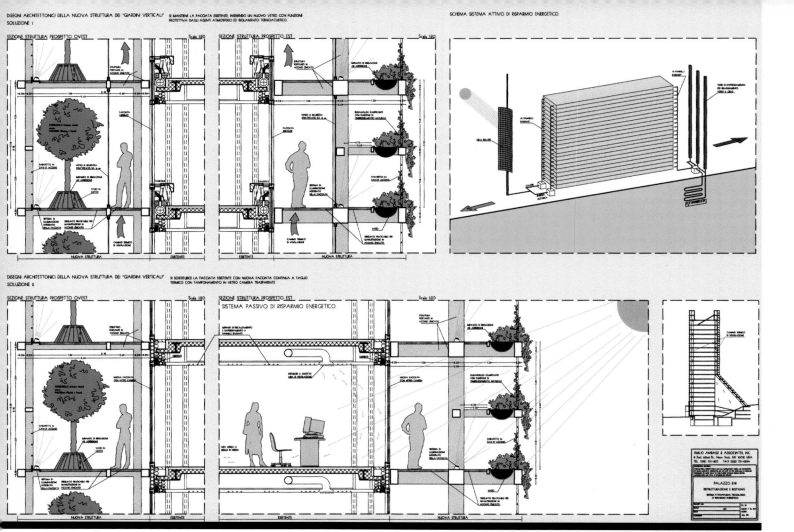

The "building of the vertical gardens" is the proposal for the transformation of the ENI office building at EUR near Rome, designed between 1960 and 1962 by M. Bacigalupo, U. Ratti, L. Finzi and E. Nova in obedience to the technological and expressive principles of the International Style.

Ambasz's idea starts out from the principle of associating the public image of the Italian energy colossus with the emerging directions of its new environmental policy: the theme of an industry that is sensitive to the problems of the ecological equilibrium and the sustainability of resources is thus reflected in the symbol of a "flowering energy", expressed by the "green" treatment of the façades. Like so many three-dimensional *brise-soleils*, these wrap around the old building with the seasonal tones of plants according to various cycles of flowering and are organically anchored to the surrounding terrain, describing a sort of unbroken natural surface.

The design of the two museums of the Polo Cultural Sur in Buenos Aires is based on the reuse of two existing buildings to be used, respectively, as an Art Museum and a Museum of Cinema: the nineteenth-century building of the Tabacalera with its characteristic use of brick and an obsolete modern building made of reinforced cement.

The transformation of the Tabacalera calls for definition of a new façade which echoes, extending it, the rhythm of the giant order of masonry pillars: the space between the new façade and the old wall allows the installation of trees that create in this way a green screen, emphasising on a large scale the traditional succession of flower-filled balconies of that part of the city.

The façade behind it corresponds instead to the condition of the fast traffic on the elevated highway that runs alongside: when viewed at speed it offers a series of images in movement that promote the activity of the two museums.

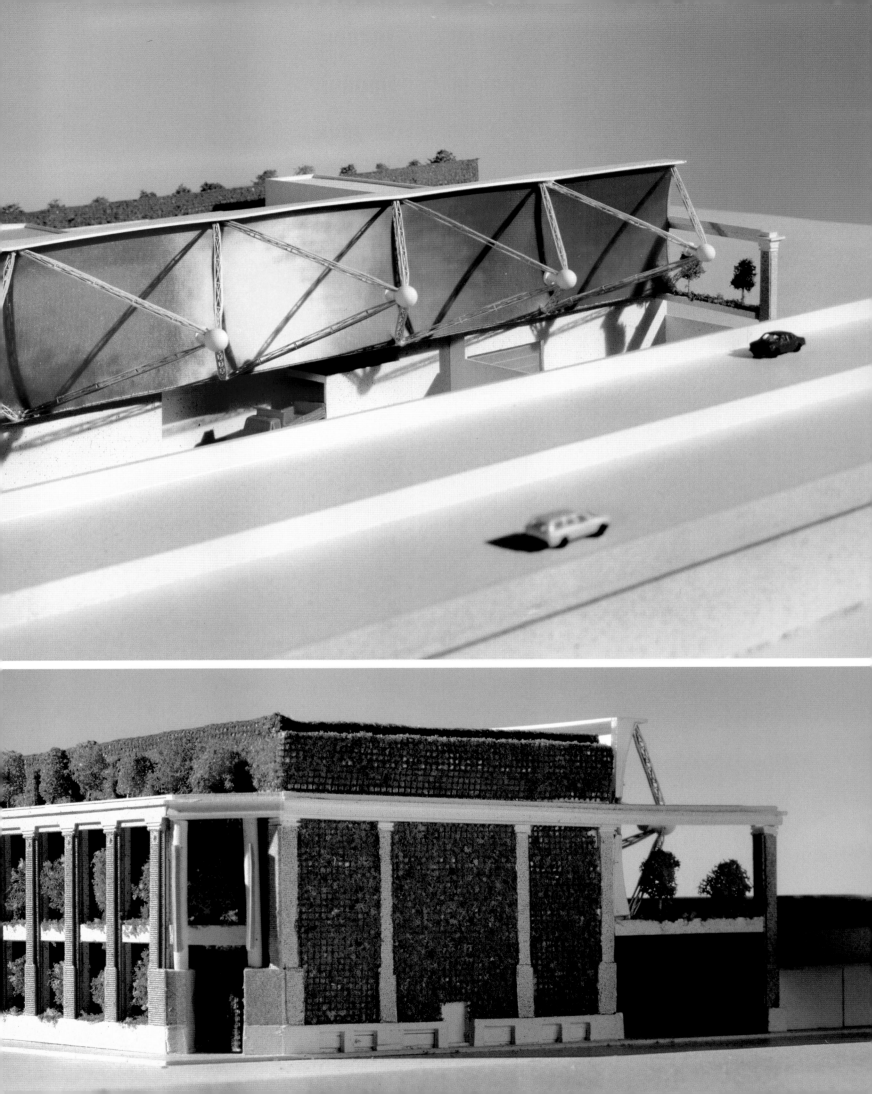

A structural grid allows each module to house a plant in a vase: a luxuriant growth of ivy conceals the structure, offering the vision of a serpentine green wall. In this way, an effect of continuity is created with the gardens below, evoking the memory of the covered verandas of traditional Japanese houses.

A shopping centre as the welcoming bridgehead of a new suburban settlement, coinciding with the boarding station for the new line of high-speed trains: serving as a screen for the farmlands behind it and for the city under construction at its back, the project offers an urban landmark of strong identity with its focal point in the colossal Torii portal with the two office towers that announce the city to those who arrive by train from the elevated station.

the green mountain

The first steps in Emilio Ambasz "voyage to the Far East" date from the second half of the Eighties: the historic destination of cultural transitions between East and West, Japan, first and foremost, is the great magnet that for almost two centuries has continually attracted the dream of modern art and architecture, which – from Wright to Taut and Mies van der Rohe – has shown that it can capture in the mystery of its tradition the tension of the modernist effort toward the ideal purity of a total "truth".

Is it simply chance that one of Ambasz's first Japanese projects – the Nichii Obihiro Department Store on Hokkaido – succeeds in transcribing in the prismatic facets of an unusual crystal façade the post-industrial echo of the utopian vision of the "Glas architektur" of Paul Scheerbart and Bruno Taut?

As if in a giant glittering piece of quartz, in fact, a faceted skin of crystal wraps around the inner perimeter of the complex, allowing the planting of the inner space with high-branch trees: this defines the image of an irregular greenhouse, shaped according to the requirements of the building regulations and by a calculation of the refractions of shadows and reflections of light.

The figure of the green mountain – so recurrent in his projects that it almost takes on the value of an archetype – here combines with that of the inhabited mountain, creating an iconography with multiple historical implications, but nonetheless opened to new meanings, as shown, for instance, by its recent reuse in the two unbuilt designs by Jean Nouvel for the Museum of Human Evolution in Burgos (2000) and for the Guggenheim Temporary Museum of Art in Tokyo (2001).

An optimistic counterpoint to the urbanisation of the second-largest city on the island of Hokkaido, the Nichii Obihiro Department Store offers a radical innovation on the recurring typology of the shopping centre: a mountain-mall, as Lauren Sedofsky suggested it might be called, which, by rejecting both the image of architecture-as-container and the image of a micro-city of merchandise, opted for a hybrid geological

[1] J. Wines, *Green architecture*, Taschen, Cologne 2000, p. 69.

[2] E. Sottsass, in *Emilio Ambasz. Architettura Naturale Design Artificiale*, Electa, Milan 2001, p. XXII.

[3] E. Ambasz, *Green Towns*, typescript, February 24, 1995.

implant, where nature and artifice pay their design debt to the Japanese art of the garden.

A large hollow centre – which can be traced back relatively directly to the organic irruption suggested in the project for the transformation of Union Station in Kansas City – houses a winter garden that however does not attempt to simulate the static order of the "palm houses" of the nineteenth century, but the pervasive effect of a "naturalistic" landscape. A symbolic reference to the interior as an organic "cavity", this centre inaugurates a family of recurring figures in Ambasz's large-scale projects, as shown by its versions in the Worldbridge Trade and Investment Center in Baltimore (1989), in the Mycal Cultural and Athletic Center in Shin-Sanda, and in the Fukuoka Prefectural International Hall (1990).

While the Baltimore complex reinforces the allegorical use of geological morphology, the Mycal Center develops the construction of a total landscape, in which the visible fragments of the functional structure are offered as retaining walls against an internal topographical explosion. In Fukuoka, the figure of the staircase – utilised in visual aphorisms as a symbol of the descent toward the depths of the ground – becomes the support for a "natural promenade" that prolongs the existing park upwards, with effects possessing a certain scenographica resonance. Stratified in low terraces that rise gradually from the park before them, the stepped profile of the Japanese "Arcadian ziggurat"[1] combines the practical expedient of the illumination of the office spaces with the symbolic mysticism of a "sacred staircase" that, by crossing the various gardens of meditation, repose, and shelter reaches the panorama of the upper terrace. In this way, the effect of the grassy carpet rising up to cover the body of the building becomes a metaphor for a progressive recognition of the uncertain identity of the city, recomposed definitively in the vision of the bay from high up in the belvedere.

To restore to the community all the green taken away by new buildings is the ethical imperative and, at the same time, the constructive expedient of a design strategy – "green over the grey" – that corresponds to a philosophy of subtraction and repositioning that is typical of landscape art and an idea of architecture "as a talismanic instrument of a wager, of a hidden ritual to fascinate some immense natural divinity", as a "liturgy performed to obtain forgiveness for the scars we inflict everyday on the planet", as Ettore Sottsass has observed[2].

But the shopping and office complexes of Shin-Sanda, Fukuoka, and Hokkaido, as well as the National Diet Library at Kansai Science City constitute as well the point-by-point elements of a pragmatic utopia – the "green town movement" – developed by Ambasz with special application to the dynamics of Japan's urbanisation: shows a very simple but profound way of "creating new urban settlements which do not alienate the citizens from the vegetable kingdom, but rather, creates an architecture which is inextricably woven into the greenery, into nature"[3].

With their various formal and functional declensions these architectural complexes give origin to that "catalogue" of urban solutions demanded by the vision of a post-industrial "Broadacre": fast trains in place of individual transportation on rubber wheels and "mountain-buildings", instead of the isolated skyscrapers imagined by Wright. Designed as a nodal element of the new science city of Kansai, the National Diet Library is the living memory of the Nation's historical culture and therefore a symbolic, as well as functional, element of the new urban landscape under construction on the hills of Keihanna: a "sacred mountain", a ritual mound, similar to those in which thousands of years ago the preservation of sacred texts was entrusted. Rewriting in a monumental key that archetype of the rock-mountain first seen in "Emilio's Folly", the earth hill of the National Diet Library is the emerging element of the territorial composition of which it summarises the need for collective symbols in the creation of definite urban identities.

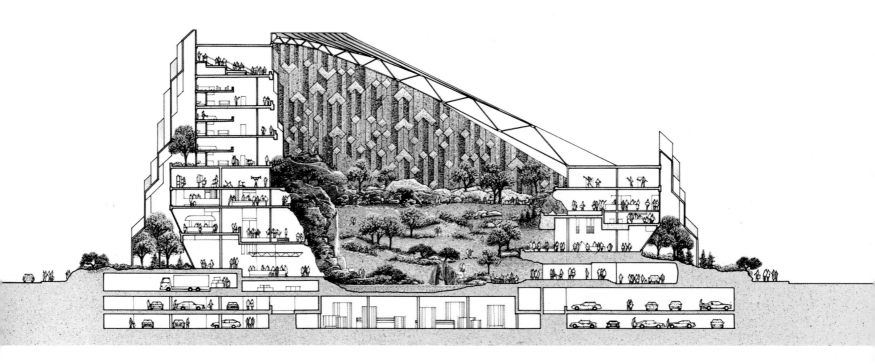

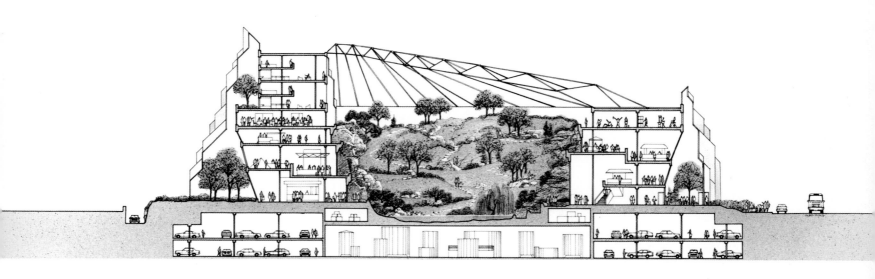

As in the alpine fantasies of the "architecture of crystal" by Bruno Taut, the Nichii Obihiro Department Store on the island of Hokkaido is a glittering mountain where the glassy transparency of the faceted surfaces allows us to glimpse the green skin of a luxuriant garden animated by the plants lodged in the space between the external layer and the insulated walls of the building itself. By interpreting the demands for social interaction in a city where the climate is reminiscent of Siberia, the shopping centre offers the inhabitants of Obihiro a suggestive transparent "grotto" animated by the continuous noise of small waterfalls and by the artificial Arcadia of a landscape dotted with trees and grassy knolls.
The unusual variety of services — from shopping to restaurants, health clubs, and so on — configures the entire centre as an urban site, midway between a covered plaza and a winter garden.

Seen from afar, the great complex offers the illusion of a flowering promontory set high on a podium of earth where the parking areas are located. The facets of its profile are dictated by a calculation of the angle of the rays of the sun and the angles of shadow, as well as by the respect for the height limitations imposed by urban regulations.

Recharting in a creative manner the topography of Maryland, the outline of the shopping centre designs, along with the underground display hall,

the balanced composition of an explosion of the ground upward and the implosion of the ground toward a minutely etched cavity.

OUTDOOR GARDEN TERRACES   ENCLOSED ATRIUM   DROP

EMILIO AMBASZ & ASSOCIATES, INC.

PACIFIC WORLD TRADE
& INVESTMENT CENTRE
SITE PLAN

0   25   50   100

INTERIOR RING ROAD   EXHIBIT HALLS- 3 LEVELS   EXHIBIT HALL DROP OFF
(100,000 SQ. FT.)

The green rind of an irregular mountain envelops and protects the surprise of an empty core, a monumental atrium shaped like a truncated cone that expands downward in an intricate landscape of rocks, greenery, and water and narrows, upward, into the luminous eye of the glass-covered roof.

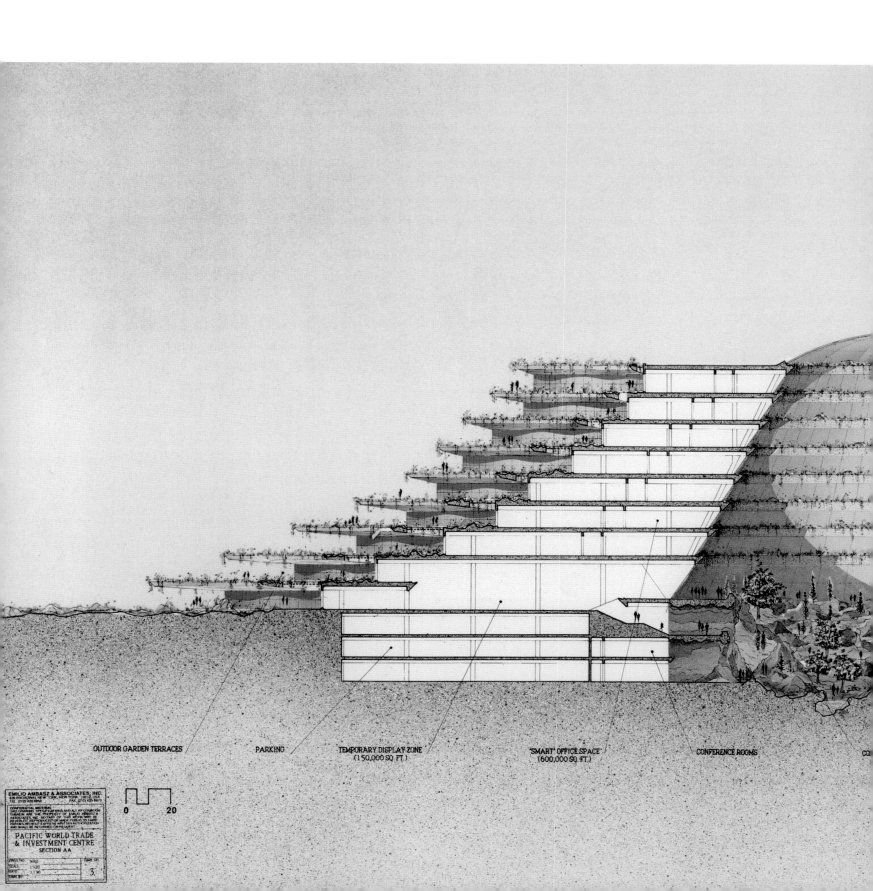

OUTDOOR GARDEN TERRACES　　　PARKING　　　TEMPORARY DISPLAY ZONE
(150,000 SQ FT.)　　　'SMART' OFFICE SPACE
(600,000 SQ FT.)　　　CONFERENCE ROOMS　　　CO

0　　20

PACIFIC WORLD TRADE
& INVESTMENT CENTRE
SECTION AA

3

Designed as a stacking of horizontal planes with undulating outlines, the office complex extends in waves around the great void of the entrance: a gap among the various floors allows the planting of the areas as gardens, conferring upon the entire volume the surreal effect of an artificial highland.

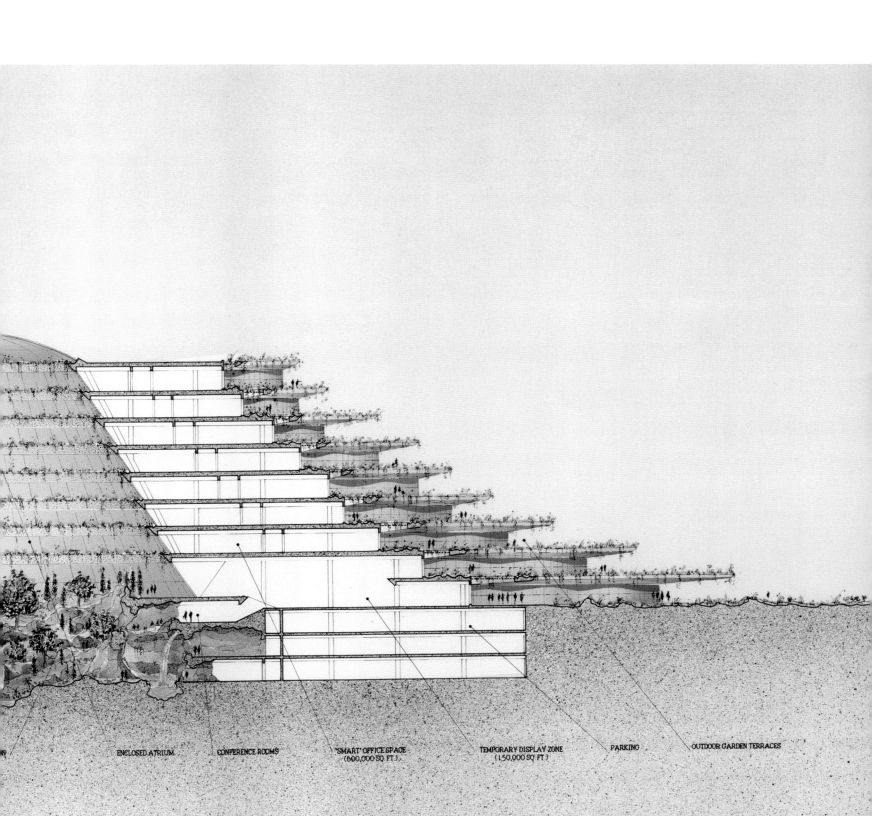

ENCLOSED ATRIUM   CONFERENCE ROOMS   SMART OFFICE SPACE (600,000 SQ. FT.)   TEMPORARY DISPLAY ZONE (150,000 SQ. FT.)   PARKING   OUTDOOR GARDEN TERRACES

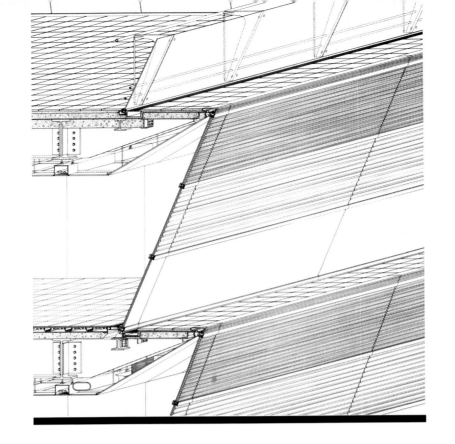

0 5 10m
0 10 20 30ft

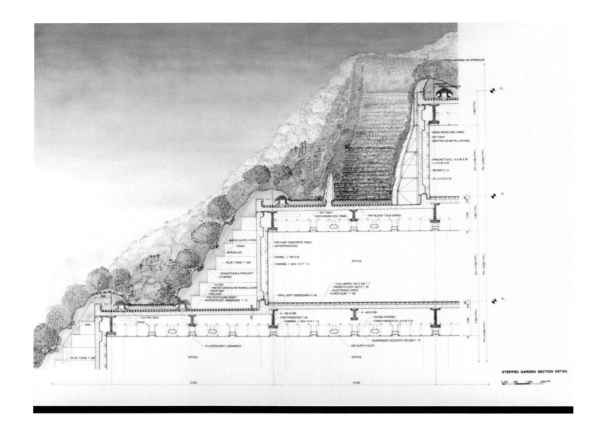

Situated in the only square in the city of Fukuoka, along a canal, the project of the government building has offered Ambasz a chance to apply in an urban setting his theory of "green over the grey": that is, to restore to the city every part of soil taken away by building. That rebate that Le Corbusier had established in the figure of the "roof-garden", then, is extended to the diagramme of the entire construction, making it become the dominant motif of its skyline. Fukuoka Prefectural International Hall expresses with vigour the message of the environmentalist culture of the twenty-first century, offering to restore a harmony with Nature without repudiating the western technological tradition.

A flowering terraced ziggurat forms, story upon story, an ascending landscape: a large Baroque machine contrasting further down by a stone wedge that contains the entrance to the building and by the glassed semicylinder that casts light onto the interior. The technological structure yields to the analogue image, overlapping in the visitor the memory of sites and places of a monumental past, from Villa Aldobrandini to the gardens of Sans Souci, from the hanging gardens of ancient times to the theatrical staircases of Baroque Rome.

Each level contains an array of gardens destined for meditation, rest, and shelter from urban congestion: once the peak has been won, the "sacred" mountain reveals its nature as an observatory upon the city, which presents itself laid out in the spectacle of bay and surrounding mountains.

An authentic *boîte à surprise*, the interior of the prism with setbacks appears as a large atrium illuminated from above and banded with long balconies that allow visitors to flow, transforming them into spectators for public evens and ceremonies.

Among the various functions housed on the interior, alongside the administrative spaces and offices there are meeting rooms, an exhibition gallery, a 2,000-seat theatre, and a museum, as well as parking and services. The visible structure reveals the technological nature of the construction, creating a deliberate counterpoint between the architecture of the scaffolding the vegetable warp and weft of the luxuriant exterior.

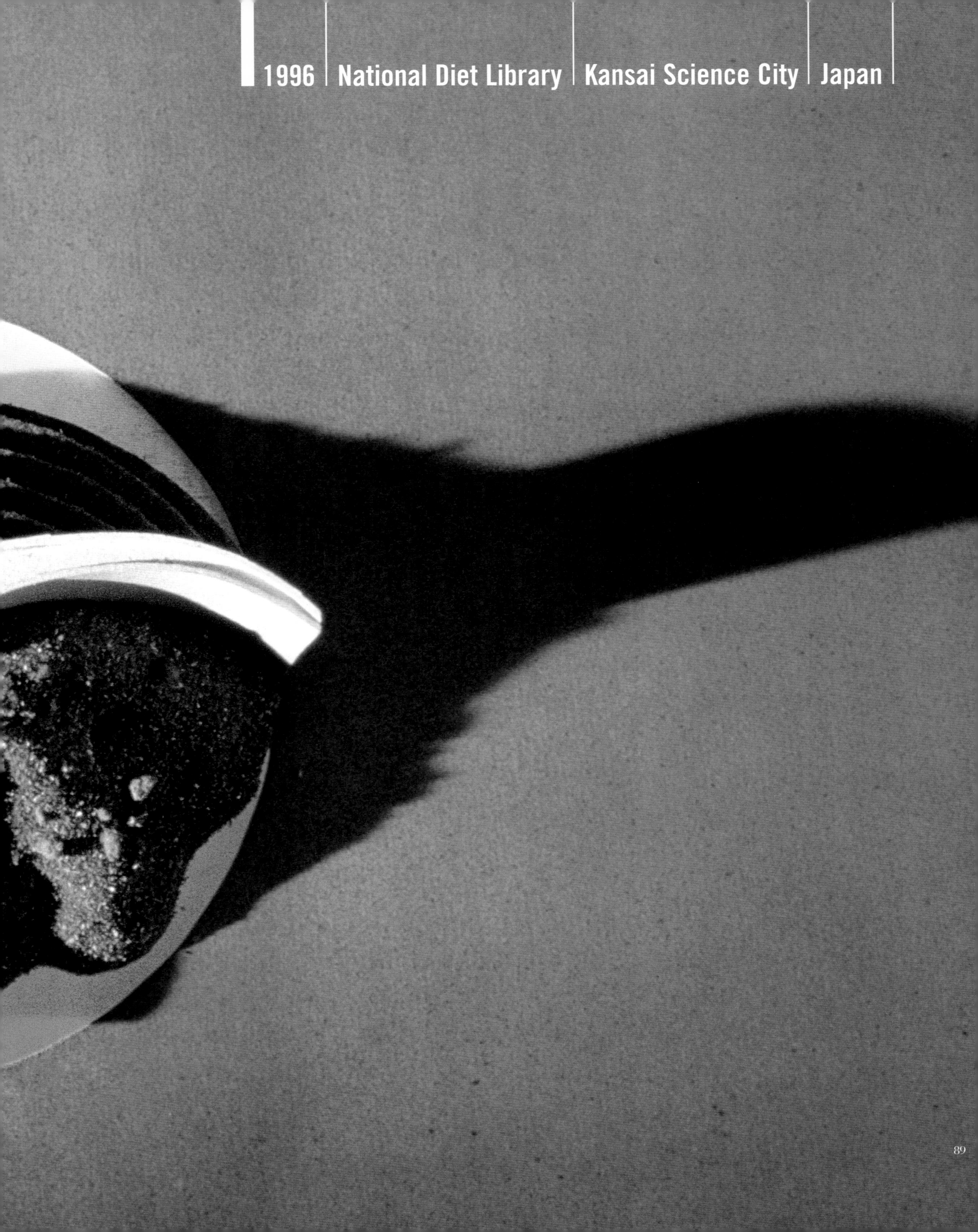

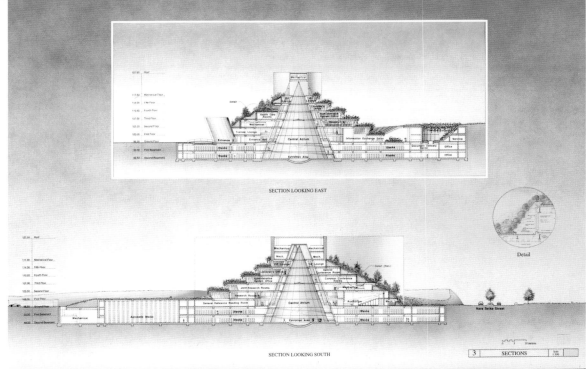

SECTION LOOKING EAST

Detail

SECTION LOOKING SOUTH

3   SECTIONS

SOUTH ELEVATION

NORTH ELEVATION

7   ELEVATIONS

Mausoleum of national culture, the grassy "mound" intended for the preservation of a number of important paper materials of the Japanese National Library has the value of a ritual temple to the memory in the new science city of Kansai on the Keihanna hills.

Taking inspiration from the primordial gesture of guarding sacred texts in the depths of the earth, Kansai-Khan offers the image of a cultivated hill: a metaphor for natural order in the threat of chaos, the sinuous trace of a wall represents the undulating border line between *natura naturans* and *natura naturata*. On the one hand, then, five stepped terraces hark back the theme of the humanised environment, on the other hand, the apparent spontaneity of the hill. An analogous symbolism inspires the interior: a large cone — geometric evocation of fire — configures the cross-section of the atrium; the crowning hemisphere evokes the celestial vault, while the shelving arrangement of the storerooms refers to the idea of the cube, a synthesis of the stability of the earth.

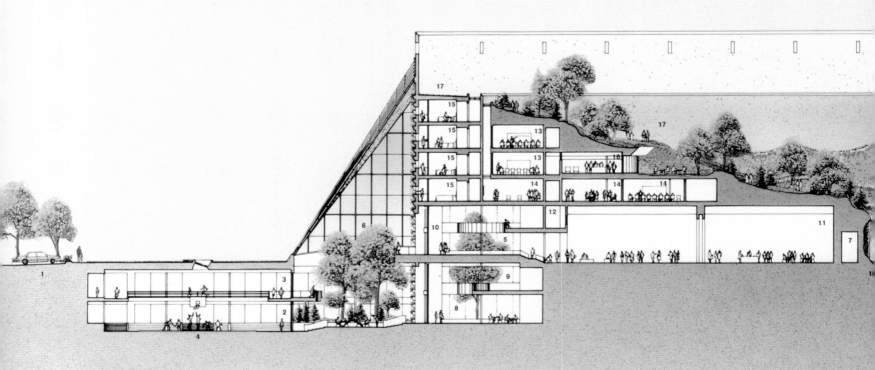

断面図　B

0　　　5　　　10　　　20M

The background for two walls that protect on their interior the picturesque landscape of a steep garden, the Mycal Cultural and Athletic Center is the surreal crown placed on a hill of the new city of Shin-Sanda, in an area located between a man-made reservoir and a golf course. From the summit of the garden enclosed between the two wings of the complex runs a stream of water that joins the basin below, while the planted terracings offer space for small theme gardens that have to do with meditation and the contemplation of nature. In this way, the challenging task of attenuating the environmental impact of the roughly 40,000 sq. m. of the construction is translated into the invention of design and urbanistic scheme that avoids solutions of continuity between the landscape in the distance and the new gardens.

As in a huge greenhouse, the glassed walls filter the natural light, creating a variety of intermediate spaces to be used for collective functions. Inclined to form a triangular section with the wall behind, these undulating membranes offer an organic rendition of a high tech structure, predisposing the visitor to the sinuous nature of the interior spaces, whose strong colours create a significant contrast with the rarefied serenity of the winter gardens.

the earth as garden

"The layers of the terrain are an endless museum. Buried in the sediments is a text that eludes rational order and the social structures that limit art."[1]

To scratch, to carve, to raise the soil are the characteristic signs of an idea of architecture as total landscape that seems to transport us into the context of construction as the aspiration to the "landscape" of the American avant-gardes of the Sixties, theorized by Rosalind Krauss in her renowned 1978 essay, "Sculpture in the expanded field". In Ambasz's design *Bildungsroman* the chapter of "collaborations" with artists is an important one, written as a protagonist and not as a mere sounding board for motifs developed elsewhere.

His friendship with Robert Smithson – as well as his admiration for all the leading figures of American landscape art, from Sol Lewitt and Michael Heizer to Richard Serra – is the spontaneous reflection of a natural conceptual brotherhood, founded upon the idea that "every act of building is a challenge to nature": "the ideal gesture would be to arrive at a plot of land so immensely fertile and welcoming that, slowly, the land would assume a shape – providing us with an abode. We must build our house on earth only because we are not welcome on the land"[2].

Characterised by a tension toward the "construction of sites", environmental art refuses to represent, duplicating it, reality and prefers instead to recreate it, intervening upon it concretely, defining "places", marking the territory, producing installations that do not appear to be anchored to the ground, but rather an emanation, in some sense, from the soil itself through operations of excavation, filling, intersection with the pre-existing natural elements. The notion of landscape – redefined in a radical manner with respect to its traditional acceptation as a

1 R. Smithson, *A sedimentation of the Mind; Earth Projects*, 1968.

2 E. Ambasz, unpublished typescript, reply to M. Sorkin, 31 July 2002.

3 *Ibid.*, p. 20.

background to contemplate – becomes a vanishing point for a way of operating that visualises the context as the scene of a total theatre that actively includes the spectator: hence derives the necessity of working on the elements of perception, conferring significance to the identification of the individual sites. The introduction of the spectator's point of view implies a temporal reality of the landscape as a place that is built through the interaction of man and nature: what derives, then, is on the one hand the impossibility of thinking of Nature as separate or pre-existing cultural anthropology, on the other hand the possibility of narrating the landscape as the product of a working process, an action, which in the case of the farming cooperative of Borrego Springs, for instance, has all the characteristics of a rite of foundation.

Like the "earthworks" of Michael Heizer or Robert Smithson, the environmental architecture of Emilio Ambasz presupposes the preparation of an imaginary orography that starts out from the importance assigned to "terrain" as the matrix of the future landscape. To detect and understand its topography corresponds to the idea of establishing a symbolic correspondence between geology and psychology, which in the "Working Fables" is expressed in the moralistic tones of the apologist and in the large-scale projects in the pragmatic tones of environmental redemption. The "allegorical" dimension of these places is perfectly legible only in their overhead representation: seen from above, the layout of the residential complex of Nuova Concordia at Castellaneta, for instance, eschews the bucolic character that we might expect from a holiday village to reveal a complex, if hermetic, configuration of signs, inscribed in the soil as traces of an archaeological dig site. The impossibility of recognizing in it sharable icons brings us back to the abstract and minimalist sensibility of Ambasz's architecture, which utilises asymmetry and geometry to convert every naturalistic

temptation into an imagination with subtly surreal tones. "I believe that in our pursuit to master Nature-as-found, we have created a second man-made Nature, intricately related to the given Nature. We need to redefine architecture as one aspect of our man-made nature, but to do we need first to redefine the contemporary meaning of Nature."[3] And so, in the proposal for the revitalisation of the wooded region of La Venta, on the outskirts of Mexico City, the theme of the reforestation of a forest on the brink of extinction becomes a point of departure for the introduction of an eccentric sampling of geometric silhouettes in the vegetal mantle: the new nurseries in fact establish a hybrid typology of terraced planes, which on the interior offer spaces for offices and on the exterior open-air nurseries for the high-branch trees. Inhabited by mysterious presences – a square, a triangle, a semicircle, etc. – the forest of La Venta is a non-mimetic landscape, almost the architectural equivalent of the "construction of a site": a marking in the landscape with interventions to the soil or through the vegetation.

In the same conceptual category, we find the hotel and recreation complex of Winnisook Lodge on the interior of Catskill Park, on the wooded crest of Belleayre Mountain. Like a three-dimensional extension of the adjoining golf course, Winnisook Lodge develops along precise curving silhouettes, reminiscent of the ruins of cities thousands of years old, buried under luxuriant vegetation. The "absence" of architecture corresponds in this way to a virtual presence: the shadow of an analogy that alludes to the triumph of nature over the ruins of the built.

A prehistoric site observable through its excavation site is the shopping centre near Amersfort which, developing as it does in a deep fault carved into the ground, seems like the appropriate homage to the environmental culture of a country whose history is nothing other than the age-old narration of the warlike relationship between sea and land.

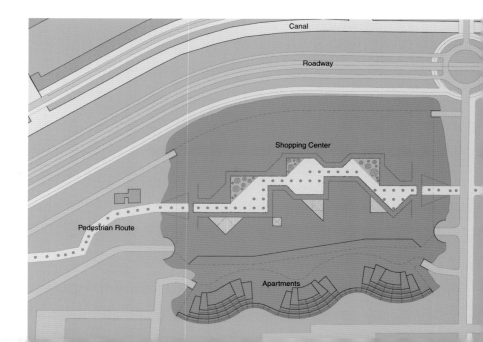

Canal

Roadway

Shopping Center

Pedestrian Route

Apartments

Vathorst, a new small town with a population of 27,000 near Amersfoort, is known in Holland as an example of a "green city": the new shopping and residential centre offers itself as a creative application of this urbanistic principle, considering the entire buildable surface area as a unitary landscape. In the place of buildings distributed over the terrain, then, an articulated grassy mantle designed in keeping with a two-fold gesture of placing and removing: on the one hand the geometric incision of the commercial spaces, and on the other, the uneven line of the alignment of the grassy terracings of the residences.

The shopping centre includes two supermarkets, a discount shop, retail sales outlets, and a covered parking area: thanks to the special design layout which gives the city a generous green area not specified in the original construction permit, it has been possible to expand the programme with the construction of 78 residential units, arranged in a scheme of terracing entirely treated as gardens.

When construction is complete, the layout of the shopping centre presents itself as an irregular fault carved into the ground: in reality, the project calls for the ground floor to rise gradually to cover completely all built surfaces, relying upon the traditional Dutch technique of the berm, a embankment used to protect the dykes against the danger of erosion.

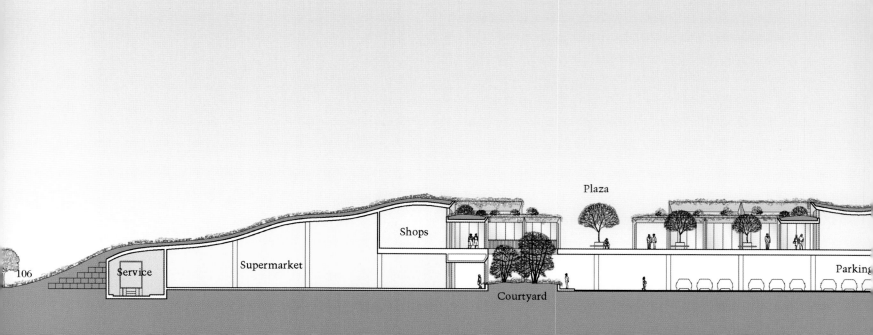

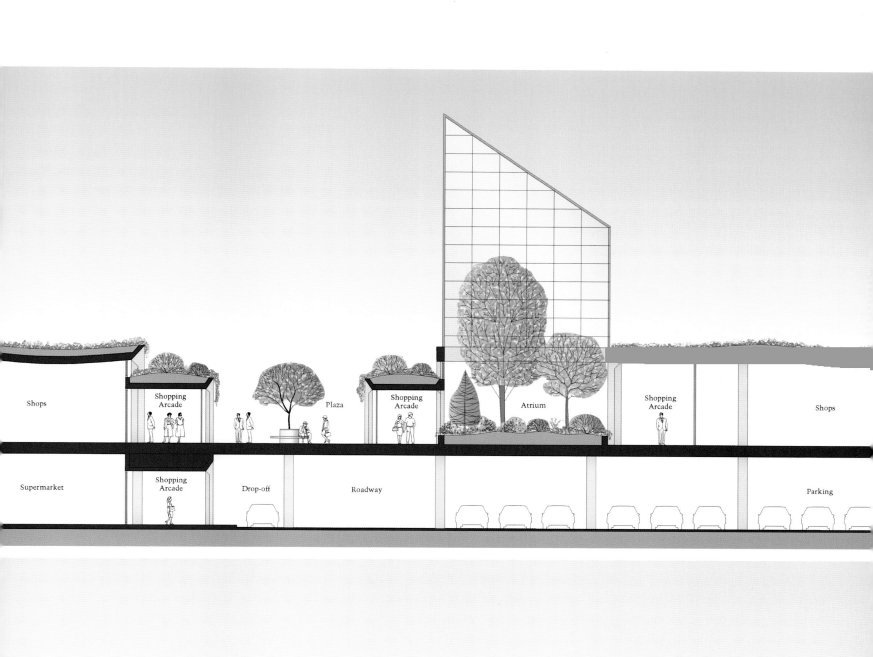

Shops

Shopping Arcade

Plaza

Shopping Arcade

Atrium

Shopping Arcade

Shops

Supermarket

Shopping Arcade

Drop-off

Roadway

Parking

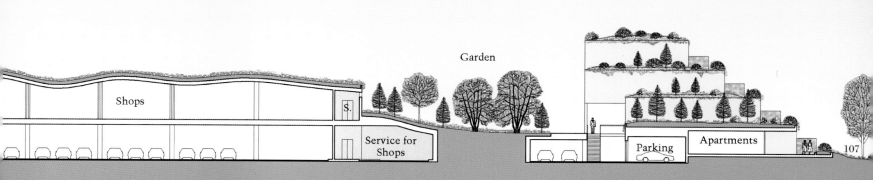

Shops

S.

Service for Shops

Garden

Parking

Apartments

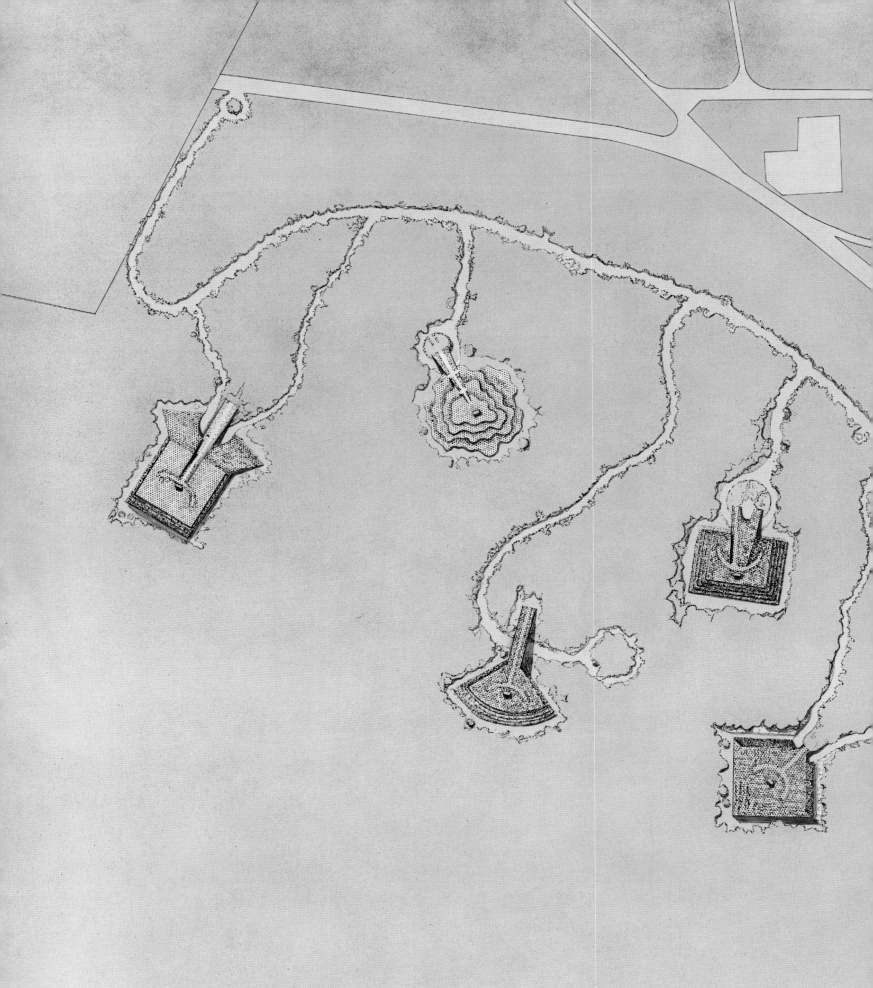

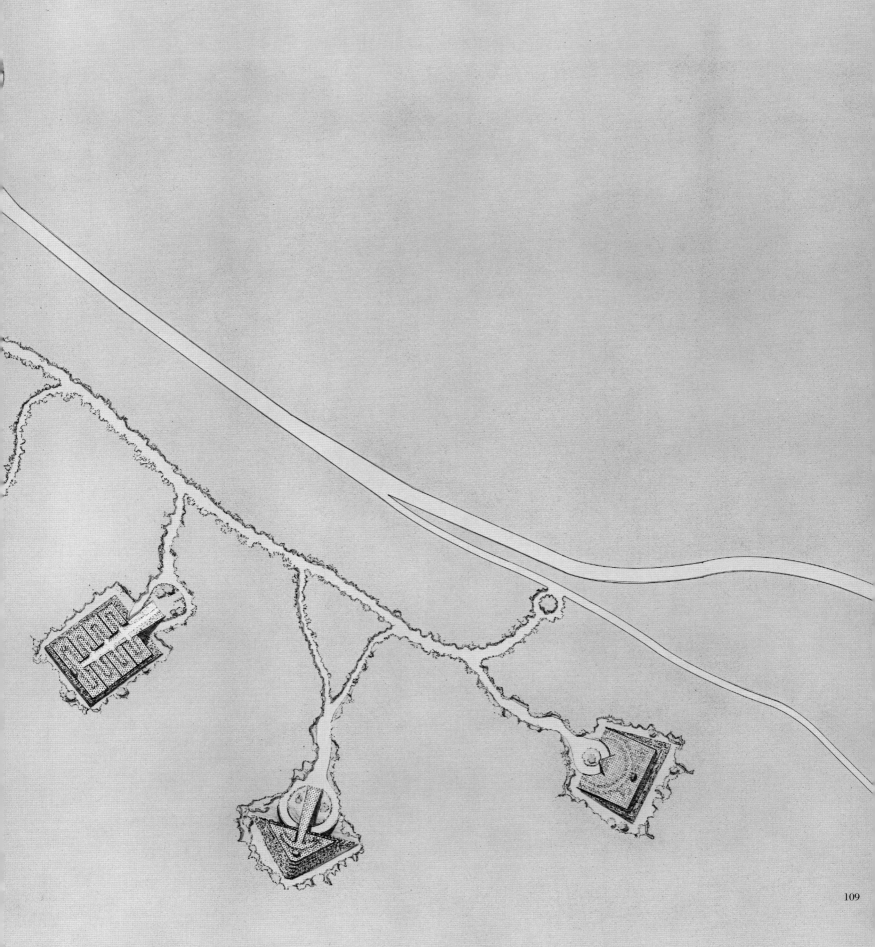

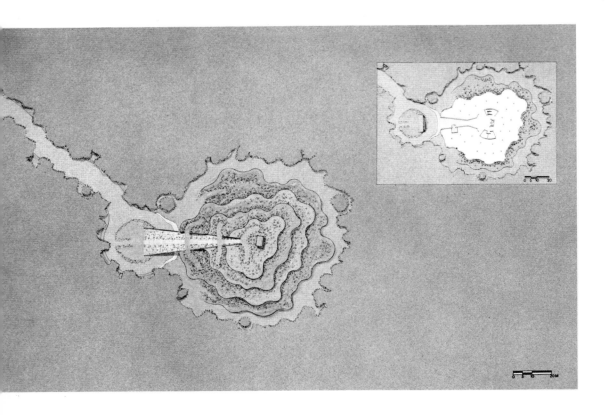

"La Venta is Ambasz's most synoptic project. It clarifies the stakes in twenty years' investment [...] The myth-making' that Ambasz has always seen as architecture's vocation arises, then, in the mythic moment of an historical threshold: the death of Nature and the emergence of its complex materiality. Or, perhaps, the death of Nature and the advent of the hybrid form: an architecture of the graft, a mutant in the age of genetic interventions, where the human hand is magisterial and the parterre everywhere."

A forest on the far outskirts of Mexico City, abandoned and gradually being destroyed by the continual deforestation of the surrounding wooded areas and the difficulty of growing new trees in the suffocating welter of old trees. The biological decay of trees, in fact, accelerates rapidly due to the impossibility of building new nurseries for replacement trees: this leads to a decline in the ability to remove nitrogen from the soil and a consequential pollution of the water tables.

The project, then, proposes a consolidation of the forest and a simultaneous development of a programme of settlement suit to obtaining new funds for the preservation of the environment and its improvement.

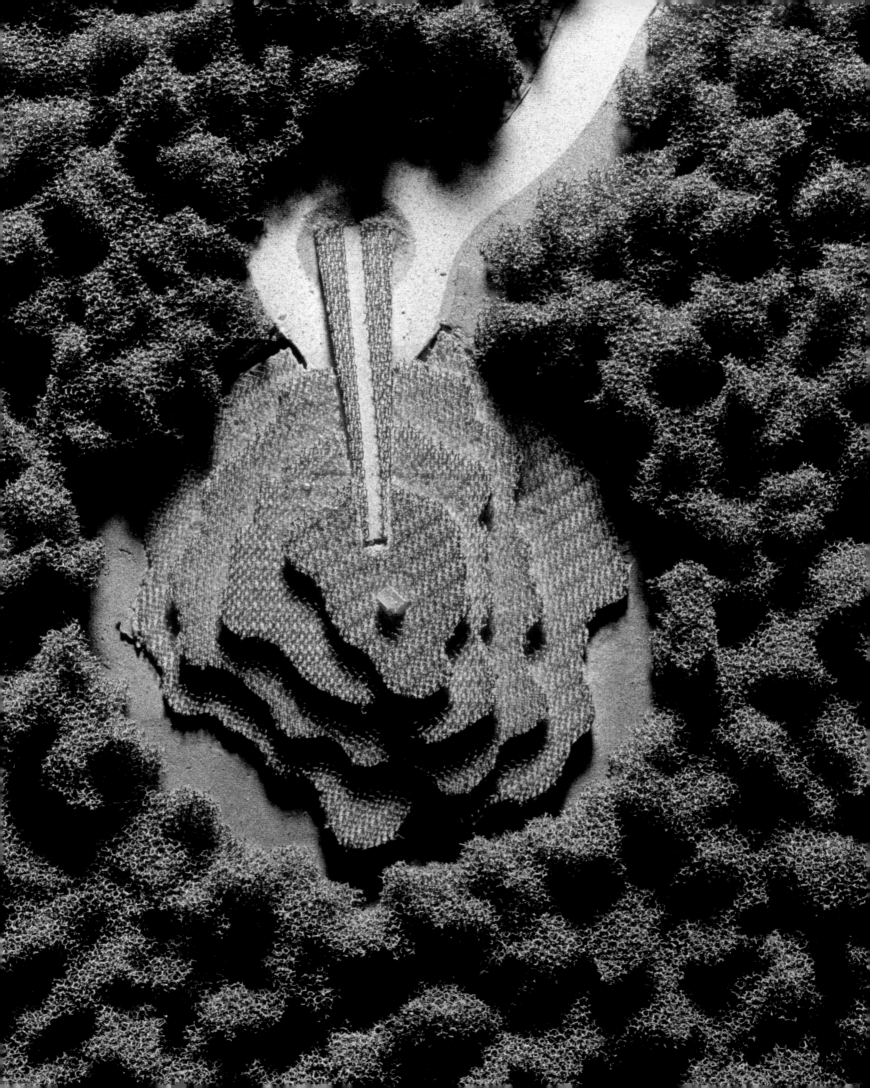

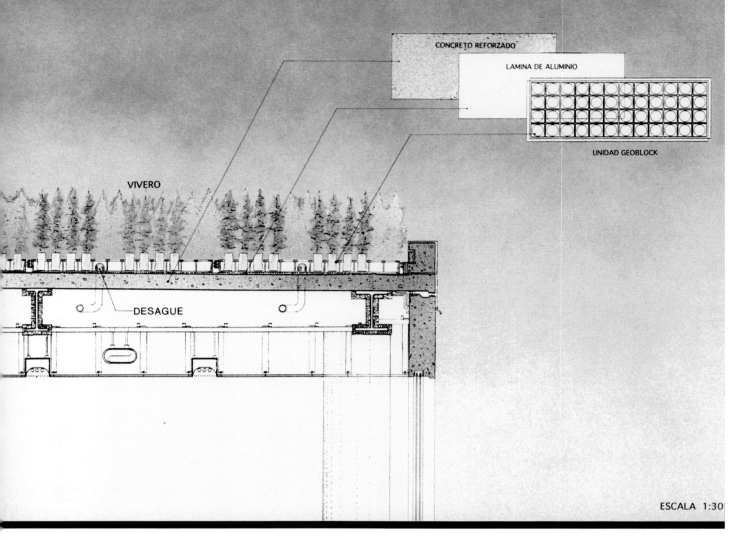

CONCRETO REFORZADO

LAMINA DE ALUMINIO

UNIDAD GEOBLOCK

VIVERO

DESAGUE

ESCALA 1:30

The design principle of the intervention consists of the creation of nurseries, arranged as stepped terraces: above are the plants, beneath are spaces for offices to be used as a source of revenue with which to maintain the area. The design of these office-nurseries varies in relation to the places, in keeping with a chart of compositions that includes the crystalline forms of the traditional geometry and the ameboidal forms of the natural organic accretions.

From this point of view, design can be considered as a didactic compendium of the resources of architecture and indicates an approach to the themes of landscape that possesses the value of a method.

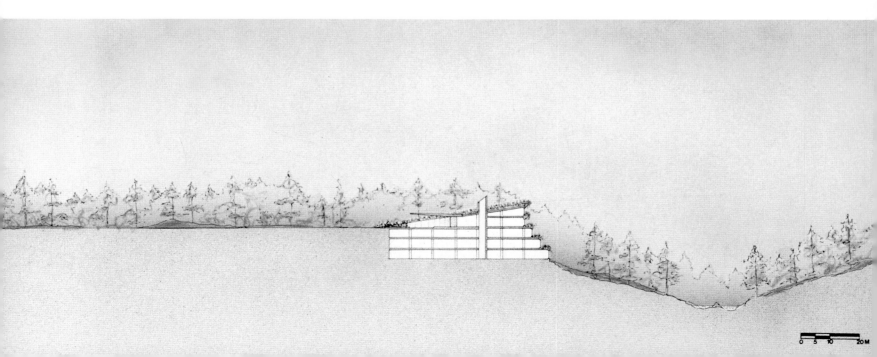

0 5 10   20M

On the plain just outside of the city of Castellaneta, Nuova Concordia is a vacation village that calls for residential structures and public structures for community life. Although it is articulated in individual units, its overall design establishes itself as the articulation of a total landscape, carving into the earth irregular crescents that almost confer upon the village the flavour of an archaeological site.

The constructions and the linking infrastructures present themselves, in fact, screened by trellises upon which the vegetation grows and protected by embankments that shape the ground with soft elevation lines. Enclosing the surface of a man-made lake, the individual villas form recognisable figures, arranged symmetrically with respect to the broken circle of the larger nucleus, where a hotel is planned.

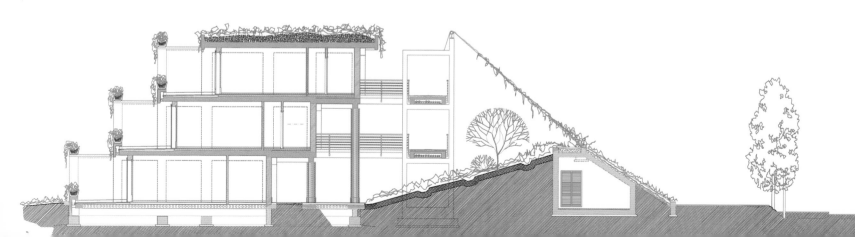

CONSTRUCTION 7-8-03

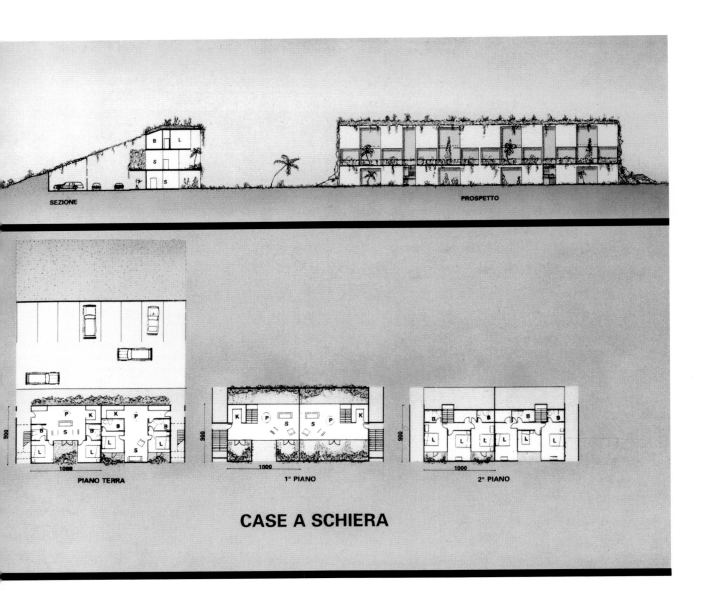

SEZIONE   PROSPETTO

PIANO TERRA   1° PIANO   2° PIANO

CASE A SCHIERA

Pedestrian bridges or a ferry service ensure connections with the shopping island, arranged in a semicircle beneath porticoes and shady galleries. Around the hotel are distributed houses and villas of various size and typology: like the strings of a broken necklace, they mark the progressive thinning out of the settlement toward the forest behind, in keeping with the principle of a progressive diminution of the heights so as to keep from obstructing the view of the landscape and minimise the environmental impact.

SITTING AREA

CORRIDOR

CLUB HOUSE

PATIO

GOLF CART STORAGE

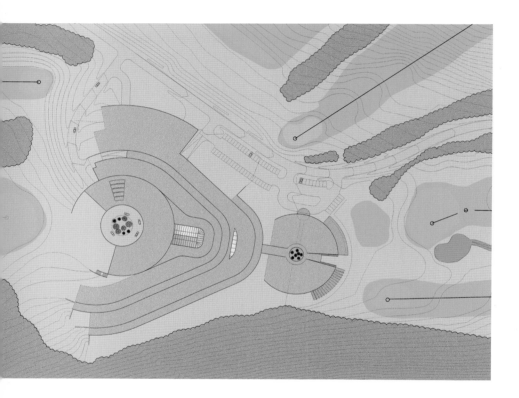

Winnisook Lodge is a 150-room hotel located on the slopes of Belleayre Mountain, in the Catskill State Park, in southern New York state. Taking advantage of the topography of the long crest, the imposing complex, covering some 6,900 sq. m., is articulated on five different levels, each of which interprets the gradient curves of the ground in such a way as to integrate organically with the environment. Complex, but at the same time compact in its recognisable figure, the new structure describes the ascending movement of uninterrupted terraces: on the higher plane, the entrance offers from the very outset the spectacular view of the mountainous landscape. Through a circular courtyard we reach the reception desk and the restaurants, while the atrium continues on the floor below to the banquet hall, the ballroom, and three conference rooms.

An open-air, five-story atrium links the lower floors, creating a protected point of view from which it is possible to enjoy artificial landscape of plants and waterfalls, recreated on the interior.

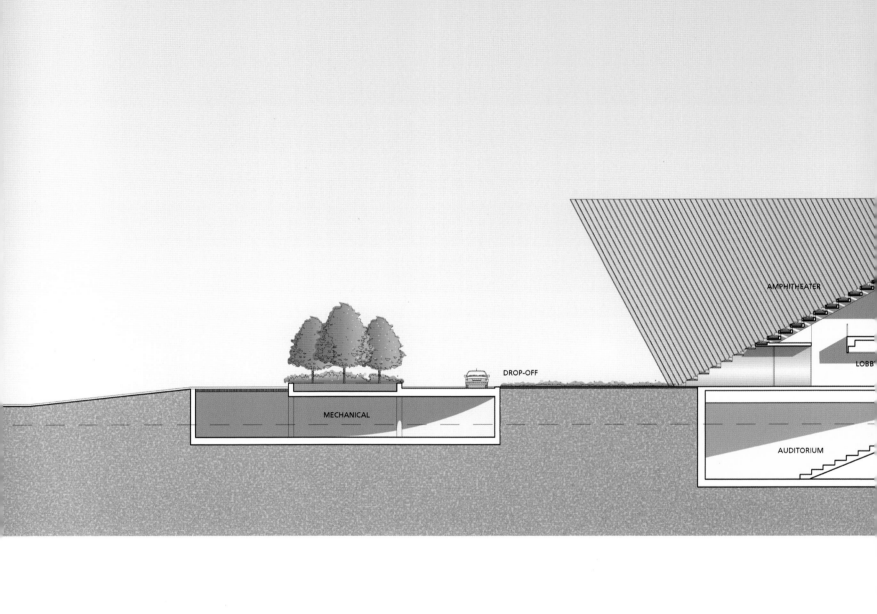

MECHANICAL

DROP-OFF

AMPHITHEATER

LOBB

AUDITORIUM

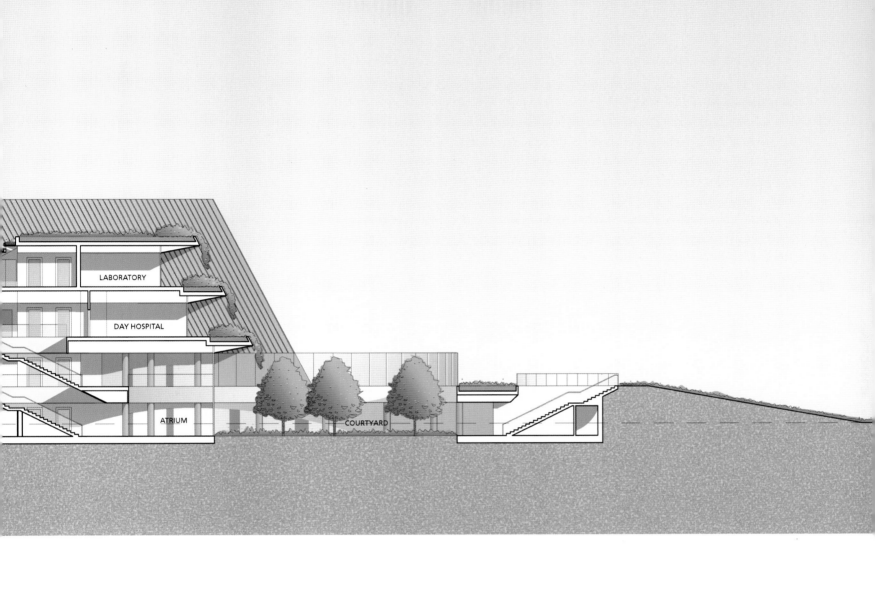

LABORATORY

DAY HOSPITAL

ATRIUM

COURTYARD

129

A 5,000 sq. m. complex will house the headquarters of Eidon, an advanced training and research centre in the field of oculistic medicine.

The layout is a triangle, two sides of which are formed by retaining walls 12 metres tall, clad in slabs of pre-patinaed copper, and the third by the terraced elevation of the three stories above ground. A metaphor for the eye, to the study of which the sophisticated research laboratory is dedicated, the tree-lined circular courtyard serves as a distribution element to the semicircle of lesson halls: the cut of a tall glass wall separates it from the large interior lobby.

The ritual of entry then calls for a theatrical approach to the complex reality of the building, which from the outside appears as hermetic as two closed eyebrows and only on the interior reveals the complex articulation of the setback planes which serve as an open-air amphitheatre.

The axial organisation of the entry routes, in fact, structures a path that runs from the narrow entrance corresponding to the summit of the triangle, expanding progressively toward the lobby and the tree-lined courtyard: through a parabolically shaped apertura it suddenly overlooks the surprise of the sharp rise of the stories set aside for administrative offices, the research laboratories, and the operating rooms of the day hospital.

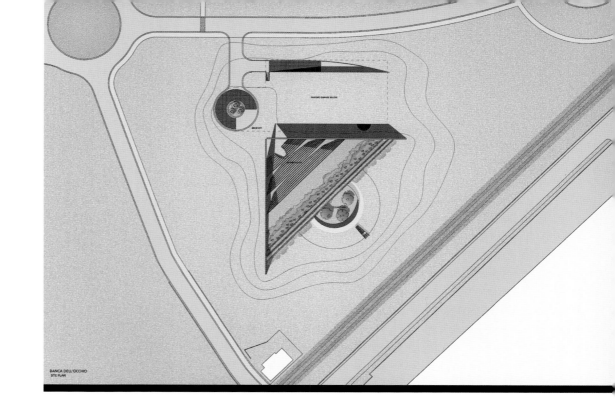

BANCA DELL'OCCHIO
SITE PLAN

building in the garden

If the garden, as M. Sorkin has written, is Emilio Ambasz's Aleph and the "biosphere of his infinite greatness of place"[1], then it is not hard to imagine the Argentine architect as a latter-day Paxton of the twentieth century. But, while the architect of the Crystal Palace summarised in the technological possibilities of the "greenhouse" construction the expectations of nineteenth-century positivism for a rational control of the world, the Argentine architect seems to attribute to it the role of the poetic iconography of his idea of "artificial nature".

A transparent display case for the creation of a climate-controlled and artificial environment, the greenhouse is the transparent refuge that serves as a counterweight to the penumbra of the grotto and the solid opacity of the underground: it is not, then, isolatable, as in the splendid glass flowerings of the nineteenth century, but an emerging element of a system of signs that – as in the Edmond de Rotshschild Memorial Museum at Ramat Hanadiv – includes the earth in order to achieve the effect of a total landscape. As Ettore Sottsass has noted, in fact, "in his architectural work there are almost never objects plainly resting on earth, as is usually the case in the more conventional architecture where buildings are just a statement, and that is all. Emilio's architectural creations are a bit outside the earth and a bit inside it. They are like stone slabs emerging from the earth, or fissures cracking the earth open, rather than attempts at controlling the universe by means of logic or agree upon signs. His is an architecture seeking, almost always, to represent the internal and eternal movement of an all encompassing planetary geology while at the same time respectfully reflecting local pulses, explosions, contractions, tempests, and deeply welled mysteries"[2]. Of this complex symbology, the Lucille Hansell Conservatory in San Antonio (1982) remains as of this writing the chief text and the generative matrix of a design family with multiple and sometimes paradoxical applications. In the hot, dry climate of southern Texas, for instance, the reliance on the greenhouse serves the function of protecting plants from the sun instead of exploiting the sun's heat and light: thus, the true element offering containment and protection of the plants is the earth, to which the variable glass prisms serve simply as covering. Depending on the study of the angle of the sun's rays, their forms vary, constituting once

[1] M. Sorkin, *Et in Arcadia Emilio*, in *Emilio Ambasz. The Poetics of the Pragmatic*, Rizzoli, New York 1988, p. 23.

[2] E. Sottsass, in *Emilio Ambasz. The Poetics of the Pragmatic*, Rizzoli, New York 1988, p. 9.

[3] E. Ambasz, unpublished typescript, replies to M. Sorkin, p. 13.

again a picturesque catalogue of geometries projecting upward as frozen fragments of a subterranean explosion. In this way, the project manages to confer upon the landscape the heartfelt and vaguely romantic tone of a picturesque garden: the gentle undulation of a meadow spangled with fragile open-air ruins, with the vegetation becoming an integral part of the construction, indeed inseparable from it, is the translation into a collective key of those obsessions expressed in *Emilio's Folly* in an autobiographical key. Vaguely anthropomorphic, the plan of the Lucille Hansell Conservatory gathers around the exposed belly of a patio – the eternal "canal of the sky" sung by Borges – a massive magnet that with its arches controls the controlled explosion of the greenhouses, attracting magnetically the verdant islands of the individual "places".

"Architecture is, for me, one aspect of our quest for cosmological models. Every one of my projects seeks to possess, at least, an attribute of the universe."[3]

Imagining the botanical gardens of San Antonio as a ceremonial path that runs over and under the level of the horizon, Ambasz all the same shows that he grasps the surreal value of the greenhouse as an expression of the desire for the marvellous in the culture of the nineteenth century: to dominate with technology the passage of time, optimise the power of the climate, gather in the expression of a virtual Arcadia all that in the real world presents itself as dispersed and fragmented; capture the pleasure, in other words, while eliminating the danger and the innate harshness of Nature.

Perhaps that is why the model of the greenhouse can be applied to apparently heterogeneous situations, as Joseph Paxton had sensed when he led its transition from the art of gardens to the gardens of goods and the desires of the masses. Under the transparent vaults of the thermal gardens of Sirmione, for instance, palm trees and high-branch trees can coexist with covered swimming pools, wedding the care of the body with the contemplation of nature. Apparently intact, the landscape of the peninsula toward Lake Garda presents itself to visitors as a pleasant garden, under whose grassy mantle lay hidden the wonders of the more refined culture of the senses, combining the benefits of nature's waters with those of the artificial cunning of man.

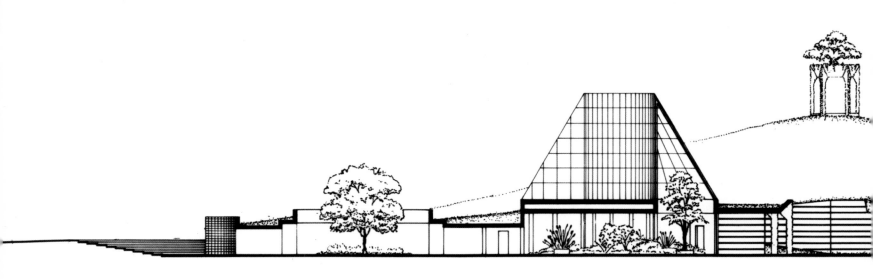

In contrast with traditional greenhouses, in this case the glass elements are simple roof structures for the earth containers and the transparent surfaces are raised to allow the arrangement of the taller plants. On the interior, a central patio, reminiscent of indigenous Mexican architecture, organises the various environments, allowing access to the greenhouses through the shadow of deep porticoes. In this way, the autonomy of the individual pavilions is assured, with their own specific requirements of space and climate control.

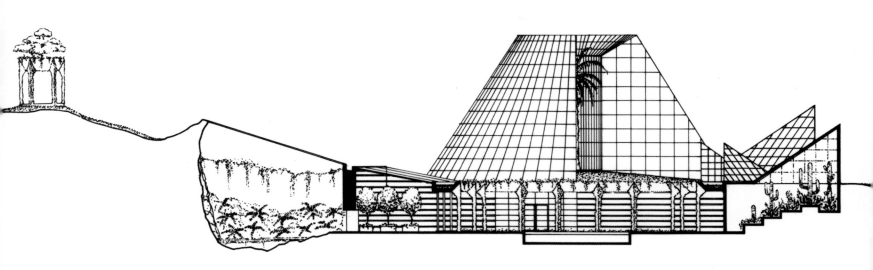

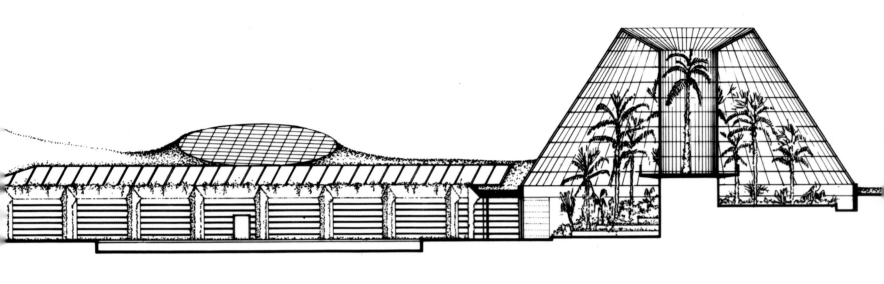

"*Emilio's architectural landscapes seem to be the remnants of a place an hour after the great cataclysm, or, perhaps, I should rather say, a thousand hours after the cataclysm; those thousand hours that will have given time to Nature to calm itself and to assume the density of silence. After a thousand hours, man, or perhaps, technological superman, will have arrived to create order, to restructure some form of physical and mental survival; after such time, after thousand hours, he may start to build a stairway leading who knows where, and to construct, here and there, some more or less useful arcade, some far away monument, some isolated little temple, and a few greenhouses to protect those last trees, those that have not been burned by the fires of the lava.*"

Ettore Sottsass, 1988

The Lucille Halsell Conservatory is a complex of green-houses on the interior of the botanical garden of San Antonio, a large park set up on the outskirts of the second-largest city in Texas, with areas for entertainment and strolling that include, aside from the landscape amenities, zones set aside for presentations on native art and architecture.

In order to protect the vegetation from the intense heat, the plants are located underground and the only elements visible from the exterior are the high-tech skylights with different geometric shapes that overlay the "natural" landscape of the greenhouses beneath with the skeletal skyline of surreal presences with a vaguely archaeological flavour. Used as a containing element, the earth lowers the maintenance costs of the technological facilities, utilising the natural resources to isolate the constructions and control the temperature by reducing to a considerable degree the quantity of sunlight.

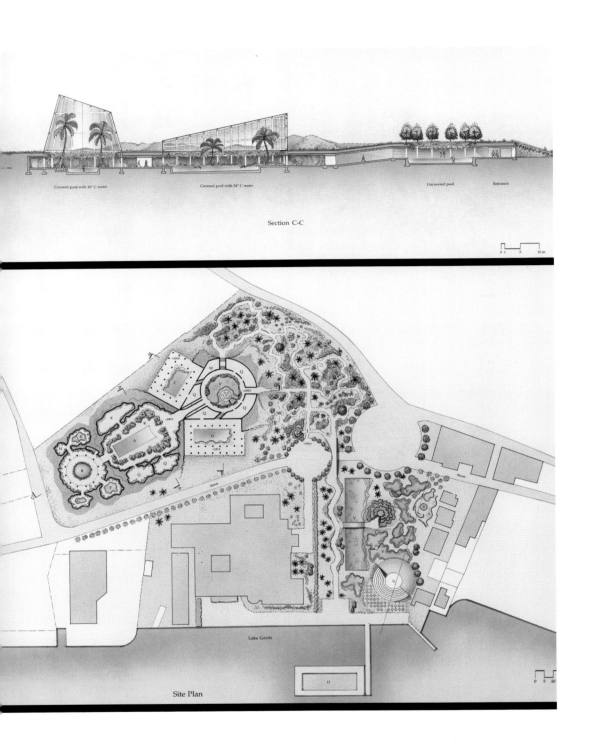

Covered pool with 16° C water   Covered pool with 34° C water   Uncovered pool   Entrance

Section C-C

0 1   5   10 m

Lake Garda

Site Plan

0   5   10

The project calls for the construction of new thermal services for 1,500 persons in an environment subject to strict urbanistic restrictions: in order to fit harmoniously into the natural landscape, the thermal pools, the dressing rooms, and the related facilities are lodged in embankments that redesign the line of the ground with a light and active progress. The two covered pools are emphasized by the geometric silhouettes of transparent greenhouses that seem barely perched on the ground, while the open-air pools, for physical therapy, are protected by a pergola, the hollow columns of which contain the roots of the olive trees planted on the roof. A complex architecture of paths develops, then, beneath the horizon line, configuring a compact and symmetrical organism, laid out along its own longitudinal axis like the wings of a butterfly.

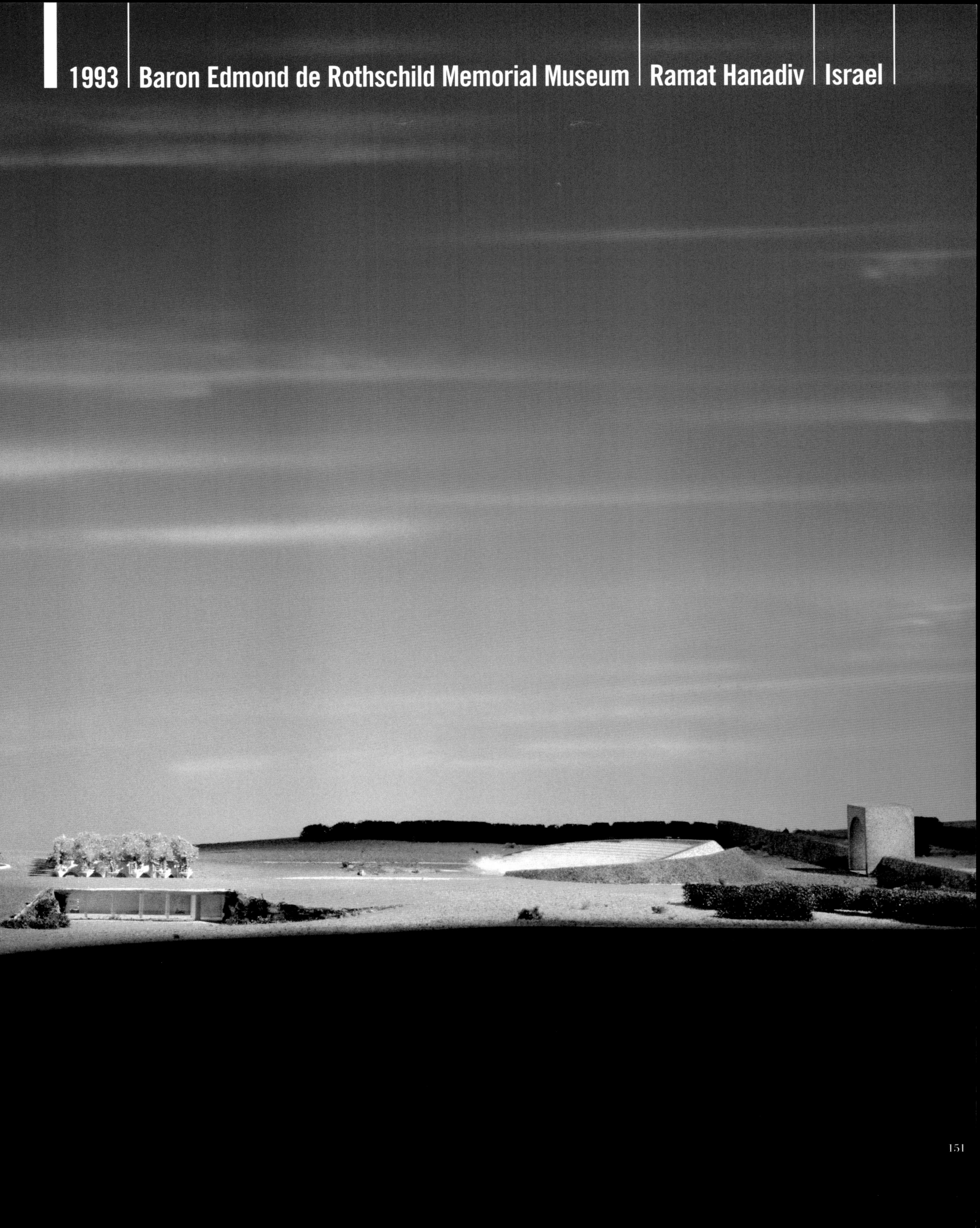

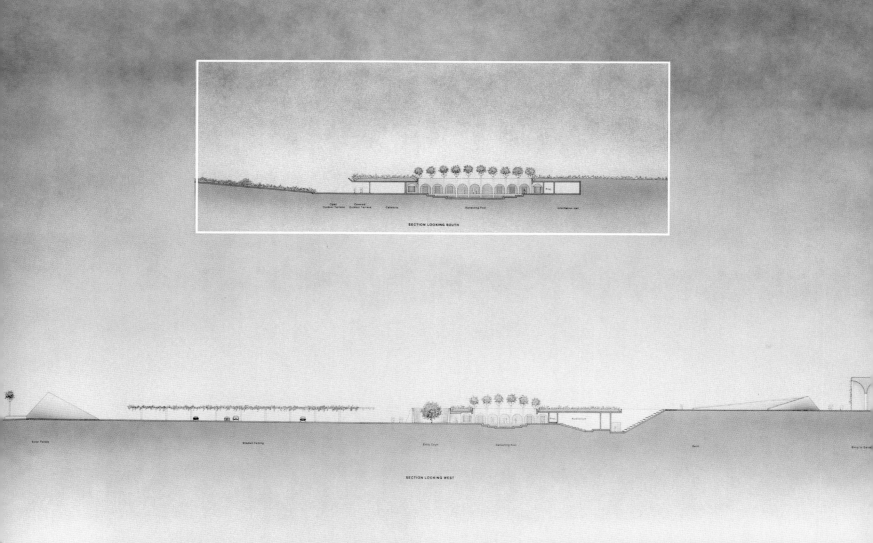

Aside from being a tribute to the founding father of Israel, the Memorial Museum is a sign of hope in the possibilities of dialogue and faith in the values of coexistence. It is inspired, in fact, by the Eastern tradition of the shadow garden, preparing for the visitors attracted by the reputation of the existing European-style gardens a ritual path of access, which exalts the awareness through the sense and invites one to the eloquence of silence in the peace of nature.

Two sloping embankments identify the entrance to the parking areas, concealed beneath the gridwork of two pergolas: on the other side of the axis, a monumental gate offers access to visitors moving toward the first courtyard where a flowering tree recalls the remarkable commitment of the founding father of Israel to render fertile and productive the arid soil. A portico arranged along the sides of a courtyard surrounds an open-air pool, while olive trees project from the sunken column area.

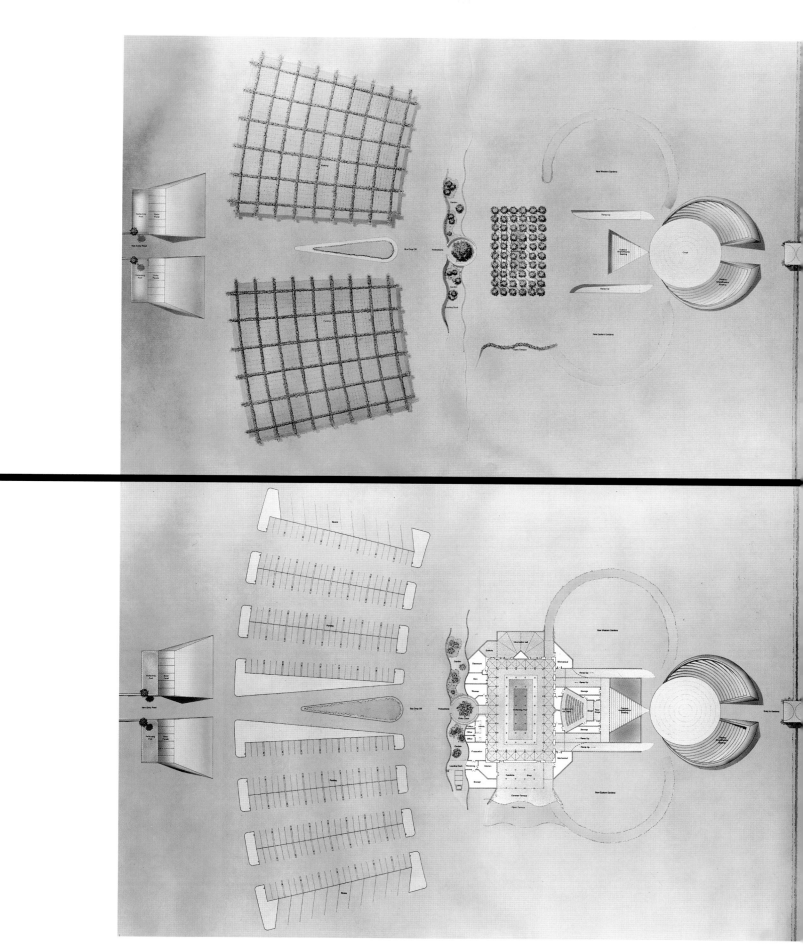

urban gardens

"The garden is the smallest particle of the world and it is also the totality of the world. The garden represents, from the earliest antiquity, a sort of happy heterotopy."[1]

The opposites of the non-places of utopias, the counter-places of the heterotopias described by Foucault mark the reality of a space where all the other places of real life "are at the same time represented, contested, and subverted".

To introduce a garden into the stone order of a historic city, as Ambasz suggests for the Plaza Mayor of Salamanca, is a manifesto of a contradiction that can only be resolved through a poetic gesture of reconciliation. To break down the perfect geometry of the square into a series of converging terraced steps in the protected, tree-lined space of a sunken courtyard, entails in fact the creation of an "other" place that interacts with the stone hierarchy of the façades of Churriguera, opening a surreal window on the blessed site of Nature.

It is no accident that the "metaphorical" value of the project allows its application to various contexts, all focused on the artificial nature of the urban landscape. One example is the Houston Center Plaza, opened in the perfect gridwork that constitutes the matrix of the city, of which it emphasises and contextualises at the same time the historic characteristics linked to the regularity and density of the blocks built.

In both projects, the functions of urban life are relegated beneath the earth, in the ample spaces dug out beneath the street level, while the presence of water and the very evident reliance on the topiary art take the roles of a marked vindication of a sensory dimension in the perception of the city.

And yet Ambasz refuses to consider himself the romantic heir to an arcadian, antiurban vision, harking back to the testimony of history: "To this day, you can go up to the top of the towers of a medieval city like Bologna, and discover that behind the

[1] M. Foucault, *Le langage de l'espace*, "Critique", No. 203, April 1964, p. 28.

[2] E. Ambasz, unpublished typescript, reply to M. Sorkin, p. 17.

[3] L. Sedofsky, *Peripheral Vision (Emilio Ambasz: Special Issue)*, in "Korean Architects", 131, July 1995, pp. 12-33.

facades defining treeless streets exist immense gardens which occupy almost 35% of the city area. Those were once vegetables gardens and places where cows grazed. Those were of outmost importance to survive a siege [...] I strive for an urban future where you can open your door and walk out directly on a garden, regardless of how high your apartment may be"[2].

As Lauren Sedofsky wrote, in reality, "in Ambasz's case, the urban/non urban distinction seems null and void. His paradigm is a prototype developed, not in the country, but in total isolation, a pure laboratory product"[3]. In any case, close to Robert Smithson's "land reclamation", his expectation of an elegiac and blessed Arcadia does not attempt to negate the reality of what exists, but only to justify the emphasis of the material idea of earth.

This aspect seems to be focused on with special care in his more recent projects which involve the transformation of strategic sectors of a city. In particular, the project of the Eschenheimer Tower in Frankfurt, to resolve the problem of traffic along the nineteenth-century circuit of the Ringstrasse, develops a solution of covering the road through the modulation of the street level: a man-made hill serves as a pedestrian bridge and joins in an organic system of greenery the park areas and the pre-existing gardens. This makes it possible to define an approach that tends to overcome the separation of the isolated object in favour of promoting fluid solutions capable of redesigning the diagrams of flows in the logic of a "green urbanism". By acting on the levels of the artificial ground, the rationalist notion of the "grid" once again acquires a reasonable and vital significance as the spinal cord of a reconnection that utilises in an extensive manner both biotechnologies and natural resources. It is no accident that the proposal for residential and commercial development along the Catharijnenbaan of Utrecht should appear to be an appropriate homage to the country that has done the most in the past decades to develop an innovative conception of the landscape as a technological Arcadia built by man.

Square and open, the Plaza Mayor of Salamanca is an island of geometric rationality in an historic centre that has a dense and irregular fabric. Defined on four sides by the splendid Baroque façades by Churriguera, the plaza establishes a magnificent but not particularly comfortable urban space that, while making enjoyable the shady path along the porticos, does not permit an equally enjoyable moment of rest and halting. The proposal calls for making a transformation of the stone square into a soft green surface: a series of concentric stairways converge downward, where a smaller plaza serves as the roof of a ballroom illuminated from above. Above, then, the location for a pause and relaxation under the shadowy vault of the trees, below the new leisure facilities, from movie theatre to gyms and offices. An air chamber between the steps and the spaces below holds fresh air in such a way as to allow the natural cooling of the plaza in the summer. In the winter, instead, with all the leaves on the ground, the sun heats the stone steps, storing a helpful heat.

Developing a strategy for environmental intervention comparable to that used for the beachfront of Rimini or the tourist centre of Castellaneta, the project for the Marina di Bellaria can be summarised, to synthesise to an extreme degree, as the development of a "hanging" meadow, a portion of earth's crust raised to house beneath it all those functions that are vital to its programme for use. Restaurants, parking areas, docking facilities for the boats are all located here, dictating the irregular form of this green curtain that joins the city with the waterfront.

1982 | Houston Center Plaza | Houston | Texas | USA

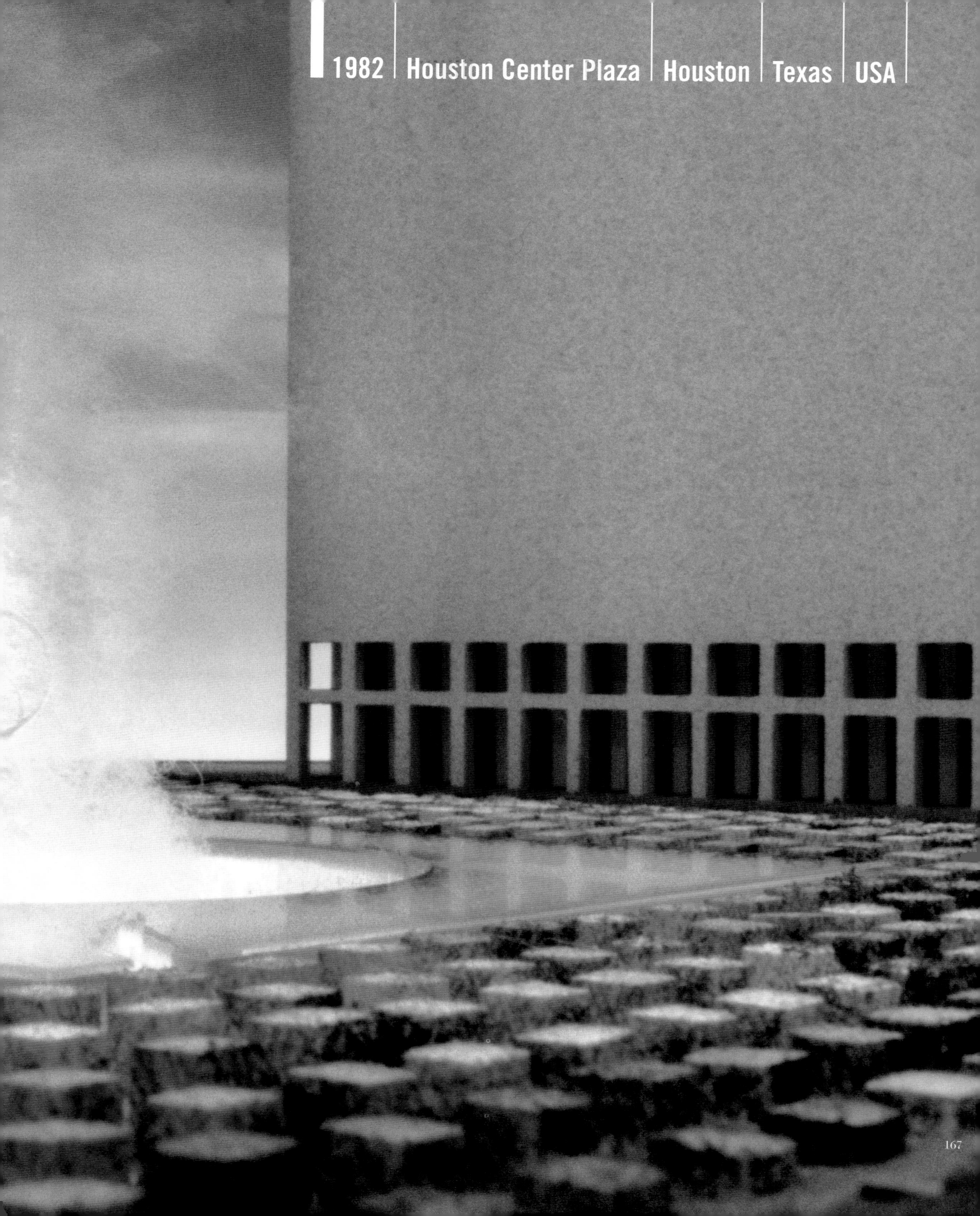

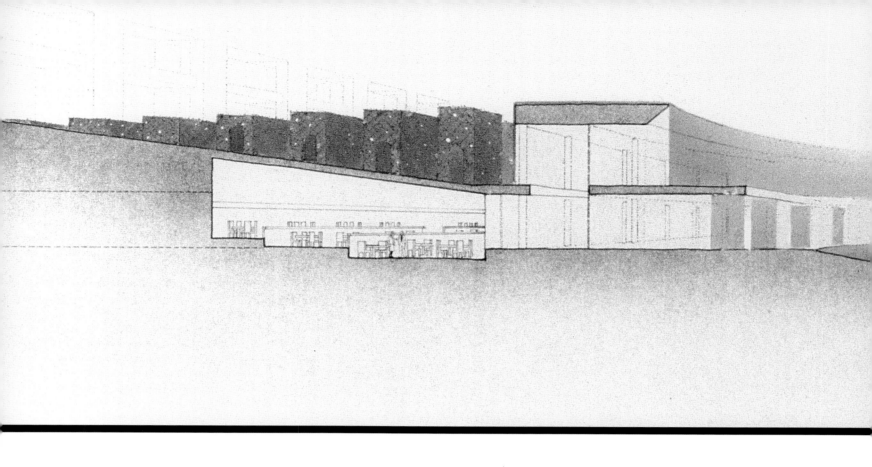

"*Sometimes from his architecture come vapors, and, sometimes, we can imagine it as if it were wrapped or covered by clouds or mist that make it appear and disappear, like the countries of the world as seen from satellite. There is non architectural project Emilio has designed that is without water nearby, without wells, without lakes or without rivers.*"
Ettore Sottsass, 1988.

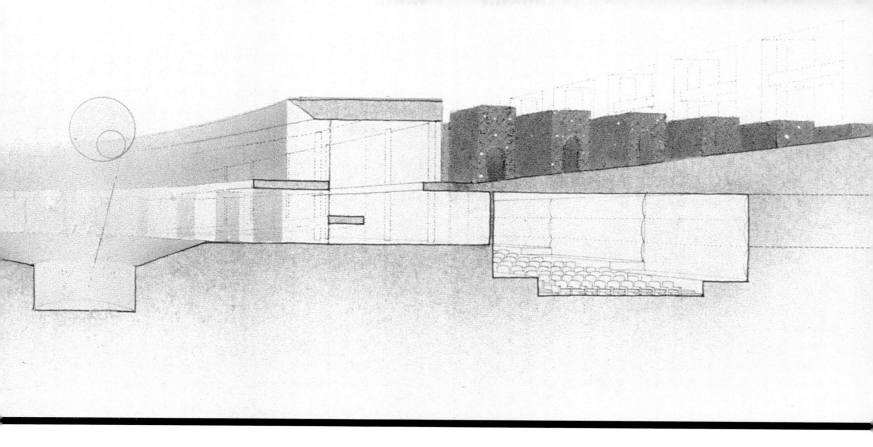

The plaza forms part of a typical block in the urban layout of Houston, which it proposes to symbolise, both physically and metaphorically. The grid is the most evident characteristic of the city: it reappears in the miniaturised design of the plaza and synthesises its purity and indeterminacy linked to the democratic dimension of American urbanistics. Theatre of urban memory, the plaza reflects its metropolitan spirit in the various aspects of its organisation: the city of culture in the theatres and the galleries; the city of shopping in the stores.

The external part of the plaza consists of a series of vine-covered trellises, which rise in correspondence to the nodes of the gridwork: the level of the soil is slightly inclined, so that it converges below toward a square pool of water with a circular aperture that establishes the comparison between the city of shadow and the city of light. The water drops in cascades along the edge of the square, running down toward the atrium beneath, which serves as a plaza of the underground city of services: utilised for cooling and for the maintenance of the garden, the water returns to the city in the form of a cloud of mist upon which a laser projection designs shifting figures.

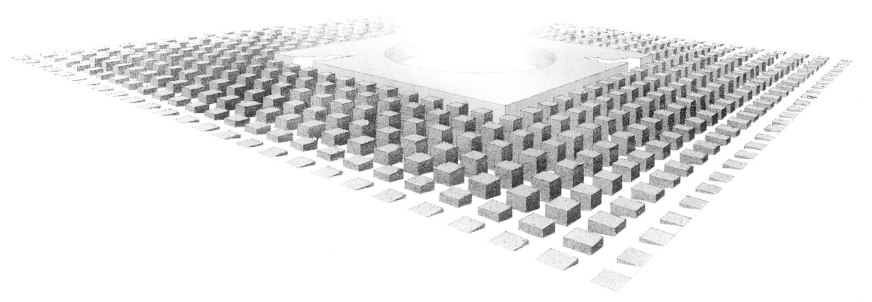

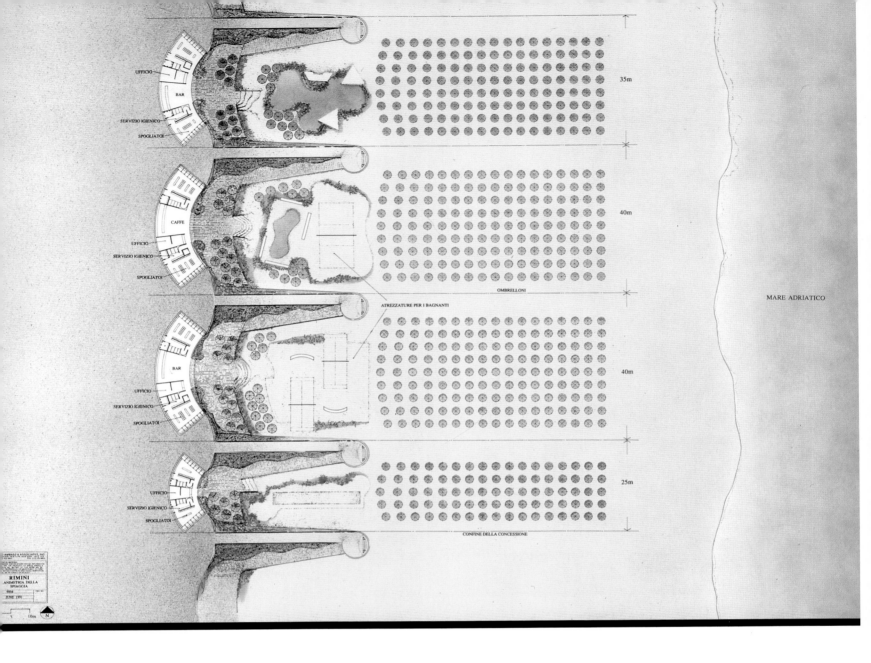

The project called for the treatment of 14 kilometres of beach front by the creation of a shaded promenade running along the sandy water-front, offering an elegant cornice to all the usual furnishings of a seaside resort. A raised walkway constitutes the backbone of a linear park punctuated by pools, bars, and cafés open all year long. In the lower part facing the sea are stored the various sorts of equipment for life on the beach, configuring the regular pattern of protected enclosures in which the beach umbrellas can be arranged all around irregular bodies of water. Certain streets of the city centre extend into the sea through the extension of moles/piers from which floating platforms can set out to take the sun, increasing the availability of concession spaces.

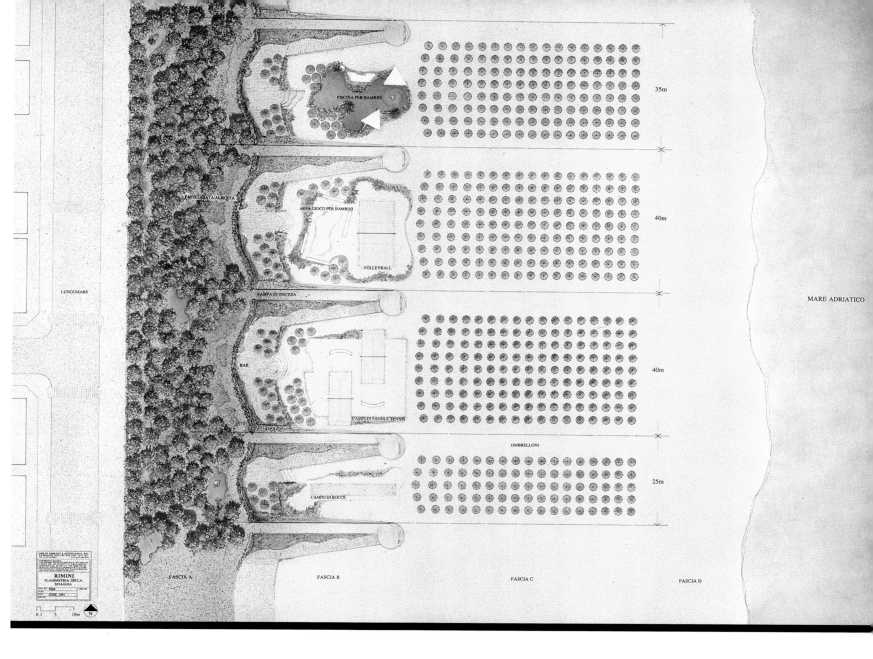

LUNGOMARE

MARE ADRIATICO

PISCINA PER BAMBINI

35m

PASSEGGIATA ALBERTA

AREA GIOCO PER BAMBINI

VOLLEYBALL

40m

RAMPA IN DISCESA

BAR

40m

CAMPI DI PADDLE TENNIS

OMBRELLONI

CAMPO DI BOCCE

25m

RIMINI
PLANIMETRIA DELLA
SPIAGGIA

JUNE 1991

0 1   5   10m   N

FASCIA A   FASCIA B   FASCIA C   FASCIA D

173

CONDIZIONE ESISTENTE DELLA SPIAGGIA

SCHEMA DELLA PROPOSTA

The city of Frankfurt was pushing for a solution that would take into consideration the possibility of a link between the old city gate — the Eschenheimer Tower — and the nearby pedestrian area, making use of the existing Schillerstrasse. The proposal wound up winning the competition because, aside from meeting the requirements of the request, it advanced a radical urbanistic solution to the chronic problem of traffic on the nineteenth century ring road known as the Ringstrasse. The proposal called for the encapsulation of the street under a vaulted covering that, once covered with earth, would appear as a hill and, at the same time, a pedestrian bridge. Extended along the entire surrounding perimeter, these bridges could enclose the city in a pleasant greenbelt, thus giving origin to a linear park that would redesign in an efficacious manner the urban perimeter of the original urban centre.

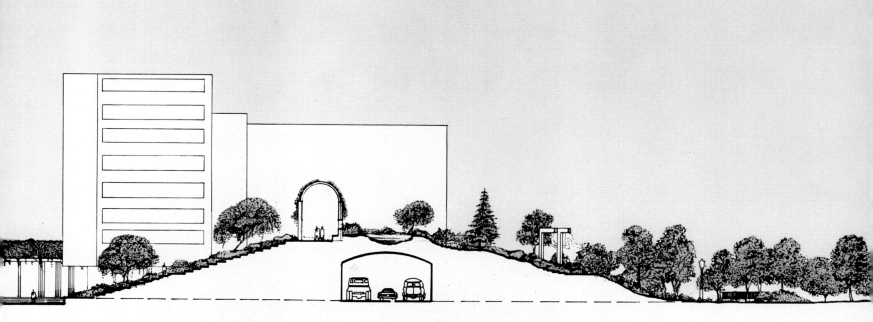

Sommer

184

Because of its extensive surrounding forests, Hilversum is known in Holland as a "green city": to that reputation the work of Willem Marinus Dudok — who worked there as the director of public works during the first decades of the twentieth century, building there some of his best known masterpieces — has added the reputation of a city sensitive to environmental quality and the elegance of its public buildings. The design for a new office complex to be built in one of the last remaining green areas available to the town government set out from these presuppositions to relaunch the theme of an integral landscape in which architecture and greenery might appear to be fused in an organic unity. As in the project for La Venta, the three blocks of spaces for offices form a terraced hillside layout, cut by a narrow glass wall that follows the track of the old hippodrome: rustic wooden pillars seem to support the slightly inclined slab so as to determine upon the ground a pedestrian passageway that links the three complexes and, running over the road, allows it to be crossed at elevation.

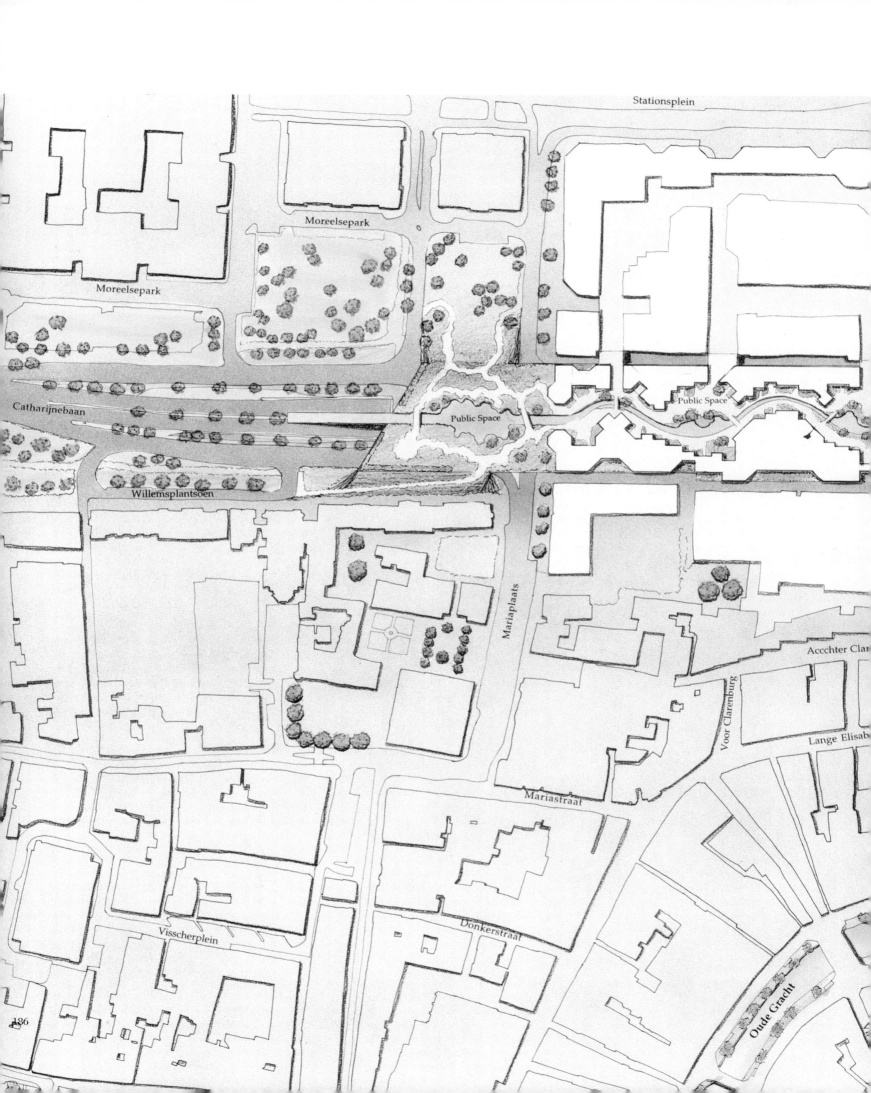

Stationsplein

Moreelsepark

Moreelsepark

Catharijnebaan

Public Space

Public Space

Willemsplantsoen

Mariaplaats

Acchter Clar

Voor Clarenburg

Lange Elisab

Mariastraat

Visscherplein

Donkerstraat

Oude Gracht

186

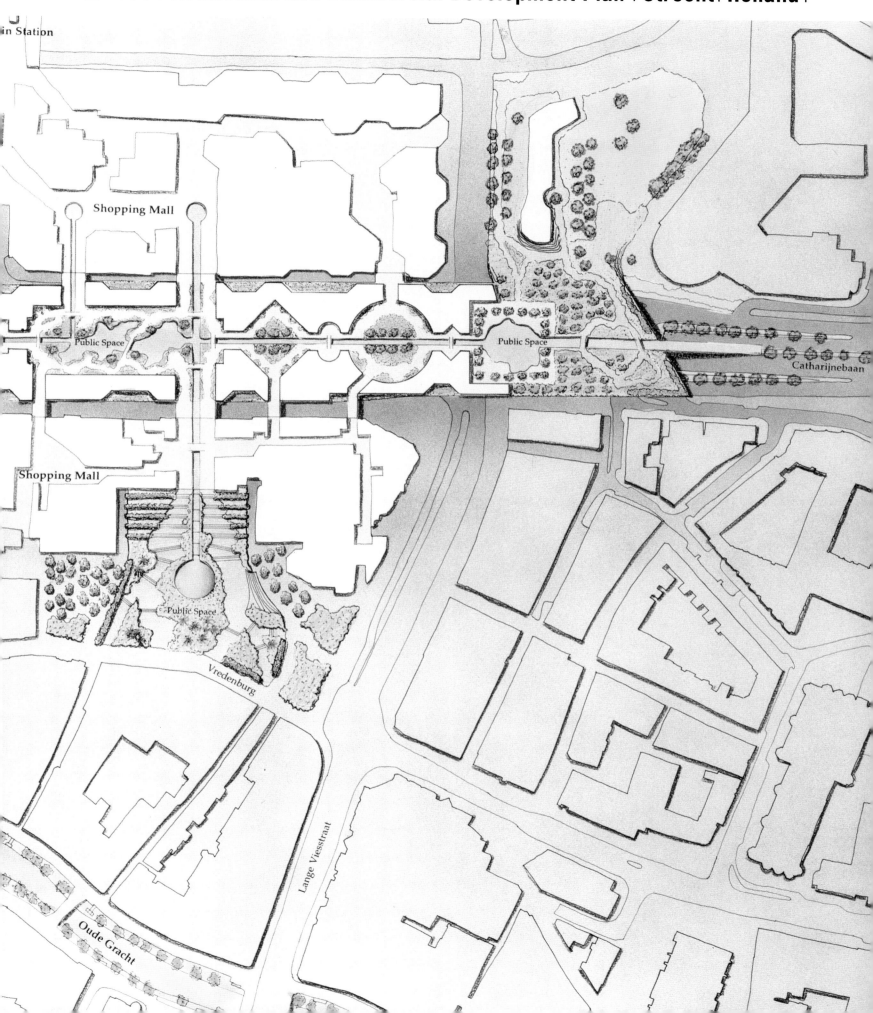

in Station

Shopping Mall

Public Space

Public Space

Catharijnebaan

Shopping Mall

Public Space

Vredenburg

Lange Viesstraat

Oude Gracht

The Catharijnensingel, in the heart of Utrecht, is one of the most durable symbols of the city's medieval identity; it is subjected to a strong daily pressure from the uncontrolled traffic of the astonishing commercial expansion. The canal still serves in part as a barrier between the traditional scene of the urban setting and the modern metropolitan expansion: in one point, all the same, the canal was filled in to make room for a highway and the consequential compression of the new buildings constitutes a visible laceration in the original continuity of the urban fabric.

The project proposes to heal this laceration by creating a platform raised 5 metres over the channel of traffic below, so as to create a hanging garden pensile that reshapes the section of street, housing it in a modern canal, redesigning the outlines with new structures with descending terraces. Covered with vegetation, the built edges of this "green" canal restore the crowded stratification of the urban scene, recomposing the demands of modernisation and those of the preservation of urban memory. The project calls for various stages of development, with the possible construction of a second platform above the rails of the station and a third platform with residences and collective facilities to hook with the playing fields of the Jaarbeurs.

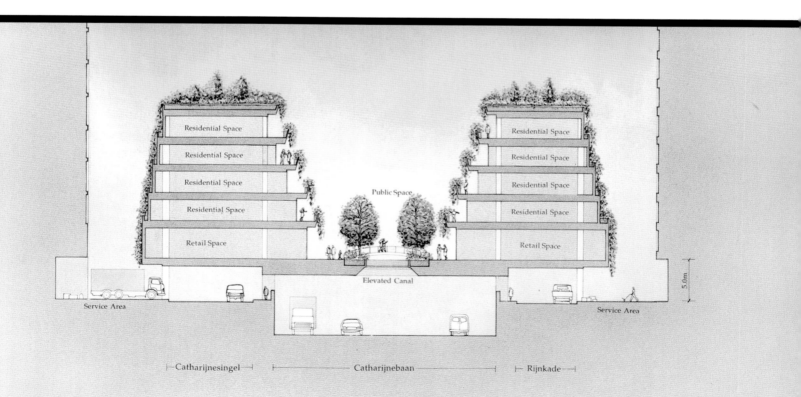

Proposed Condition 1
Section

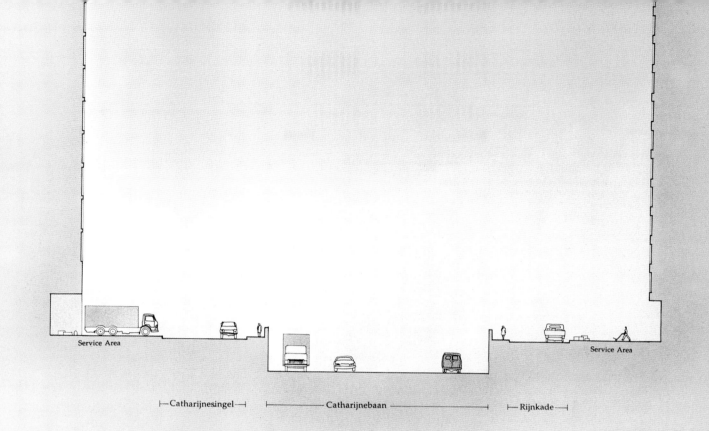

Existing Condition
Section

├─ Catharijnesingel ─┤ ├───── Catharijnebaan ─────┤ ├─ Rijnkade ─┤

0   5   10m

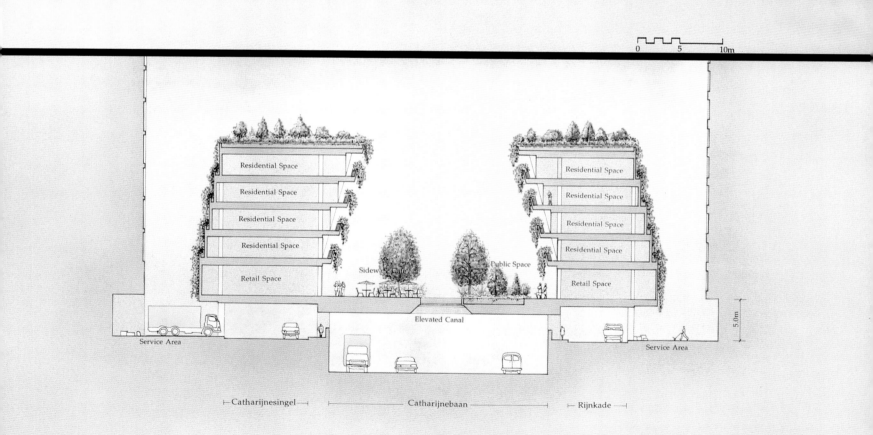

Proposed Condition 2
Section

├─ Catharijnesingel ─┤ ├───── Catharijnebaan ─────┤ ├─ Rijnkade ─┤

domestic gardens

"You always have the sense that behind the walls of these projects are absent presences or present absences. The notion of that which is in front of you and what happens behind the walls has always appealed to me. There is a certain anima or spirit behind the wall" (E. Ambasz).

The theme of the original home, the dream of the "house of Adam", the search for what preceded the rise of built forms, all return, in the wake of a millennial-old tradition, to occupy a central position in Ambasz's research, in his "metaphysical" concern with returning to the "origin" of things.

With its extreme reduction to those few elements in which the drama of the architecture that celebrates its liturgy is reflected, the Casa de Retiro Espiritual near Seville, Spain, has the absolute value of a manifesto: the house as "abode", in fact, is the poetic response to the rooted intimacy of the space: Ambasz emphasises that it "is not an answer to the pragmatic needs of man (that is, the task of building), but a response to his passion, his imagination".

Two walls at right angles announce from a distance the invisible presence of the house; two steep stairways join up high in the belvedere for meditation; two streams run down along channels in the walls, meeting in the centre of the patio in a semicircular basin.

The architecture is reduced to a pure "simulacrum" and the earth emerges as a protagonist in the serene void of the patio. Rejecting a static representation of

[1] G. Durand, *Les structures antropologiques de l'Immaginarie*, Paris 1960.

space, Ambasz conceives the house as a voyage on the interior of the habitat, a venturing into the mystery of what lies behind the wall: "the axis of the descent – as Durand recalls – is an intimate, fragile, delicate axis […], you descend to ascend (in time) and rediscover the peace that precedes birth"[1].

In the triangular patio the narrative of the descent is stripped of its drama and a filter is established between the exterior reduced to a mask and the reconquered dimension of habitation. Eternal return, ritual of the beginning; nothing monumental on the interior of the house: an irregular and organic space that is articulated by sudden recesses and unexpected jutting projection that mark off the places where the members of the domestic community celebrate the daily rites of existence. A diffuse light pours down from the serpentine skylights that transmit to the interior the cyclical passage of the seasons, curved walls move forward and back, like membranes, opening out to reveal hidden receptacles. Restored to the pure condition of landscape, the Manoir d'Angoussart is like a still life of geometries made up of earth, the image of a field with changing perspectives: an ivy façade greets the visitor as the last goal of a dissemination of mute volumes, solid embankments. Set in a gorge, this house is entirely built in the earth: grass, plants, and ground features are its introduction and ornament, while the house and the garden are fused in a single entity.

Swallowed up by the landscape, the house in Montana also emerges reluctantly from the grassy plane with the scaffolding of a detached façade: a picturesque garden simulates the primary scene of an American Arcadia. Marked by the rustic order of the wooden columns, the rustic "cabin" of the refine art lover who will live in it is the first element of a complex of three "follies", destined for the family, the watchman, and to house an art gallery.

194

As in Baroque architecture or in the wooden buildings of the traditional historic city of the American West, the façades extend over the construction itself, masking the volume behind. Partially covered by ivy-lined trellises, the façades seem to be held up by a colonnade of leaning "poles", ironically allusive to the mythical origins of the ancient orders and the wooden prototype of the Greek temple. Atop each pole, a golden capital joins with the spectacular cornice on top that functions as an elongated mirror to reflect the sunlight and increase its effects on the surfaces of the façades.

Articulated in three distinct units — the watchman's house, the museum, and the master villa — distributed over a site of 1,400 sq. m., the residential complex enjoys a view of a valley cut by a river, with the charming surrounding of large expanses of woods in a landscape with strongly mountainous features. The "rustic" order of the façade with the wooden columns made from fallen tree trunks refers, in fact, immediately to the special nature of the area.

The deployment of the various episodes is functional to the construction of a landscape perceptible especially through movement. Thus, for instance, the concave curve of the main residence describes a rural *cour d'honneur*, and is echoed, in contrast, from the convex curve of the art gallery, reachable only on foot, like an eighteenth-century "follie" in the gracious setting of a meadow.

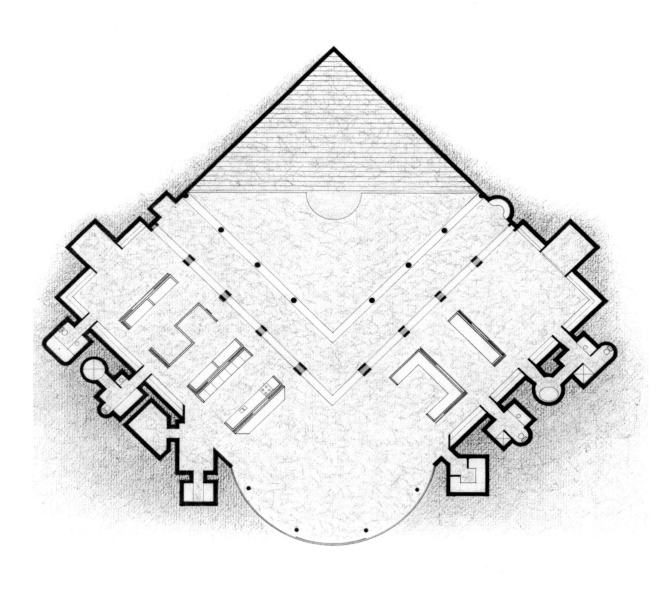

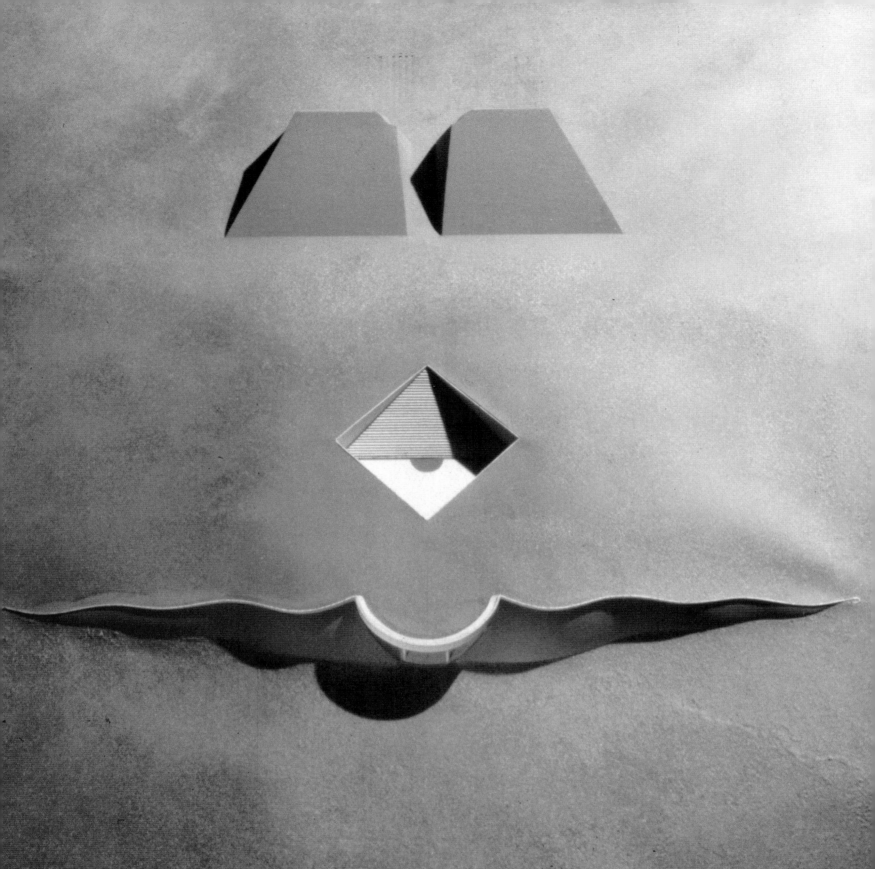

Two massive embankments equipped with solar panels mark off the entrance to the house, lining the axis of access to the sunken courtyard overlooked by the rooms. A staircase divides the triangle of descent from that of resting, which provides the residence with a sheltered patio below the ground level. A careful study of the ventilation has made it unnecessary to rely upon air conditioning systems, increasing the use of passive solar systems and allowing a reduction of more than 70 percent in the normal energy consumption. The large windows along the southern façade capture the sun's rays and the house's thick walls store and distribute them to the rest of the residence. The plan of the house is conceived in keeping with a flexible scheme of use for the interior organisation and, in the angle opposite to that of the patio, a porticoed courtyard offers shelter to the rooms and at the same time provides a gracious entry courtyard.

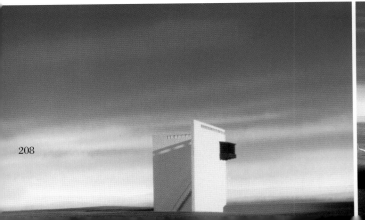

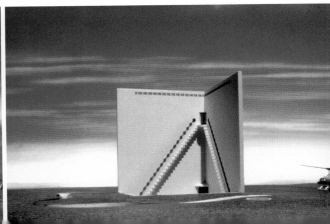

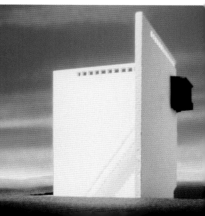

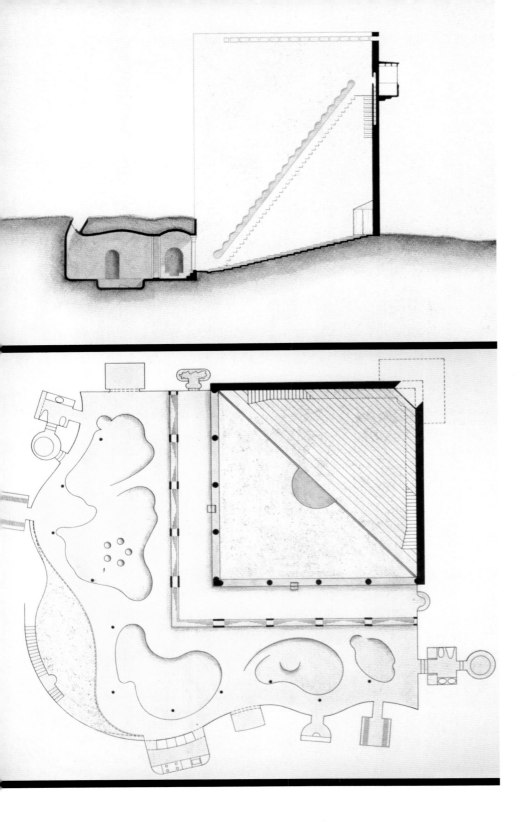

Situated not far from Seville, this vacation home reinterprets in a non-vernacular manner the prototype of the Andalusian house, with a central patio which all the rooms look out on, where the earth is also used as an insulation system against the heat of the sun. Making extensive use of the local construction techniques, the building utilises a cement and brick structure. A glass wool sheathing, sealed at the joints, wraps around all interior surfaces: double insulated walls and slender columns support the roof vault which defines the various rooms and which a series of horizontal panels render waterproof, to prevent moisture seeping upward from the ground.
Seen from a distance, the house disappears like an optical mirage, leaving a view on the horizon of only the two empty backdrops arranged at right angles like an open book.

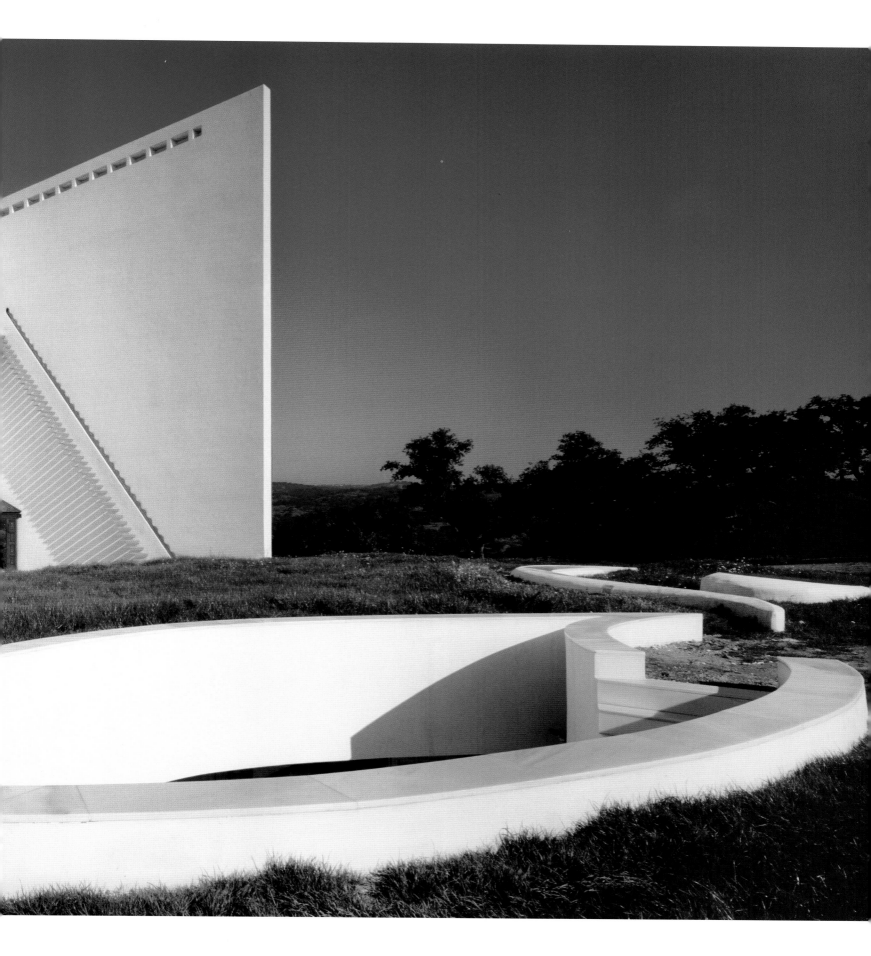

Two long handrails mark the walls alongside the steep staircase: along the hollow cut into the water a stream of water runs down to the patio, gathering in a basin of water at the end of the steep staircase. As the visitor climbs toward the top of the stairs, the noise of the water fades, merging with the view of the countryside from the high belvedere.

The house in fact is a single fluid and continuous space, bounded by the walls and screened from the patio with an ambulatory that provides an effective transition filter. Irregular cavities along the interior perimeter define the various areas of activity, receiving light from above through sinuous skylights and apertures carved like deep cuts into the ground.

the gardens of memory

224

"An inexhaustible inventor of metaphors",

Emilio Ambasz has always claimed a belief in architecture as an "act of the mythopoetic imagination": "it is not hunger, but love and fear – and sometimes wonder – which make us create" .

Concentrating on the representation of primary principles, his architecture focuses upon a reflection about memory: an ancestral memory that brushes History to draw directly upon the eternal question about birth and death.

The "Pro Memoria Garden" (1978) is a title and a programme that govern the project of a living memorial of the horrors of war, its anguish, its charge of destruction. The birth of every child in the small town of Ludenhausen, south of Hanover, is greeted with a symbolic gift: a small patch of land with a marble slab bearing an engraving of the name. Upon a death, the little garden is assigned to a new life and the name of the new owner is added to that of the old owner: a living reflection of the history of the village, the garden will follow in its growth the destiny of its inhabitants, a testimonial to the need for reconciliation that all men have in common, aside from any ideological and political divisions. The geometric arrangement of the infinite garden follows the

[1] A. Mendini, in *Emilio Ambasz. The Poetics of the Pragmatic*, Rizzoli, New York 1988, p. 15.

[2] E. Ambasz, unpublished typescript, replies to M. Sorkin, p. 11.

[3] E. Sottsass, in *Emilio Ambasz...* cit. p. 9.

organic design of a form that is neither predictable, nor fixed: reflecting "a perception of existence as an ever changing process" wrote Ettore Sottsass[3], Ambasz's work communicates the quest for "a constant state of fluidity", where dreams, aspirations, and fears can be recounted as rituals and ceremonies of everyday life.

There is also a hill of memories at the park-museum (1995) dedicated to the latest icon of the eternal dream of beauty and youth: the Barbie doll. Reinterpreted as a postmodern version of the classic feminine ideal – a Californian Kore – Barbie Knoll is the protagonist of a family-style Erechtheum on the hills of Pasadena: a sort of mass-market Sans Souci dedicated to the myth and the history of the famous doll, recounting the phases and episodes of her shifting popularity.

After entering an open-air courtyard, the visitors pause in the irregular hypostyle hall of the museum of toys, where each column corresponds to an effigy of the doll, representing a moment and a fashion in its long history. At the end of the tour, the enclosed museum space opens up to the exterior: sweetly buried in a luxuriant carpet of flowers and leaves, they are greeted by the sleeping image of "Sleeping Beauty": the sensual metaphor of eternal youth, the American Beauty of children's dreams, emerging like the evanescent Morgana of an eternal desire for beauty.

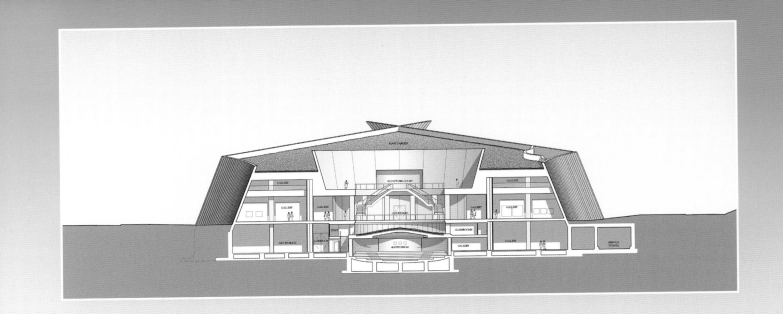

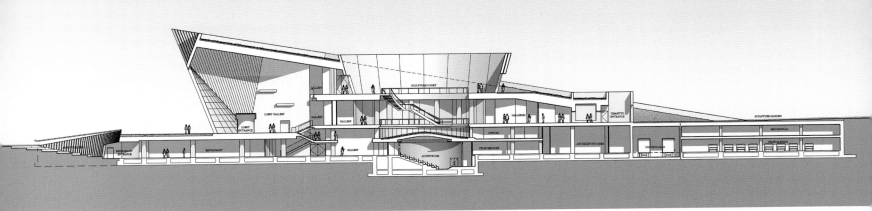

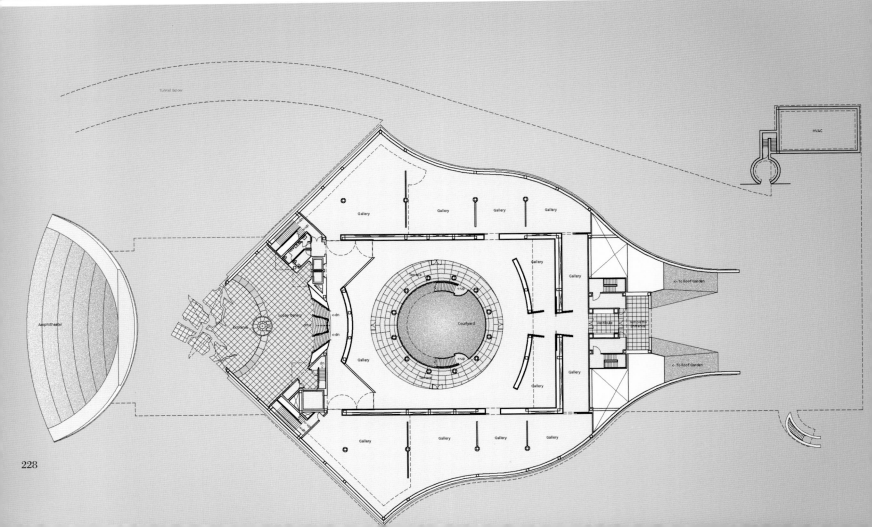

Commissioned by one of the most important collectors of avant-garde Chinese/Taiwanese art — Glory Yeh —, the Glory Art Museum — 10,000 sq. m. of highly flexible spaces — will be built in the capital of Taiwan's Silicon Valley: Hsin-Chu.

As in the Italian project for the Eye Bank, the entrance to the museum is place at the apex of a triangular plan, connected to the ground by two sinuous walls that, taken together, are reminiscent of an eagle's wings. If, on the one hand, this allows the harmonious insertion of the structure into the environment, on the other hand it makes it possible to use the roof surface as a fifth façade, destined for use as a sculpture garden. A circular courtyard occupies the empty heart of the museum, permitting access to the terrace and to the upper garden. From the ground level entrance to the free plane of the roof-façade, there is thus determine a spatial continuum that confers upon the movements of the spectators an almost ceremonial order, emphasising the important cultural role that the museum intends to play in the context of the society of Taiwan.

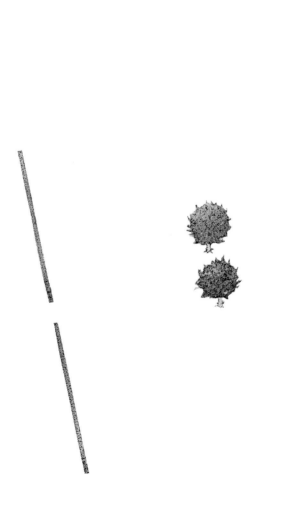

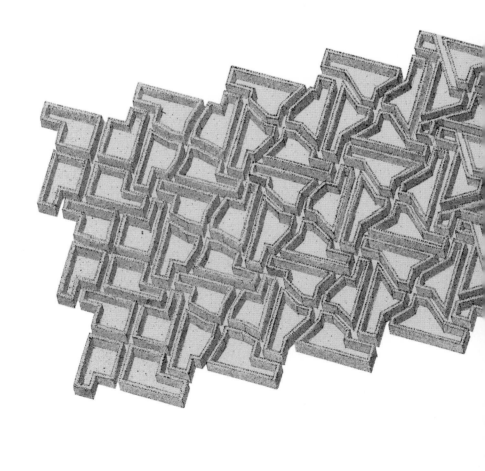

232

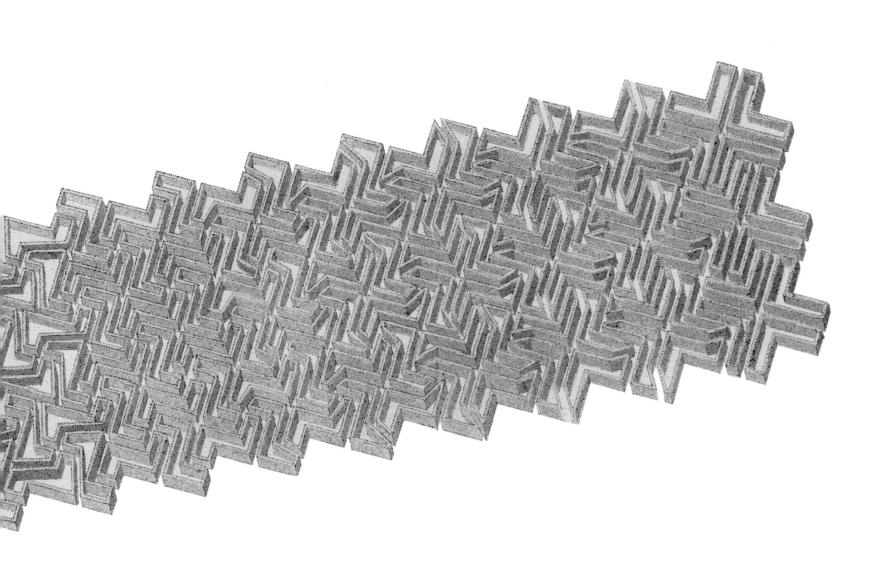

Ludenhausen is a small city to the south of Hanover, completely rebuilt after the Second World War: strongly encouraged by the local population, the project of the memory garden is meant to be at the same time a warning and a beacon of hope for the younger generations in the context of a full awareness of their own dramatic past.

In order to exorcise the horrors of war and to encourage growth in peace, Ambasz's proposal sets out from the regional tradition of Lower Saxony of the truck gardens of pensioners, relaunching it in a design open to the dynamics of local society: every garden, in fact, consists of a small irregularly shaped patch of earth, bounded by hedges and narrow footpaths. Every child is assigned, from birth, a patch of earth, with its name carved into a marble plaque: at the age of five, the child will be taught the basics of the art of gardening, in the hope that it will learn to recognise the cycles of nature to take care of the plants and flowers entrusted to their care. Upon the death of each owner, the plaque is turned over to be carved with the name of another child, which will gather the inheritance, committing to preserve it and increase it with the help of his or her enthusiasm and new ideas. The hope is that sooner or later the owners of the gardens will decided to cut down the border hedges, establishing a single, symbolic garden open to one and all.

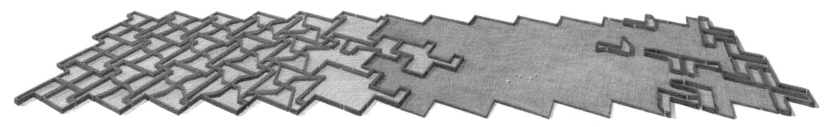

235

The "Barbie Knoll" is a garden dedicated to the memory of the Eternally Feminine: the celebration, at once ironic and popular, of the image of the Nymph restored from an artificial condition to the state of Nature. The symbolism of the depictions is integrated with the ceremony of touring the museum's collections via a route that smacks of an initiatory process, from the luminous world of life to the penumbra of memory. Pillar and banner, the silhouette of Barbie welcomes visitors with the fixity of an archaic statue: stripping itself of all and any historic connotation, it alludes to the abstraction of Myth, colouring the childish world of dolls with the sacred tone of a collective Rite. An austere cell under the open sky serves as an entrance to the "organic" space of dreams, properly gathered in the penumbra of the underground museum, punctuated by the intermittent network of giant caryatids: between one column and the next it is possible to install exhibitions on the theme of toys, transforming the tour of the museum into an active interplay of knowledge and participation. The blinding exit toward the valley of the "Sleeping Barbie" celebrates the sublimation of the Past into an eternal Present.

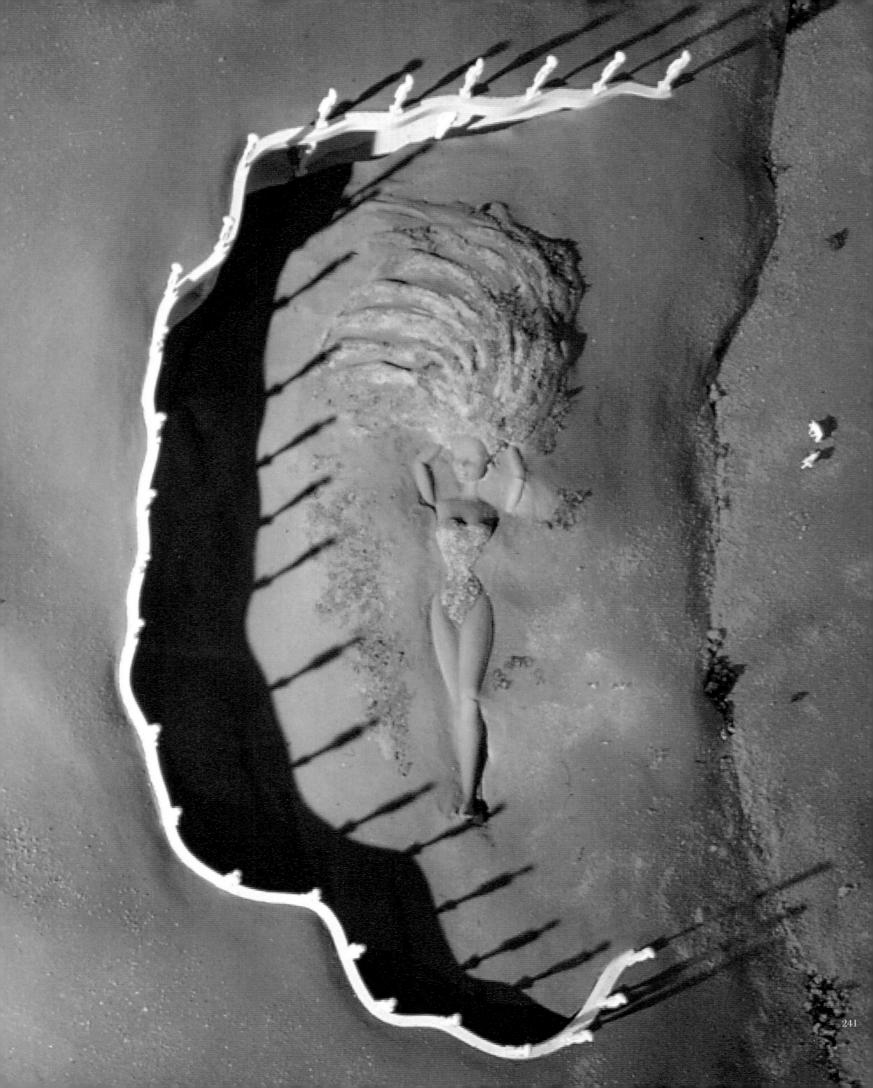

Emilio's Folly

Folly

Man is an Island

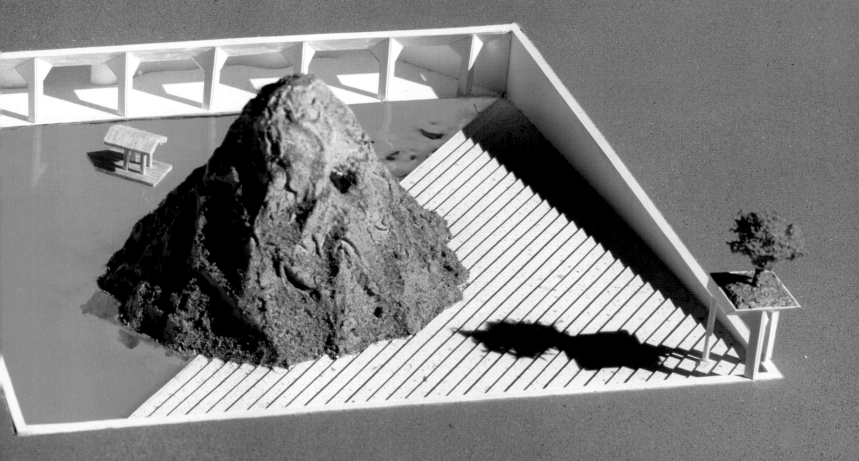

Emilio's Folly
Man is an Island

No, I never thought about it in words. It came to me as a full-fledged, irreducible image, like a vision. I fancied myself the owner of a wide grazing field, somewhere in the fertile plains of Texas or the province of Buenos Aires. In the middle of this field was a partly sunken, open-air construction. I felt as if this place had always existed. Its entrance was marked by a baldachin, held up by three columns, which in turn supported a lemon tree. From the entrance, a triangular earthen plane stepped gently toward the diagonal of a large, sunken square courtyard which was half earth, half water. From the center of the courtyard rose a rocky mass that resembled a mountain. On the water floated a barge made of logs, sheltered by a thatched roof and supported by wooden trusses that rested on four square-sectioned wooden pillars. With the aid of a long pole the barge could be sculled into an opening in the mountain. Once inside this cave, one could land the barge on cove-like shore illuminated by a zenithal opening. More often, I used the barge to reach an L-shaped cloister where I could read, draw, or just think, sheltered from the wind and sun. The cloister was defined on the outside by a water basin, and on the inside by a number of undulating planes that screened alcove-like spaces. Once I discovered their entrances, I began to use them for storage. Although I am not compulsively driven to order and

thrive, instead, on tenuously controlled disorder, I decided to use these alcoves in an orderly sequence, storing things in the first alcove until it was full, and then proceeding clockwise to the next one. The first items I stored were my childhood toys, school notebooks, stamp collection and a few items of clothing to which I had become attached. Later, I started moving out of the house and into the second alcove gifts I had received while doing my military service, as well as my uniform. I became fond of traversing the water basin once in a while to dress up in it, to make sure that I had not put on too much weight. Not all the things I stored in these alcoves were there because they had given me pleasure, but I could not rid myself of them. In time, I developed a technique for using these things to support other objects. I often wondered whether I was going to run out of space, but somehow always found extra room, either by reorganizing things or because some objects had shrunk or collapsed because of their age or from the weight of the items that had accumulated on top of them. On the diagonal axis passing the entrance canopy, but directly above it, an undulating plane was missing. Instead of a storage alcove, there was an entrance to a man-height tunnel that lead to an open pit filled with a fresh mist. I never understood where this cold-water mist originated, but it never failed to produce a rainbow.

Emilio Ambasz

248

Afterword
Paolo Portoghesi

In recent decades, after the optimistic interlude of the Eighties, architecture seems to have chose as its role that of the seismograph, registering every slightest shift of the earth, predicting earthquakes. Even before the twin towers collapsed in New York on 11 September 2001, creating a nightmarish landscape of twisting iron bars sticking out of mountains of dust, architects had foreseen the sinister scene, showing us collapses, explosions, disintegrations, virtual structural failures, repeated as a rite, and it is unclear whether that was propitiatory or to ward off evil.

And yet, in the firmament of the international star-system, there remain personalities above the fray, who continue their work without allowing themselves to be disturbed by the virtual hurricanes, by the cult of buildings "with a fever of 103" and by the countless other fashions induced by the prevailing nihilism.

One of these fixed stars is unquestionably Emilio Ambasz, Argentine, born in 1943, active in the United States, but equally tied to Europe, who certainly agrees with what Luis Barragán once said: that "any work of architecture which does not express serenity is a mistake". This belief of his can be understood from the way in which he describes the birth of architecture, roughly as follows: in a village, seized with terror at the wrath of the divine and the passions of humans, a man began to construct a circular building covered by a dome. Once he had finished the building, he told the inhabitants of the village that it had the shape of the universe and contained all the gods and persuaded them to build around the village a circular wall to enclose it. Inside the wall, near the temple, he built a house for himself, which then became his tomb.

Ambasz's "fabula rasa" contains an important message on the role of architecture: it hypothesises an epochal transformation from the principal agent of conflictual transformation of the earth to an instrument of a "new alliance," in the sense that was given to this expression by I. Prigogine and I. Stengers in their book of that name (1979). Ambasz is unquestionably a technician, one of the architects – indeed – most endowed with technical skill, and his work as a designer shows it, a designer who has created some of the objects of greatest propriety and elegance in the repertory of recent years; but his architecture does not exhibit technology as a value; on the contrary, it speaks to us, with persuasive force, of a holistic world: what a considerable portion of contemporary scientists allow us to glimpse in increasingly surprising depictions.

The new holistic paradigm (that sets out from the principle that the whole is something more than the sum of its parts) is gradually transforming the field of action of science, leading it to explore problems that once seemed like the exclu-

sive domain of philosophy and poetry. Man and nature, from this viewpoint, are parts of a single coherent system, just as mind and matter are complementary aspects of the same reality in continual development. Quantum physics has revealed that quanta are instantaneously involved, independently of their distance and of time. The fact that they can manifest themselves both in the form of material particles and in the form of waves, and that it is our very observation that determines which of these aspects reveals itself in each case, has triggered a gripping discussion of how this can be the case. Bohm's hypothesis is the existence of a subquantum level, a field that pervades all space and time, an undivided totality, a deeper order of existence that is concealed from us, but which lies at the origin of that world of appearances in which we live our everyday lives.

The manifestation of all the forms in the universe, then, is nothing more than the result of a continuous concealment and revelation of the two orders, the explicit one and the implicit one. When a particle seems to have been destroyed, it is not really lost, only concealed in the deeper order from which it had emerged. This mysterious dual order suggested to Bohm the use of the metaphor of the hologram: a three-dimensional image that is obtained with two rays of light, sending one toward the holographic film and causing the other to bounce off the object that we wish to reproduce. On the exposed place an unsettling image is formed, in which we do not see, as we do in photographic negatives, the image recorded, but only a configuration of interference, that is, a pattern of overlapping concentric circles, which reminds us of the waves created when you toss a handful of pebbles into a pond. A fundamental characteristic of a hologram is that only a small fragment of the plate is needed to reconstruct the entire image, even though the level of definition is proportional to the size of the fragment.

The metaphor of the hologram was used by Bohm to convey the possibility of the undivided totality in which everything is in everything, independently of space and time. Recently, Ervin Laszlo also made use of it in proposing the hypothesis of the existence of a field, which he calls the "Psi field," after the Greek letter, that he briefly explains as follows.

There is significant evidence of the existence in nature of a light, yet efficient field, that links every thing and every event. The presence of such a field could be the explanation of the astonishing consistency found throughout the cosmos, of the strange "involvement" of quanta, of the equally enigmatic and practically instantaneous consistency of organisms, and the notable transpersonal connections discovered in certain branches of psychology and consciousness research.

In order to illustrate fully the disconcerting aspect of research deriving from the paradoxes of quantum physics, which has reached formulations that are reminiscent of the visions of mystics and poets, we may quote the statement of Michael Talbot: "If we knew how to access it we could find the Andromeda galaxy in the thumbnail of our left hand. We could also find Cleopatra meeting Caesar for the first time, for in principle the whole past and implications for the whole future are also enfolded in each small region of space and time".

The new paradigm of science brings to a state of crisis many of the foundations of the technological society and, in particular, the nihilistic conclusion that the system of technology is actually hegemonic, invulnerable to human consciousness, destined to dictate law in the future of humanity. Bohm's theory of an implicit order that continually conceals and reveals itself seems to confirm Heidegger's view of "abandonment in the face of things" and "opening to mystery". "But", he said in 1955, "if we always and expressly take into count that everywhere a hidden sense of the technical world comes toward us, we stand at once within the realm of that which hides itself from us, and hides itself just in approaching us. That which shows itself and at the same time withdraws is the essential trait of what we call mystery. The way in which we hold ourselves open to the sense of the technical is what we call: openness to mystery."

Now Ambasz's position, the sense that emerges from his images, seems to mirror the hope for a "turning point" that Heidegger theorised. "We can make use of the products of technology and at the same time prevent them from coming to dominate us, from 'deforming, confusing, devastating our being'"; in any use that we make of them we can keep ourselves free so as to be able, in any moment, to do without them. This is the "abandonment in the face of things" that allows us to glimpse a new way that man has to establish roots in his own terrain. This new way might probe to well suited to summon up – though in changed form – the old world that is now so quickly vanishing.

Ambasz – as we have made clear – is a builder of machines and there can be no questions about his technique; his objects are often designed not to be noticed and in close consonance with the body. When he designs architecture, however, what comes onto the field and becomes a protagonist is the relationship with the earth, while technique is concealed, allowing the archetypes of the collective memory to re-emerge. When figures with technological connections appear (for instance, the skylights, where light solidifies) these are placed in dialogue with the "meadow", the "inhabited" elementary natural entity. This architectural hypothesis presuppose

253

a genuine "turning point". It nourishes itself on collective memory, moving from a detectable awareness of the characteristics of the places, it does not aim to unsettle, but to bring serenity, and yet, it is today among the most charged with the future, if by future we mean something to build, not something to accept passively.

Ever since – at the turn of the 1980s – Ambasz's projects began to appear frequently in the pages of the international magazines, it appeared clear that these were alternative ideas, that could not be relegated to the fads of fashion, endowed with a great power of image and a personal "sign" for which the most appropriate adjectives were: magical, surreal, oneiric. In effect, they seemed, in certain aspects, like paintings by Magritte, minutely detailed accounts of things seen in a dream. A medium, the dream, that was at the time triumphant in the movies, but which seemed impossible to convey into the rigid realm of architecture. "When a film is not a document", Ingmar Bergman wrote, "it is a dream. That is why Tarkovsky is the greatest of them all. He moves with absolute confidence in the space of dreams, he does not explain, and, for that matter, what should he explain? He is an observer who has succeeded in depicting his visions by making use of the heaviest and the most malleable of the media." Ambasz's dreams were recounted with realistic drawings. More often, they made use of the style that computers would later make much more common, or else scale models, in vivid colours, halfway between naïve realism and cunning abstraction. It was possible to doubt that they would become reality without losing their allure; but doubts dropped away in the face of the completed works, in which there was the same freshness, the same disarming simplicity and even, difficult thing to explain, the total extraneous nature with respect to the current motifs of contemporary architecture.

As designs and works increased in number, scale, vastness, there emerged clearly from the recurring themes, the predilections, and the repetitions that helped to reconstruct the thought that confers, upon this body of seductive images, a profound unity. The principal themes that can be identified are: accessible earth, the axial sequence, the inclined column, solidified light, and the vegetal wall.

ACCESSIBLE EARTH

Like his compatriot Lucio Fontana, Ambasz loves the absolute nature of the sign and often uses cuts as a metaphor for inhabiting. Instead of cutting the canvases stretched on a frame, so that the edges of the cut extend from the surface like the edges of a wound, Ambasz cuts the earth to make it accessible, modifying its level along the edges of the cut. The operation is prefigured in the 1976 operation for the Cooperative of Mexican-American grape growers, where a small apsed space is obtained by subtraction, excavating the earth to the level of the water table, where a crucifix appears against the background of a small body of water.

Two years later, in the Casa de Retiro Espiritual in Seville, the surface of the earth is cut in such a way as to create a curving sinusoidal fissure and a square space: a courtyard closed on two sides by a portico with columns and, on the other side, by high corner walls, crisscrossed by stairs which, from opposite sides, reach a windowed loggia. "Waterfalls", the architect recounts in a fairytale tone, "descend from both these high walls along the handrails. The noise of the water fades gradually as the visitor climbs toward the top of the stairs." The house is sheltered in the heart of the earth, like the houses of the gypsies of Guadix, but not to be concealed from view, because the two walls stand out in the landscape, unsettling it with their ambiguity, speaking to us, like a painting by Magritte, of a reality that is mixed with dreams, undermining the very credibility of the image.

The cuts reappear in the project of the House for Leo Castelli in 1980 and in the Schlumberger Laboratories at Austin in 1982, allowing the spatial structure to reveal itself in fragments that seem to allude to a military encirclement, a centripetal movement. In the Lucille Hansell Conservatory, in San Antonio, Texas (1982), the spatial structure plunges into the earth because it was necessary that the greenhouses protect the plants from excessive sunlight; thus, around a porticoed courtyard faithful to the Mexican tradition, there project from a field the pointed volumes of the pyramids in which the light – as we shall see – seems to solidify.

The cut in the ground is always reminiscent of an incision done with a scalpel, one might call it a "caesarean cut"; it serves to separate, to create a place through a break in the continuity even if, in the cut, violence and gentleness are combined through symmetry, curvature, equilibrium; the attempt to include the laboratories in the de-constructivist wave appears immediately as inappropriate and naïve. What comes to mind, while observing images of the San Antonio building, is an anthropological definition of building as offered by Daniela Vigna and M. Silvana Alessandri in their book, Antropologia della casa: "When you build", they wrote, "you chose a site, you isolate it from nature with an unnatural act that separates and divides: precisely because it is an unnatural act it requires an explanation and a justification. Human existence is punctuated from the prenatal phase by the dualism of separating and reuniting, the engine of the development of civilisation. You separate a place in order to establish there a residence, a city; the same is true for man, who is born with an uprooting, an expulsion that separates him from his *mother: and it is by rebuilding the next, the shell that in a hallucinatory manner recomposes the unity. It is a symbol of a return to one's mother's womb, it is a sacred element that permits the reappropriation of the unity". The "reappropriation of unity" is the final result also of Ambasz's compositional operations, which draw upon a primordial vision from which timeless, placeless archetypes emerge, like those that this author has described in the book, Natura e Architettura, as: the temple, the cloister, the gate/door, the façade, the apse, the column, the staircase.*

AXIAL COMPOSITION

Whether with excavations, or cuts, or projecting volumes, the preferred method for connecting them, for Ambasz, is to identify an axis of symmetry, at times corrected or contradicted, but clearly traceable. The axis, in fact, does not connect in an obvious way adjoining elements, but composes distant elements, taking advantage, as in music, of the value of the pause. Hence the original and surprising character of the spatial figures of the architect, not uncommonly paratactic in appearance only. Let us observe the Schlumberger Research Laboratories mentioned previously. Here the axes indicate three directions of penetration into the earth; they are, however, divergent one from another and one, focusing upon a circular colonnade, presents a number of anomalies: the asymmetrical façade, the caesura that interrupts the colonnade, the rotation of the apse that concludes the spatial sequence. In the School of Forestry and Environmental Studies of Yale University, the axis of the addition is rotated by 45 degrees with respect to the adjoining building, while in the Manoir d'Angoussart, at Charleroi (Belgium), 1979, the interplay of the axes becomes even more subtle: the curving silhouette of the projecting structure (a treillage covered with vegetation) emerges into a circular courtyard enclosed in a prismatic enclosure with a square plan. One of the corners of this volume overlooks at the end a small valley, offering a view, on the axis shifted by 45 degrees, of the circular courtyard that serves as a matrix for the entire composition.

Axiality is a dominant feature as well in the Memorial Museum of Baron Edmond de Rothschild in Ramat Hanadiv, Israel (1993). The architect designed the access to the park and museum, pre-existing, and an expansion of the gardens. The new access is a sequence of spaces in which the memory of Mannerist and Baroque gardens mixes with the features of Gaudí's Parc Guell. Two columns crowned by trees mark the boundary from which you reach the parking area, covered by two pergolas. On the background, there is an interplay of curving walls reminiscent of the flights of a staircase, while the path of axial penetration runs across the circular patio in the middle of the undulating walls, built around a venerable old tree, symbol of the agricultural passion of the Baron Rothschild, great sponsor of the state of Israel. From here, you pass into a hypostyle hall with sixty-six columns crowned with olive trees and inclined, "in order to suggest double-vault roof" against the sky. Beyond this you reach, through an underground passageway, a triangular courtyard and then the circular plataea of an open-air theatre, and at the far end stands a sort of cubic triumphal arch. The four new pavilions of the garden abandon the solemn tone of the entrance and, while still obeying a symmetrical organisation around a curvilinear cloister, introduce, with their diversity and asymmetry, an element of pleasurable surprise. It is incredible how this project, although it arbitrarily utilises conventional forms, succeeds in eliminating any feeling of déjà vu in virtue of the simplicity of the signs, exalted by the continual alternation of light and shadow, compressed and expanded spaces. Paths and sequences of spaces governed by axes of symmetry appear as well in the project for the thermal gardens of Sirmione (1996) where, on the model of the Roman trident of the Piazza del Popolo, the central axis is flanked by two lesser axes upon which are linked the cloisters opened in the structures covered by fields.

A new meaning is conferred upon the axial composition in the Glory Museum (1998), which will house a large art collection at Hsin-Chu, on the island of Formosa. Here the interplay of the levels of the site will make it possible to bring out of the land a volume that is at the same time a closure wall and a roof, composing, in a persuasive synthesis, the fluidity of the curvilinear walls immersed in the soil and hardness of the flat walls, intersecting at a right angle, designing at the intersection a large gap for light.

The multiplicity of compositional axes, already observed in the Schlumberger laboratories, attains in some cases the character of a list and rejects all symmetrical organisation. This is the case with the office complex and park at La Venta, Mexico City: a fanciful project that intends to create the conditions for the survival of a forest threatened by its own growth. The threat consists of the impossibility of developing for young plants, thus blocking the indispensable process of replacement. Ambasz imagined platforms rising to the height of the treetops, making it possible to establish nurseries above them, destined to supply the forest with new young trees. The axiality, in the logic of the architect's compositions, produces frontality and thus façades, usually obtained in a curve on the gap created by the two levels of the sloping terrain; but often the façade is constituted by a convex dihedron that, like an arrowhead, divides the land and establishes itself, in all its artificiality, in the lay of the landscape. This diagonal wedge, one of his great compositional inventions in which Gothic and Baroque inspirations converge, is already found in the Casa de Retiro Espiritual (1978), in Leo Castelli's house and then in the Schlumberger Laboratories, in the Manoir d'Angoussart, in the Argentine pavilion of the "Venice Biennale" (1994) and in the Air Force Memorial in Arlington (Virginia, 1994), where it appears inclined upwards and, like an arrowhead, indicates the axis that links the Capitol in Washington D.C. with the Lincoln and Washington Memorial.

THE SINUSOID AND THE AMOEBA

On several occasions, Ambasz has made use of the curve line in its sinusoidal version, where the convex and the concave alternate and are transformed one into another; here too a Baroque, indeed Borrominian discovery, because we find it for the first time in the façade of the church of San Carlo alle Quattro Fontane; but Ambasz takes it to extreme consequences, enclosing it on itself in a ring-like form to the point of suggesting the profile of one of the most enigmatic living creatures: the amoeba, whose incredible social capacity has recently been discovered. The amoeba is a single-celled organism with an elusive shape, in constant movement, because of its convex projections in continual metamorphosis. Amoebae move by demolishing their structure made of microtubules and reconstructing it on the other side. They build it by adding protein rings and they destroy it by splitting it lengthwise, the way you would "peel a banana", to use Ian Stewart's metaphor. The oddest thing is that amoebae, when they associate in colonies, they form the Myxomycetes (Dictyostelium discoideum), a mathematical animal, capable of constructing one of the most spectacular forms in nature: a sort of large helicoidal snail that contains within it slowly rotating crumpled surfaces. The mathematical biologists Thomas Hofer and Martin Boerlijst have discovered a system of equations that produce a very similar form. Ambasz adopted the amoeboid profile, formed by a closed sinusoid ring, in Baltimore (1989), at La Venta (1993), and in Lisbon (1995). In all these cases the ring-like silhouettes are repeated, becoming smaller higher up, with a system of terraces that call to mind Poelzig's project for the Festspielehaus of Salzburg. What derives is a sort of man-made hill that reminds one of the topographic curves that describe the orographic lay of the land the scenographic terraces of the Isola Bella on Lake Maggiore and the castle of Frederick II in Potsdam. This man-made hill is one of the way in which the architect's favourite nature-architecture relationship is expressed, in which abstraction and imitation are indissolubly intertwined.

In the Archives of the Japanese National Library, in the City of Science of Kansai, the sinusoid appears as a giant wall that cuts in two a man-made hill, dividing, according to the architect, the part pertaining to natura naturalis from the part having to do with natura naturans which assumes the geometric form of circular steps. The idea of this two-headed image inserted into a circular basin of water, derives from a reinterpretation of archaic Shintoistic symbolism, whereby the sacred texts were to be placed inside a ritual mound in which the most precious scroll was found, having to do with the myth of the sacred mountain. This symbolism was successively translated into the sequence of geometric figures: a cube, symbol of the earth, a sphere for water, a cone for fire, and a hemisphere for the vault of the sky; figures that Ambasz has introduced into his fantastic green treasure chest. The sinusoid already appeared in the design for the house of Leo Castelli, in a symmetrical edition as a slowly fading wave; we find it again in the project for the port of Monte Carlo (1998) and, in a continuous and asymmetrical version, in Phoenix and in the ironic Barbie Museum, in Pasadena, California (1995), where the icon of the doll is proposed repeatedly as a caryatid in a huge hypostyle hall placed beneath a sloping meadow and in a small temple that gives access to the hall from the other side of the hill. The side of the hall is sinusoidal and it calls to mind the canopus of Hadrian's Villa, surrounding on three sides a sloping meadow upon which is carved, in bas-relief, the figure of Barbie with her long flowing hair.

Finally, proposing quite literally the sinusoid of San Carlino, Ambasz designed not far from Castellaneta (1994), Italy, the tourist complex Nuova Concordia, made up of a horseshoe-shaped structure and two facing structures, one straight and the other curvings, in keeping with Borromini's model. Here, too, the environmental impact is minimised by shaping the surrounding earth and accommodating the forest facing the sea.

THE INCLINED COLUMN

Inclined surfaces enter Ambasz's lexicon not to exalt the oblique or to "destabilise" the structure, but in order to better anchor the building to the ground and to accentuate its relationship with natural forms, never rigidly vertical. The Mycal Cultural Centre, in Shin-Sanda, Japan (1990), is one of the most successful experiments in this sense. The arrowhead-like convex dihedron is joined to the ground in a different way from the convex part and from the concave part. Where the "L"-shaped element presents itself in all its geometric power, the connection is created by a sinusoidal glass surface that, like a wave against a pier, designs a continuous curve to *the attachment. On the other side the earth rises and wedges itself between the two walls, upon which you can glimpse four sinusoidal incisions, running up to the top at the centre. The architect used for the Mycal centre the metaphor of hands crossing at the wrists "to protect and care for the earth", where it is possible to see the reflection of the renowned page by Heidegger in which living – through the revealing mirror of language – is identified with being and with taking care.*

In the Montana estate (1991), another built project, we see for the first time the inclined columns, inspired by that "rustic classicism" that is often found in the American countryside and derived from the historic tradition of Montana where the typical wooden cabins have roofs covered with earth and the planes of the façade extend over the volume which remains partly concealed. Of the three constructions located on the farm, the house and the art collection develop the same theme: a curving wall covered by a trellis, made to hold up the creeping vegetation, crowned by a copper cornice that is separate from the volume below, as if suspended against the background of the sky. While in the residence, the curvature is concave toward the exterior, in the gallery it is convex and it opens toward the centre in a conical space or expanding upward. In the watchman's house, on the other hand, the façade is flat. In all three cases, a number of wooden logs leaning toward the façade suggest the theme of the classical peristyle, but in a new and persuasive manner, because they seem to be meant to support the thrust of the earth, and, in the same they mediate, through the material selected, the relationship with the landscape. A magical intervention has rendered the earth inhabitable by transforming one of those rocky crags that often interrupt the slope of the fields and obtaining, in the gap, a welcoming, protected space. The inclined columns, delicately set upon the meadow with their knotty shafts, are reminiscent of Bramante's columns for the cloister of St. Ambrose in Milan, or those of the wooden etching illustrating the treatise on architecture by Philibert Delorme; in place of the capital is a little copper hood, connected to the façade behind with a small hinged arm. This is unquestionably an architectural intervention that is entirely extraneous to the logic now prevailing in research and experimentation, and yet it might well claim a place among the architectural masterpieces of recent decades: as if opening toward a hoped-for future of reconciliation between man and earth. A clear contradiction can be sensed between the ephemeral character of the treillages and the sense of the eternal induced by the system of temples and by the Arcadian serenity of the site. But perhaps it is precisely this mixture of the ephemeral and the eternal, humility and tension, ingen-

uousness and wisdom, that accomplishes the true "turning point" toward an architecture that is no longer self-referential.

The inclined columns reappear, along with the sinusoidal system of the amoeba, in the office complex at Hilversum in Holland (1998), the city made famous by Dudok's architecture. A podium built by Dudok identifies the axis of penetration of the terraced hill in which the space of the offices is immersed. A glass wall, buttressed by the inclined columns, runs through the building volume and covers an interior path that maintains the geometric silhouette of the old hippodrome. Attention to historic memory does not prescribe a fetishist conservation of the existing, but rather its integration as a "sign" in a new context that takes on and solves current problem. The inclined columns reappear in a very different interpretation of the bridge designed in Columbus, Indiana (1989), to celebrate the 500th anniversary of the discovery of America. The placement, up high, in place of the capital, of green shrubs, is an indicator of the relationship with Gaudí's Parc Guell, but the Gaudí theme is enriched here by a series of perceptive attentions with respect to the role of entry gate that the bridge is called upon to perform. As one approaches the city, the columns are arranged musically to create a "crescendo" obtained with oscillations in height and a variation in the sounds (produced by the wheels of the vehicles) obtained through the irregularity of the street axis.

SOLIDIFIED LIGHT

The love at once of transparent and reflective structures, the love, then, for crystal architecture in the sense given to the definition by Scheerbart and Bruno Taut (and by Mies in his design for the Friedrichstrasse), filters into Ambasz's architecture through the form of its skylights, now pyramidal, now faceted, which, unlike the vertical façades, cause light to be reflected with the pluridirectional logic of precious stones. The most spectacular case is the Lucille Hansell botanical centre, where a rectangular patio, inspired by vernacular Mexican architecture, is surrounded by the crystalline projections of the skylights which offer reflecting surfaces to the light, mixing the image of the earth with the image of the sky. By night, in the projecting geometric figures, light seems to solidify with spectacular effects.

The theme of luminous solids returns in the thermal gardens of Sirmione (1996) and, in an especially innovative form, in the electric power plant of Hekinen in Chubu prefecture in Japan, in 1994. The client, based on the architect's well-established sensitivity to ecologic problems, asked him to reduce the environmental impact of an existing electric power plant, consisting of two very tall smokestacks and var-

ious factory buildings, built, with no attention at all to the landscape, in proximity to the ocean. The architect was nothing daunted by the virtually insoluble problem and put to work his entire magic repertory of allusive forms; he linked the summit of the smokestacks with the earth via cables that formed a conical surface that was partially materialised by an imposing curtain structure (velarium) and he enveloped the old buildings behind another such velarium, partially covered by climbing plants that, along with the cone of the smokestacks, formed a profile similar to that of Fujiyama. It is to be hoped that the ambitious project is put into construction because it might well become a model for the attenuation of the environmental impact of many industrial plants built with no concern for the landscape.

THE GREEN WALL

This last theme, which runs throughout Ambasz's work, is complementary to that of the accessible earth because, once the path of minimising (not, hypocritically, annulling) the visual impact of the built volume has been chosen, it becomes logical that what is erected should be in continuity with the natural landscape or, where this setting has been erased, that it should evoke it or recreate it. Here too memory has the value of a stimulus. We can all bring to mind the fascinating effect of the massive ivy-covered walls of castles or villas, or the magic of pergolas that create virtual volumes, surfaces that breathe and change with the seasons, alternating veiled transparency with luxuriant mass, charged with colour. Vegetation "applied" to architecture constitutes a world of its own, close to that of gardens, but endowed with an identity all its own. That which in the closed system of built architecture is entirely marginal and occasional becomes, for Ambasz, the primary mode for conceiving the volume alternating with the use of glass that appears in the blemishes of green or looms above it, in the pointed shape of the large skylights. The transformation proposed in 1998 for the ENI headquarters in the Roman neighbourhood of EUR is the most brilliant operation to impose the green wall as a screen in front of a curtain wall designed in the Sixties, which did not fit in with the Piacentini-esque setting of the lake. With the new façade proposed, which expands in the centre and joins with the water through an inclined plane, Ambasz links the great vertical volume to the handsome gardens by De Vico which stretch out on the hill, solving the problem of the anonymous vulgarity of the previously existing building.

The most audacious experiment, which develops the theme in a three-dimensional sense, is the International Hall of Fukuoka (1990), in which the greenery cov-

ers a terracing that rises toward the sky along the back of a gigantic multi-use building, continuing the green of the previously existing park beneath. A proposal that seemed unbuildable in both technical and economic terms was instead built in a short time and with a very positive outcome, even if the idea of entry fissure and the virtual cascade, suggested by the spray from the fountains, had to be sacrificed. Here too Ambasz's creative memory triumphed in the spontaneous chain of images that the work suggests, from pre-Columbian pyramids, to eighteenth-century gardens, the Trevi Fountain, the roof-gardens of Le Corbusier. It is a courageous response, which reacts to the logic of large building volumes that occupy only space, without any compensation for the citizens, who little by little see the free spaces of their city disappear and in the replacements of volumes they see nothing but a loss of livability in their environment. In the process of urban growth, in which economics prevails and architecture is downgraded to the role of merely overlaid decoration, Ambasz was able to restore to architectural design its power as an alternative.

Alongside the examples that we have commented upon of the green wall that lightens the volume and allows it to breathe, we could also mention the examples in which the dematerialised wall is made up of filiform or lamellar elements and creates an analogous transparency and spatial ambiguity. A typical example, for the interior space, is the offices of the Financial Guaranty Insurance Company in New York (1984), where silk threads hanging from the ceiling divide the space and, depending on the point of view, take on the consistency of luminous walls, fog barriers, or waterfalls, suggesting the glass columns that Terragni had imagined for his Danteum. An analogous effect, in an external volume, might be that created by the horizontal fins that screen the sun in the Monument Tower, Phoenix, Arizona (1998). Here it is the theme of the sacred mountain that is powerfully set forth, in an urban centre, with all its oneiric potential. No project does as much as this one to illustrate the distance between Ambasz's design and the architecture of recent years. There is a superficial similarity between the twisted volumes that pullulate in the pages of fashionable architecture magazines and triumphed in the recent competition to replace the Twin Towers. But in Ambasz's mountain there is nothing destabilising, publicity oriented; on the contrary, there is a reaffirmation of the Vitruvian triad and the link with the collective memory, utilising the universal value of a metaphor – that of Monument Valley – in which the recognition of a human imprint in the landscape corresponds to the transfer of a natural imprint in the heart of the city.

263

EMILIO'S FOLLY

In 1983 Ambasz interrupted his continuous production of concrete designs, always tied to a client, a competition, or a well defined occasion, and began to design or describe a "vision", or rather a "fable", which has for that matter the same characteristics as the designs and works completed and which could be built, perhaps in a garden like the "follies" of French gardens of the eighteenth century. Folly, of course, in the sense Erasmus of Rotterdam gave the word, while praising it.

"There are two types of folly. One is the horrible offspring of the inferno, which the cruel Furies scatter over the earth, every time that they hurl their horrible serpents into the hearts of mortals [...] the other, quite different from the first, which is destined to render men happy. It consists of a certain delightful illusion which takes hold of the soul, allowing it to forget all cares, all disquiet, all the miseries of life and immersing it in a torrent of pleasure." "I saw myself", wrote Ambasz, "as the owner of a broad meadow, somewhere in the fertile prairie of Texas or in the provinces of Buenos Aires. In the centre of the field was an open-air construction, partially buried. I had the feeling that this place had always existed. Its entrance was characterised by a baldachin, supported by three pillars, each of which supported a lemon tree. From the entrance, a triangular earth ramp sloped gently down toward the diagonal of a large square sunken courtyard, made half of water and half of earth. At the centre of the courtyard, a rocky mass that resembled a mountain. On the water floated a raft, protected by a straw roof supported by beams resting on square-section wooden pillars. With the help of a pole, the raft could be pushed into an opening in the mountain. Once you were inside the grotto, you could moor the raft on the beach, as if in a bay illuminated by an opening in the zenith. More often I used the raft to reach an L-shaped cloister, where I could read, draw, or just think, sheltered from the wind and the sun. The cloister was bounded on the outside by the body of water, and the interior by a certain number of undulating planes that sheltered spaces similar to niches. Once I discovered the way into the niches, I began to use them for storage. Despite the fact that I am not necessarily inclined to be orderly and I relaxed into a barely controlled disorder, I decided to use these alcoves in an orderly sequence, crowding things into the first niche until it was full, then proceeding clockwise to the next one. The first things that I stored were toys from my childhood, my school notebooks, my stamp collection, and the few items of clothing I was still fond of."

The vision could be interpreted as a self-analysis that explains Ambasz's way of thinking, imagining, and designing. "Every man is an island", is the subtitle of the story and therefore the island is the architect, the cave-port is his inner life, the two shores are two moments of life, either side of straight-line boundary that corresponds with the hypotenuse of the triangular basin of water. The raft is used to land at a shady portico where one can "read, draw […] think, while sheltered from the wind". The storehouses, behind the undulating wall, suggest the techniques of mnemonics, the art of the memory set forth in the Latin treatise Ad Herennium *and perfected and transformed by such authors as Cicero, Quintilian, Thomas of Aquinas, all the way up to Lully, Julius Camillus, Giordano Bruno, and Robert Fludd. "Constat igitur artificiosa memoria", we read in the Latin treatise, "ex locis et imaginibus". The loci are easily remembered places, such as a house, an intercolumnar space, a corner, an arch, while images are forms, distinctive features, symbols of what we want to remember. It is essential that places form a series and can be remembered in order, so that it is possible to set out from each locus of the series and move forward and back from there. Mnemonics is based on the interaction of visual and conceptual memory and, prior to the invention of printing, it served a fundamental role, comparable in a certain sense to that of the computer. But let us return to Ambasz and his description. "Later on, I began to move from my house to the second niche the gifts I had received while I was in the military, such as my uniform. I began to enjoy crossing the water every so often to put it on, with the purpose of reassuring myself that I had not gained too much weight. Not all the objects that I was storing in these niches were there because they had brought me happiness, but I could not get rid of them. With time, I developed a technique for using these things as supports for other objects. Often I wondered whether the space was about to run out, but somehow I always managed to find more space, either by reorganising the objects or because some things had shrunk or been ruined by the passing years or by the weight of the other objects stacked on top of them. Along the axis of the diagonal, beyond the entry baldachin, but precisely above it, an undulating plane was missing. In the place of the niche-storehouse, there was the entrance to a tunnel, the height of a man, that led to an open cavity filled with a cold mist: I never understood where this vapour came from, but it always managed to produce a rainbow." The storehouses located behind the cloister clearly represent the patrimony of experience that each of us carries with him and which are compressed with the passing of the years; the tunnel that opens up in the place of the missing storeroom might symbolise invention, which requires forgetfulness (the tunnel the height of a man), but it is resolved in an opening to the sky in the midst of a myriad of drops of water that creates a rainbow, an image of hope and a bridge to the "new alliance" between man and the earth.*

Of the many who have tried to define Ambasz's architecture, the one who has hit 265 the bulls eye in terms of its character and the secret meaning that it emanates is Ettore Sottsass, who has spoken correctly of "rites" and "liturgy", defining his architecture as so many "propitiatory projects that attempt to evoke the presence of architecture". For Sottsass each element of his buildings is a little like the vehicle of a bet to ward off evil, a mysterious ritual to propitiate a great natural deity. Perhaps they are parts of a liturgy recited to ask forgiveness for the scars that we inflict daily upon our planet, or perhaps they are tatters of a magical ritual staged to re-establish a harmony with those mysterious astral spheres that the Greeks and Indians first intuited so long ago. The truth is that, along with a select few, who may be considered in fifty years the refounders of a discipline on the verge of extinction, Ambasz took seriously the hypothesis of Lovelock and Margulis that our planet is also, itself, a living being, capable of maintaining its equilibrium through a sensibility that has nothing to envy in a thinking being. How do we human beings behave toward this "mother" that allows us to live? The same that microbes behave when, multiplying and entering into conflict with the living body, they threaten its survival. Tommaso Campanella had already realised this in the seventeenth century, when he asked that we respect the earth.

"The world is a large and perfect animal
Statue of God, that praises and resembles
God: We are imperfect worms, and vile family,
And within its belly we have life and shelter.
If we ignore its love and its understanding,
Neither does the worm in my belly
Try to understand me; but devotes itself
To doing me harm.
And so we must proceed with great respect."

Lovelock in fact did nothing more than to return us to a way of considering the earth that permeates the origins on the history of humanity and has never died out in poetry and art. Ambasz's proposal is to express with architecture the awareness of living with renewed respect and "poetically" the rediscovered "Mother Earth."

Publications and articles by Emilio Ambasz

2004

Architetture di Vetro, La collezione Corolle d'Autore Rex, Editoriale Domus (2003), Italian/English.
"Creatori di Utopie." *Dove* (October 2004): 49-52.
"Fuoriluogo." *Casamica* (October 2004): 248-250.

2003

Casciani, Stefano. *MONUMENTS, Oggetti e Soggetti 1979/2003*, Milano, Vol. 12 marzo-maggio. 2003: 44-45.

2002

Elements of Design (Foreword by Emilio Ambasz) New York, NY: Princeton Architectural Press (2002): 8-9.
Natural Architecture – Artificial Design: Emilio Ambasz Milan, Italy: Elemond-Electa Publishing, 2001.

2001

"*Shigeru Ban.*" (Foreword by Emilio Ambasz) New York, NY: Princeton Architectural Press (2001).

2000

"Emilio Ambasz." *Cantico 2000, Società per le Belle Arti ed Esposizione Permanente* Milan, Italy: Stampa Inedita/ Etica Europa/Banca Europa, 2000: 84-87.
"Green Towns." *Sustainable Architecture, White Papers* (November 2000): 83-90.
"Manhattan: Capital of the XXth Century." *Dialogue* (June 2000): 142-143.

1999

Architecture as Nature: Emilio Ambasz – Projects and Objects Milan, Italy: Elemond-Electa Publishing, 1999.
"Fiabe al lavoro. Racconti sull'architettura per bambini scettici." *Etica e Ambiente* Milan, Italy: Stampa Inedita, 1999: 31-40.
(epigraph) *Modelmaking: A Basic Guide* New York, NY USA: W.W. Norton & Company, Inc., 1999.

1998

"2000: Fine Secolo." *Abitare* 379 (December 1998): 53, 166.

"Vecchi rigori per ritrovare nuove vie." *Il Sole-24 Ore* (April 12, 1998): 27.

1997

"Design of the Imagination." *Ottagono* 122 (March-May 1997): 26-27.

1996

"Centro cultural y deportivo Mycal en Japón, El." *Mercado de Materiales* (April 1996): 7-9.
"Fabula Rasa." *MODO* 171 (April 1996): 17.
"Green Cities. Ecology and Architecture." *Architecture for the Future* Paris, France: Terrail, 1996: 141-145.
"Modo di Fax, A." *MODO* 172 (May-June 1996): 17, 19.
"Muro ha muerto: que vivan los muros, El." *CPAU (Consejo Profesional de Arquitectura y Urbanismo* (January 1996): 26-29.

1995

"Anthology for a Spatial Buenos Aires." *Abitare* 342 (July-August 1995): 21-22.
"Interroga se stesso (I Ask Myself)." *Ottagono* 114 (March-May 1995): 81-87.
"Sogni infranti sopra Berlino?" *Il Sole - 24 Ore* (July 9, 1995): N. 182, 35.
"Why Not the Green Over the Gray?" *Domus* 772 (June 1995): 82-84.

1994

(and Radice, B.) "Angels of History: Chimerical Milanese Faxes." *NEOS* Vol. 4, No. 1 (June 1994): 10-14.
(advertisement for the Triennale di Milano exhibition) *Domus* 796 (December 1994): viii.
"Frank Lloyd Wright on Show (Frank Lloyd Wright in mostra)." *Domus* 761 (June 1994): 82-84.
"Green Towns." *Strategy of Environment for Communities and Local Governments* Japan, 1994: 229-252.
"To Travelling Wisdom from Friends Around the World." *Hamano Concept Index* Venice, CA, USA: Hamano Concept Inc., 1994: 357.
"Working Fables: A Collection of Design Tales for Skeptic Children." *Atelier Mendini: una utopia visiva* Milan, Italy: Fabbri Editori, 1994: 7-12.

1993

Emilio Ambasz Architecture and Design 1973-1993 Tokyo, Japan: Graphic-sha Publishing Co., Ltd., 1993.
"Modern Design Drawings. Christopher Dresser to the Present." *The Metropolitan Museum of Art* (Spring 1993).
"Quattro Progetti di Gabetti el Sala." *Eden* 2 (November 1993): 20-21.

1992

"Alphabets for Aesthetes." *Igarashi Sculptures* Japan: Robundo Publishing, Inc., 1992: 9-15.
Emilio Ambasz: Inventions. The Reality of the Ideal New York, NY USA: Rizzoli International Publications, Inc., 1992.
"FAX." *ID* 1 (February 1992): 50-51.
"FAX." *ID* 3 (May-June 1992): 28-29.
"FAX." *ID* 5 (September-October 1992): 49.
"FAX: Could a Design Magazine Become the Theological Review of the 21st Century?" *ID* 2 (March-April 1992): 50-51.
"Curved Sewing Needle." *Industrial Elegance* Steelcase Design Partnership for VECTA (March 1992): 11.
"Melodie di Carton." *l'ARCA* 65 (November 1992): 76-78.
"Soft Tech." *Innovation* 5 (Fall 1992): 64-65, 102-103.
"*Stichthandling.*" *ID* 2 (March-April 1992): 74-75.
"Unbuilt Projects: Unforgettable Images." *SD* 333 (June 1992): 121-130.

1991

"Emilio Ambasz: Works and Projects." (Zevi, B., ed.) *L'architettura* (November 1991): 889-905.
"Luca Scacchetti Architetture." *Borrowed Lives* Milan, Italy: IDEA Books, 1991: 42-43.
"Robertos Wilson, Luminarios (Premier Régisseur) et Maître." *Robert Wilson* Paris, France: Editions du Centre Pompidou, 1991: 23-28.
"Visual Monologues." *Collages* (Chermayeff, I.) New York, NY USA: Harry N. Abrams, Inc., 1991: 24-25.

1990

"Algunas notas sobre una correspondencia mental que mantuve a traves de los ultimos veinticinco años con Delfina Galvez de Williams sobre la obra de Amancio." *Amancio Williams* Buenos Aires, Argentina: Gaglianone Establecimiento Grafico S.A., 1990: 13-16.
"Exhibition Recap." *SD* 2 (1990): 102-112.
Houses for the Steles New York, NY USA: Ulysses Gallery, 1990: 22-23.

"Italian Radical Architecture and Design 1966-1973."
(Radice, B.) *Terrazzo* 5 (Fall 1990).
"Oficinas para una Empresa de Seguros." *Tecnologia y Arquitectura* 10 (October 1990): 34.
"Who Owns Design?" *Metropolis* 3 (October 1990): 62.

1989

(and Foscari, A.) "All the Lagoon's a Stage..." *Marco Polo* 61 (February 1989): 49.
"Dear Friends, Wish You Were Here." *Marco Polo* 61 (February 1989): 50.
Review: New Product Design London, UK: Design Museum, 1989: 37.

1988

"Da un addetto ai lavori: breviario per un..." *Modo* 108 (September 1988): 22-24.
"Elegy for Italian Design." *International Design* (November-December 1988): 55.
Emilio Ambasz: The Poetics of the Pragmatic New York, NY USA: Rizzoli International Publications, Inc., 1988.
(des.) *Mimar* 27 (January-March 1988): cover/concept.
"Mycal." *Nikkei Architecture* (August 8, 1988): 94-95.
"San Antonio Botanical Conservatory." *Deconstruction – Architecture* 3/4 (April 1988): 46-47.
"Tadao Ando." *Ando by Ando* Bordeaux, France: Arc en Rêve Éditeur, 1988: 55.

1987

"Carrelli Elevatori a Wall Street." *l'Arca* 1 (January-February 1987).
(des. and prod.) "Design Review." *AXIS* 23 (Spring 1987): 105, excerpts 9, 18.
(des. and prod.) "Design Review." *AXIS* 24 (Summer 1987): 57, excerpts 9.
(des. and prod.) "Design Review." *AXIS* 22 (Winter 1987): 105.
"Emilio Ambasz: A Decade of Architecture, Industrial and Graphic Design." *Emilio Ambasz* (Tironi, G., ed.) Geneva, Switzerland: Halle Sud Institute of Contemporary Arts (March 1987).
"Design Review: Italian Design: Requiem for Memphis." *AXIS* Vol. 22 (Winter 1987): 105, excerpts 19.
"Emilio Ambasz and the Memesis of Nature." *AU: Arredo Urbano* 23 (December 1987): 72-76.
"Interior Advantage." *Brutus* 172 (January 15, 1987): 188-189.
(des.) *Mimar* 23 (January-March 1987): cover/concept.
(des.) *Mimar* 24 (April-June 1987): cover/concept.

(des.) *Mimar* 25 (July-September 1987): cover/concept.
(des.) *Mimar* 26 (October-December 1987): cover/concept.
"Nota Biografica/Textos/ Obras y Projectos." *Summarios* 109 (1987): 8-15.
"Siviglia si riflette nel mondo." *l'Arca* No. 8 (July-August 1987): 40-47.

1986

"The 1986 Design Zoo." *The International Design Yearbook 1986/87* (Sudjic, D., gen. ed.) London, UK: John Calmann and King Ltd. and Cross River Press Ltd., 1986.
"Ancient Court Music Beaten Up!" *Space Design* 8601 (1986): 57.
"Chi è Luis Barragán." *Casa Vogue* (June 1986): 94-109.
"Design Review: Italian Design: A 15 Year Perspective." *AXIS* 21 (Autumn 1986): 50, excerts 8.
Il Giardino d'Europa. (Vezzosi, A., ed.) Milan, Italy: Mazzotta, 1986: 202-204.
"Italian Design. A 15 year Perspective." *AXIS* (Autumn 1986): 50.
"The Italian Influence." *Interior Design in the 20th Century* (Tate, A. and Smith, R.C., eds.) New York, NY USA: Harper & Row, 1986.
"La citta del design." (Cornu, R., trans.) *Halle Sud Magazine* (1986): 4.
"Luis Barragán." *House and Garden* (February 1986): 18-28.
(with Smith, P.) "A Millenarian Hope: The Architecture of Emilio Ambasz." *The Harvard Architecture Review* New York, NY USA: Rizzoli International Publications, Inc., 1986: 96-103.
(des.) *Mimar* 19 (January-March 1986): cover/concept.
(des.) *Mimar* 20 (April-June 1986): cover/concept.
(des.) *Mimar* 21 (July-September 1986): cover/concept.
(des.) *Mimar* 22 (October-December 1986): cover/concept.
"Spain: Columbus Expo." *TWA: Ambassador* (December 1986): 9.

1985

(des.) "Contract and Residential Furniture Logotec Spotlight Range." *Industrial Design Excellence USA* USA: The Design Foundation, 1985: 13.
"Ambasz, Emilio." *Contemporary Landscape from the Horizon of Postmodern Design* Kyoto/Tokyo, Japan: The National Museum of Modern Art, 1985-1986.
"Design Review." *AXIS* (Autumn 1985): 3, 38-41.
"Emilio Ambasz: Botanical Pleasures." *Domus* 667 (December 1985): 14-17.
"Ensayos y Apuntes para un Bosquejo Critico." *Luis Barragán* Mexico City, Mexico: Museum Rufino Tamayo, A.C., 1985: 23-25.
"Exhibition & Lecture Series of Work by Young Architects:

Competition Winners." *Rough Drafts 85* New York, NY USA: Urban Center Galleries, 1985.
"Exhibition." *The Commercial Architecture* 6 (June 1985): 244-245.
(des.) "Furniture and Furnishings: Dorsal Seating Range." *Industrial Design Excellence USA* USA: The Design Foundation, 1985: 44.
"Introduction." *Intercepting Light* (Ando, T.) Japan: Designer's brochure, 1985.
"Manoir D'Angoussart." *The Princeton Journal* (Beeler, R., ed.) (1985): 128-131.
"La libreria nel Giardino." *Gran Bazaar* (December-January 1985): 140.
(des.) *Mimar* 15 (January-March 1985): cover/concept.
(des.) *Mimar* 16 (April-June 1985): cover/concept.
(des.) *Mimar* 17 (July-October 1985): cover/concept.
(des.) *Mimar* 18 (November-December 1985): cover/ concept.
"New Work of Shiro Kuramata." *AXIS* (Summer 1985): 60-61, 63.

1984

"Dar forma póetica a lo pragmático: notas sobre mi obra de diseño." *Diario* 16 (May 11, 1984): 5 (Hogar 16).
Emilio Ambasz Italy: Grafis Editions, 1984.
"Emilio Ambasz: The Innovator for Aiming at Utopia." *Idea: International Advertising Art* 187 (November 1984): 88-95.
"Fabula Rasa." *Via 7: The Building of Architecture* Cambridge and London, UK: The MIT Press, 1984: 87.
"Houston Center Plaza." *AD: Architectural Design Profile (Urbanism)* 12 (January-February 1984): 46-47.
"La Folly de Emilio: El Hombre es una Isla." *Follies: MOPU Arquitectura* (May-June 1984): 34-37.
"La piazza interminabile: il caffè della città." *Domus* 649 (April 1984): 14-19, 116.
"L'art dans l'eau: New Orleans Museum of Art." *Domus* 651 (June 1984): 30-31.
(des.) *Mimar* 11 (January-March 1984): cover/concept.
(des.) *Mimar* 12 (April-June 1984): cover/concept.
(des.) *Mimar* 13 (July-October 1984): cover/concept.
(des.) *Mimar* 14 (November-December 1984): cover/ concept.
"Notes About My Design Work." *IDEA* 187 (November, 1984): 90-93.
"Notas acerca de mi labor de diseño." *Diseño* (May 1984): 71-75.
Obras y Proyectos, 1972-1984: Entre la Arcadia y la Utopia Madrid, Spain: Colegio Oficial de Arquitectos de Madrid, 1984.
"Plaza Major, Salamanca." *Architectural Design – Urbanism* (January-February 1984): 44-45.
"Popular Pantheon." Article on James Stirling. *The Architectural Review* 1054 (December 1984): 35.
"Three Projects by Enzo Mari..." *Domus* 649 (April 1984): 14-19.

1983

"Automatisch-Dynamisches Sitzen." *MD: Moebel Interior Design* (October 10, 1983): 56-57.
Dal cucchiaio alla città: nell'itinerario di 100 designers (Venosta, C.) Milan, Italy: Electa, 1983: 26-27.
"Emilio Ambasz: dieci anni di architettura, grafica, design in un Multivision realizzato da Domus." *Centrodomus* (October 24, 1983).
"Emilio's Folly: Man is an Island." *Follies: Architecture for the Late-Twentieth Century Landscape* (Archer, B.J., ed.) New York, NY USA: Rizzoli International Publications, 1983: 34-37.
"Houston Center Plaza, Houston: Metaphoric Image of the City." *Lotus International* Venice, Italy: Gruppo Electa S.p.A. 1983: 65-69.
(ed.) "Italy: The New Domestic Landscape, Exhibit, MOMA 1972." *Domus* (1983): 27.
(and Jakobson, B.) "La Casa Bifronte / Janus's House." *Domus* 635 (January 1983): 34-39.
"La Mostra 'Italy: The New Domestic Landscape' presentata... ebbe un forte e profondo impatto." *Domus* 1983.
(des.) *Mimar* 7 (January-March 1983): cover/concept.
(des.) *Mimar* 8 (April-June 1983): cover/concept.
(des.) *Mimar* 9 (July-October 1983): cover/concept.
(des.) *Mimar* 10 (November-December 1983): cover/ concept.
"Premios Kones 1982 – Artes Visuales." *Diploma al Merito: Libro de Oro de las Artes Visuales Argentinas* Buenos Aires, Argentina: La Fundacion Konex, 1983: 86.
"Review on Herbert Muschamps." *Man About Town* Cambridge, MA: MIT Press, 1983.
"Salamanca: The Plaza Mayor. A Garden in the City, a City in the Garden." *Lotus International* Venice, Italy: Gruppo Electra S.p.A., 1983: 62-64.
"Skin and Bones." *Alcantara* (Confalonieri, F.G., ed.) Milan, Italy: Electa 1983: 20-29.
(des.) *The Dorsal Seating Range: Innovation* McLean, VA USA: Industrial Designers Society of America 1 (Winter 1983): 23-25.
"Visual Monologue." *Collages* (Chermayeff, I.) Vienna, Austria: Galerie Ulysses, 1983.

1982

"Ambasz: Los que Conozco Diseñan los Domingos." *Vivienda* 235 (February 1982): 8.
"Ambasz to Consult at Cummins Engine." *ID: Industrial Design Magazine* 4 (July/August 1982): 30.
"Beyond Metaphor, Beyond Form. Meanings of Modernism." *Design Quarterly* 118-119 (1982): 4-11.
"Il design oggi in Italia tra produzione, consumo e qualcos'altro" Naples, Italy: Museo Villa Pignatelli June, 1982: 27.

"La città del design." *Skyline* (November 1982): 24.
"Milano, 1920-1940." *Skyline* (November 1982): 18-19.
(des.) *Mimar* 3 (January-March 1982): cover/concept.
(des.) *Mimar* 4 (April-June 1982): cover/concept.
(des.) *Mimar* 5 (July-September 1982): cover/concept.
(des.) *Mimar* 6 (October-December 1982): cover/concept.
"P/A Second Annual Conceptual Furniture Competition." *Progressive Architecture* 5 (May 1982): 158-169.
(pref.) *Precursors of Post-Modernism* New York, NY USA: The Architectural League, 1982.
Introduction to discussion of Architectural League Exhibition, *Precursors of Post-Modernism* (November 1982).
"Reportaje: Emilio Ambasz." *Summa* 174 (May 1982): 21-22.
Wait Until You See the Next Olivetti Machine: Memphis 82 Milan, Italy: Stampa Nava Milano S.p.A., 1982: 4.

1981

"Columbus il Mito." *La mia casa* 141 (October 1981): 106-107.
"Farewell, Caro Maestro." *Progressive Architecture* 5 (May 1981): 117.
"La Proposta di Ambasz." *Domus* 622 (November 1981): 49.
(des.) *Mimar* 1 (July-September 1981): cover/concept.
"P/A First Annual Conceptual Furniture Competition." *Progressive Architecture* 5 (May 1981): 150-155.
"Post Modernism, the Social Aspect." Extract: *Performing Arts* 3 (1981): 59-60.
"The Four Gates to Columbus." *Artists & Architects Collaboration* (Meritet, M., illus. and Diamonstein, B., ed.) New York, NY USA: Whitney Library of Design, 1981: 130-135.
The Return of Marco Polo (with Vignelli, M., des.) New York, NY USA: Rizzoli International Publications, Inc., 1981.

1980

"A Cooperative of Mexican-American Grape Growers, California, 1976." *Design Quarterly* 113/114 (1980): 26-27.
"Ambasz." *Domus* 610 (October 1980): 20.
"Notes About My Design Work." *Architecture and Urbanism (Special Issue: Emilio Ambasz)* 5 (May 1980): 33-60.
"Imponderable Substance." *Progressive Architecture* 9 (September 1980): 138-141.
"Projet d'une maison pour un couple, a Cordoue, Espagne." *Techniques et Architecture* 331 (June/July 1980): 118-119.
"Working Fables: A Collection of Design Tales for Skeptic Children." *Architecture and Urbanism* 5 (May 1980): 107-114.

1979

"CIESP: Núcleo de Desenho Industrial." *MOMA Design: Exposicão* New York, NY USA: The Museum of Modern Art, 1979.

"Deux Propositions Alternatives." *Techniques et Architecture* 325 (June-July 1979): 101-104.
"Favolette di Progettazione (Working Fables)." *Modo* (September-October 1979): 56.
"House & Atelier for Luis Barragán and San Cristobal." *GA: Global Architecture* 48 (1979): 2-7.
"Luis Barragán." *GA: Global Architecture* 48 (1979).

1978

"Architecture is the Reply to Man's Passion and Hunger." *The AIA Journal* (Mid-May 1978): 231.
"Ambasz, Emilio." *Global Eye '78 7 New Design Powers* (Kamekura, Y.) Japan: Japan Design Committee, 1978.
(fore.) *High Tech: The Industrial Style and Source Book for the Home* (Kron, J., and Slesin, S.) New York, NY USA: Clarkson N. Potter, Inc. Publishers, 1978.
"Views Credit: Chair Development." *Progressive Architecture* 2 (December 1978): 8.

1977

(des.) *Architecture I* (Apraxine, P., org.) New York, NY: Leo Castelli Gallery, 1977.
"Centros Comunitarios Educacionales y Agrarios." *Summarios* 11 (September 1977): 8-19.
"Centro Mexicano de Cálculo Aplicado SA." *Summarios* 11 (September 1977): 17.
"Community Art Center." *Summarios* 11 (September 1977): 28.
"Conjunto de Viviendas en un Establecimiento Agrícola." *Summarios* 11 (September 1977): 26-27.
"Cooperativa de Viñateros Mexicano-Norteamericanos." *Summarios* 11 (September 1977): 20-22.
"For Sale: Advanced Design, Tested and Ready to Run." *Design* 346 (October 1977): 50-53.
"La Univerciudad (Borrador)." *Summarios* 11 (September 1977): 17.
"Le designer comme réalisateur." *l'Architecture d'Aujourd'hui* (October 1977): 64-66.
"Moral: una condición de prediseño." *Summarios* 11 (September 1977): 16.
"Una Declaración Sobre mi Obra." *Summarios* 11 (September 1977): 15.
"View of Contemporary World Architects, A." (December 1977): 186-187.
"Working Fables: Sleepwalker's Dream." *Modo* 3 (September-October 1977): 56.

1976

"Commentary." *Princeton's Beaux Arts and Its New*

Academicism (Wurmfeld, M., ed.) New York, NY USA: The Institute for Architecture and Urban Studies, 1976: 25.
The Architecture of Luis Barragán New York, NY USA: The Museum of Modern Art, 1976.
(ed.) *The Taxi Project: Realistic Solutions for Today* New York, NY USA: The Museum of Modern Art, 1976.
"Up-and-Coming Light: Emilio Ambasz, His Works and Thoughts. A Statement About my Work." *Space Design* (Special feature) (October 1976): 4-44.

1975

"Anthology for a Spatial Buenos Aires. A Selection from 'Working Fables': A Collection of Schematic Design Tales for Skeptic Children." *Casabella* 389 (February 1975): 6-7.
"Coda: A Pre-Design Condition: A Selection from 'Working Fables': A Collection of Design Tales for Skeptic Children." *Casabella* 401 (May 1975): 4-5.
"Manhattan, Capital of the 20th Century: A Selection from 'Working Fables': A Collection of Schematic Design Tales for Skeptic Children." *Casabella* 397 (January 1975): 4.
"Ultimately, a Flower Barge." *Progressive Architecture* 5 (May 1975): 76-79.
"The Univercity: A Selection from 'Working Fables': A Collection of Design Tales for Skeptic Children." *Casabella* 399 (March 1975): 8-9.
(ed.) *Walter Pichler: Projects* New York, NY USA: The Museum of Modern Art, 1975.

1974

"A Selection from Working Fables: A Collection of Design Tales for Skeptic Children." *Oppositions* 4 (October 1974): 65-74.
"Design im Zeitalter der Aufklärung." *Form* 68 (March 1974): 32-33.
"La città del design: A Selection from 'Working Fables': A Collection of Schematic Design Tales for Skeptic Children." *Casabella* 394 (October 1974): 4-5.
"The Enlightened Client: A Selection from 'Working Fables': A Collection of Schematic Design Tales for Skeptic Children." *Casabella* 396 (December 1974): 4-5.

1972

(ed.) *Italy: The New Domestic Landscape* New York, NY USA: Museum of Modern Art, 1972.

1971

"Instituciones y Artefactos para una Sociedad Postecnológica." *Summa* 37 (May 1971): 30-36.

1969

"The Formulation of a Design Discourse." *Perspecta* 12 (1969): 57-71.

Publications on Emilio Ambasz

2004

Buchanan, P. "El Pais (Arquitectura)." *Un sueño, una casa*, September 4, 2004: 20.

De Palma A. "A Boon for the Catskills, Or Something in the Water?" *The New York Times* New York, NY (February 8, 2004): 25, 32.

De Palma A. "America America." *Modulo* 299 (March 2004): 122-131, 202.

Giacomini, L. *Cosmo e Abisso: Pensiero mitico e filosofia del luogo,* Milan, Italy, Guerini Scientifica, 2004: 157, plates 22, 160, 169, 170.

Grossman, L. *Arquitectos Made in Argentina.* Buenos Aires, Argentina: Arquitectos Argentinos en el Mundo Editores, 2004: 24, 52-57.

Grossman, L. "Indian Architect & Builder", *International: Embanking on Design* (Volume 17 No. 10), 2004: 96-103.

— Sin fronteras: Argentinos que viven y trabajan en el exterior, *Arquitectura: Diseño & Urbanismo* (June 2, 2004): 1, 3.

Lessard, C. *Concours International d'Architecture: Complexe Culturel et Administratif de Montréal,* Québec, Canada: Société immobilière de Québec, 2004: 24.

— "Construction Europe" *News (The Grand Embrace),* (Volume 15 No. 2, March 2004): 6.

— "Pasajes" *Noticias: Monument Towers,* (Número 52 2004): 14.

Redhead, D. *Electric Dreams Designing for the Digital Age,* London, UK: V & A Publications, 2004: 14-16.

"Sarà una grande fabbrica della salute", *Il Gazzettino* Venice-Mestre, Italy: (February 21, 2004): 1.

Scott, F. *Grey Room*, Cambridge, MA, USA: The MIT Press, 2004: 46-77.

Sorkin, M. *Analyzing Ambasz,* New York, NY: The Monacelli Press, 2004.

— "Without Green I Cannot Breathe", *Colorfulness* (April, 2004): 102-105.

Ten Years/The Monacelli Press, The Monacelli Press, New York, NY 2004: 20 (Book Review – Analyzing Ambasz).

Valle, P. "Frammenti di Arcadia." *Mestre/ Idee per una città possibile,* periodico quadrimestrale, Marsilio, Venice, Italy 2004: 4-10.

2003

Antonelli, P. *Objects of Design*, New York: The Musuem of Modern Art, 2003: 115.

"Architect grows on a skeptical world." Geraldine O'Brien. Sydney, Australia: *"The Sydney Morning Herald"* (April 28, 2003): 2.

Blasi, C. & Padovano, G. *The challenge of sustainability*, Naples, Italy: Foxwell & Davies Italia S.r.L., 2003: 33-40.

Botta, M. "Quasi un diario." *Frammenti intorno all'architettura,* Florence, Italy: Le Lettere 2003: 39, 272.

— "Correspondant's File: Costa Rica", *Architectural Record* (September 2003): 79-80.

Celant, G. "Arts & Architecture, 1900-2000", Milan, Italy: Skira 2004, italian/english.

Cooper, P. Interiorscapes / Gardens within Buildings, London, UK: Octopus Publishing Group 2003: 64-65.

Dujovne, B. "Naturaleza y Paisajes." *Contextos*, 12, Buenos Aires: Facultad de Arquitectura, Diseño y Urbanismo, 2003: 140-143.

Grossman & Casoy. *Arquitectos Argentinos en el Mundo/Colección 2003*, Buenos Aires. 2003.

Grossman & Casoy. "Industrial Initiatives: Desktop & Personal Accessories", *Indian Architect & Builder* (Volume 17, 2003): 92-93.

Johnson, C. *Greening Sydney: landscaping the urban fabric*, Sydney, Australia: Government Architect Publications, 2003: 132-35, 188-93.

"Just picture the hanging gardens of… Sydney." Chris Johnson. Sydney, Australia: *The Sydney Morning Herald* (April 28, 2003): 11.

"Last Word… for now! (Green Towns)." *Indian Architect & Builder* (17 Anniversary Issue, 2003): 32-35.

Meijenfeldt, E. von. *Below Ground Level: Creating New Spaces for Contemporary Architecture,* Basel: Birkhauser Publishers for Architecture, 2003: 16, 44-49.

Morgan, Conway Lloyd. *Mauk Design*, Ludwigsburg, Germany: avedition GmbH, 2003: 152-153.

Querci, A. *16 tisaniere*, Florence, Italy: Alinea editrice, 2003: 14-15.

"Reportajes/Argentinos en el Exterior", *Summa* (June/July 2003): 224-231.

Riley, T. *The Changing of the Avant-Garde: Visionary Architectural Drawings from the Howard Gilman Collection*, New York, NY: The Museum of Modern Art, 2003: 126-127.

Tommasini, M. C. *Glass Architecture: The Corolle d'Autore Collection,* Milan, Italy: Editoriale Domus, 2003: 28-29, 170 and cover.

MAK "Zielen – elewacja/ Prefektura w Fukuoce", *Architektura* (July 2003): 100.

2002

Arcila, M. T. *Contemporary Houses Of The World,* Spain: Atrium Internacional de Mexico, 2002: 318-327.

Asensio, Paco. *Product Design,* Spain: Loft Publications, 2002: 48, 244, 246, 249, and 281.

Betsky, Aaron. *Landscapers: Building With the Land,* New York: Thames & Hudson, 2002: 22, 48-49.

"E adesso mambo: ristoranti, balli e un po' di Ambasz." *Il Resto del Carlino* (September 5, 2002).

McQuaid, M. *Envisioning Architecture: Drawings from The Museum of Modern Art*, New York: The Museum of Modern Art, 2002: 200-203.

"Piano Ambasz: parliamone." *Corriere di Rimini* (September 5, 2002): 7.

"Per tetto il prato e la casa respira." Servadio L. *Avvenire* Milan, Italy (July 16, 2002): 25.

Facciotto P. La spiaggia del futuro: il piano Ambasz: "il rimpianto piu grande", *La Voce*, Rimini, Italy (July 14, 2002): 15.

2001

"The 2000 Saflex Design Awards", *Architecture* (May, 2001): 57.

Le Journal de l'Architecte (Architetecture naturelle), 2001: 7.

Architectuur als natuur "Architecten krant." (December 2000-January 2001): 7.

Capella, J. *Tiny Architecture. Designs by the twentieth-century architect* , Bacelona, Edicions UPC, 2000: 155, 179.

— "De Cara a La Historia." *Arquitectura*, Buenos Aires (August 6, 2001): 12.

Marino, S. "Montañas de Metal y Vidrio". Buenos Aires *"Arquitectura"* (July 16, 2001): 6-7.

Madia, E.H., Arq. "La Arquitectura Poetica de Emilio Ambasz.", *Ibero Americana*. Quaterly 17 (2001): 10, 11.

2000

"Business Week/Architectural Record Awards.", *BusinessWeek* (November 6, 2000): 140.

"Business Week/Architectural Record Awards.", *Architectural Record* (October, 2000): 94, 95.

Cranz, G. *"The Chair" Rethinking Culture, Body and Design* New York 1998: 84

de la Vega, M. "El sueño de un ecologista*", El Mercurio*: 14-17.

Earth P. *Sustainable Architecture White Papers*, New York, NY: Earth Pledge Foundation, 2000: 4.

Fiell, C. & .P *"Design of the 20 Century"*: Taschen, 2000: 37.

— *"Industrial Design A-Z"* Taschen, 2000: 26-27.

— *"1000 Chairs"* Taschen, 2000: 513.

"La scena della città." *Interni* (La rivista dell'arredamento No. 507) (December 2000): 46.

"La scena della città." *Interni* (Il magazine del design No. 10) (November 10, 2000): 43.

McDonough, M. *"Malaparte: A House Like Me"*. New York: Verve editions, 1999: 190.

Pile, John F. ed. "Ambasz, Emilio." *The Grove Dictionary of Art,* http://www.groveart.com/ (March, 2000).

Rizzi, Ivan., "Emilio Ambasz." *Cantico 2000*: 84-87.

Salvadori, L. "La scena della città."*Casabella* No. 684/685
(December 2000-January 2001): intro pages.
"Architetture Sotterranee: casa unifamiliare - Montana"
Modulo (June 2000): 32-35.
Wines, J. *Green Architecture*. Taschen, 2000: 69-73, 74, 75,
80, 83, 97, 108, 130, 188.
Toto, S. *581 Architects in the World,* "Emilio Ambasz"
(Japan 1995): 344.

1999

Ando, T. *Architecture as Nature: Emilio Ambasz – Projects
and Objects* Milan, Italy: Electa 1999: XXVI-XXVII.
Bach, C. "Making Space for Nature." *Américas* 51/1
(February 1999): 6-15.
"Architecture as Landscape: Emilio Ambasz." *Archi-Tech*
(April 1999): Profile: 42-49.
Bellini, M. *Architecture as Nature: Emilio Ambasz – Projects
and Objects* Milan, Italy: Electa 1999: XX-XXI.
Botta, M. *Architecture as Nature: Emilio Ambasz – Projects
and Objects* Milan, Italy: Electa 1999: XIX.
Burkhardt, F. "Un guanto deve adattarsi alla mano." *Domus*
819 (October 1999): 72-79.
Caotorta, F.M. "E ora germoglia la città che non c'è."
Il Sole-24 Ore (January 17, 1999): Tempo liberato
Section, 39.
Fujimori, T. "Green Architecture – Fukuoka and Mycal
Sanda." *MY HOUSE* Tokyo, Japan: Asahi Shimbun, 1999:
42-43.
Innovation. Award-Winning Industrial Design – Industrial
Designers Society of America 1999: 32-33, 98, 100, 102,
154, 182.
Krampen, M., Schempp, D. "Of Sun, Light and Shade:
Bioclimatic Interests." *Glass Architects* Ludwigsburg,
Germany: avedition GmbH, 1999: 102-113.
"La conferencia del arquitecto Emilio Ambasz." *Consejo
Profesional de Arquitectura y Urbanismo* No. 0327-3997
(1999): Jornada de Arquitectura: 40-41.
Maki, F. *Architecture as Nature: Emilio Ambasz – Projects
and Objects* Milan, Italy: Electa 1999: XXIV-XXV.
Mendini, A. *Architecture as Nature: Emilio Ambasz –
Projects and Objects* Milan, Italy: Electa 1999: XXVIII-XXIX.
Pastore, D. "Mycal Cultural and Athletic Center, Japan."
Argentina Architecture 1880-2004 Rome, Italy: Gangemi
Editore, 1999: Section 2, The Contemporary Protagonists:
156-159, 203.
Pahl, J. "Skulpturale Architektur." *Architekturtheorie des
20. Jahrhunderts; Zeit-Räume* Munich, Germany: Prestel
Verlag München, 1999: 255-256.
Pavarini, S. "At EUR, Rome." *L'ARCA* (September 1999):
14-21.
Riley, T. "Landscape of the Marvelous, The." *Architecture
as Nature: Emilio Ambasz – Projects and Objects* Milan,

Italy: Electa 1999: IX-XVI.
Sottsass, E. *Architecture as Nature: Emilio Ambasz –
Projects and Objects* Milan, Italy: Electa, 1999:
XXII-XXIII.
"Terrasse de l'hôtel Résidence-au-lac, à Lugano, Suisse,
La." *ARCHICRÉÉ – Revue d'Architecture et de Design* 285
(Summer 1999): Cover, 3.
Villa, Marzia "The overnight bag by Emilio Ambasz."
Italian Life (August-September 1999): Dream Destination
Luggage: 51.

1998

Canabal, B.F. "El jardín del arte." *Experimenta* 23
(November 1998): Buenos Aires: 65-68.
Celaya, C. "Un museo verde para San Telmo." *Clarin* (May
4, 1998): Arquitectura.
Dagna, C. "Una villa nel Montana." *Firenze* 4362 (February
1998): 84-87.
De Giorgi, G. "Emilio Ambasz.*" The Third Avant Garde in
Architecture* Rome, Italy: Diagonale s.r.l., 1998: 2nd Part,
Profile Architects on the Cutting Edge: 68-71, 108.
Edelmann, T. "'Kompass' zum Sitzen." *Design Report*
(December 1998): Orgatec, 64.
"Emilio Ambasz, Internationale Präfekturhalle, Fukuoka."
Schwäbisch Hall AG Annual Report 1998 (1998): Bausteine
für die Zukunft: 15.
Garcia Navarro, S. "Inventar Buenos Aires." *La Nacion*
(April 30 to May 6, 1998): Vialibre Section 4, 1.
Glusberg, J. "El Mamba empieza a tener ritmo." *La Nacion*
(May 6, 1998): Section 5, Arquitectura 3.
Gradara, M. "Vola la darsena di capitan Ambasz." *Riccione
e Cattolica* (February 15, 1998).
King, G.K. "Foretelling Architecture of the Next Millennium."
Dialogue (September 1998): 26-55.
Lazzarini, M. "Nel 2000 con la darsena." *Corriere Bellaria*
(February 15, 1998): 16.
"Museo de Arquitectura (Torre de Agua)." *SCA-Noticias*
(March 1998): 9.
Newhouse, V. "Towards a New Museum: A Provocative Book
Assesses Recent Experiments in Exhibiting Art."
Architectural Digest 7 (July 1998): 58, 62.
"The Cabinet of Curiosities: An Update." *Towards a New
Museum.* New York, NY USA: The Monacelli Press, Inc.,
1998: 30-31.
Servadio, L. "Metti l'albero sul tetto." *Avvenire* (June 8,
1998): Agora.
Symmes, M. "Fountains as Commemoration." *Fountains:
Splash and Spectacle.* New York, NY USA: Rizzoli
International Publications, Inc., 1998: 135.
Villani, L. "Emilio Ambasz." *Futurshow Design: Un taglio
al passato* (1998): 8-11, 40.
Zunino, M.G. "Shopping Mall in Fukuoka." *Abitare* 373

(May 1998): 190-191.
"Environment Park in Turin." *Abitare* 379 (December
1998): 70.

1997

Alvarez, C. "La torre abandonada." *El Fantasma de
Recoleta* (October 1997): 1, 8-9.
Barbero Sarzabal, H. "Invenciones para las oficinas del
Mañana." *Arquis* 12 (June 1997): 10-13.
Colonetti, A. "Cultural Worlds." *Ottagono* 122 (March-May
1997): 25.
"Emilio Ambasz: un pragmatico visionario." *FuturShow* 1
(1997): 43-48.
Flagge, I. "Der Garten als Gesellschaftsaufgabe." *Der
Architekt* 6 (June 1997): 366-369.
"Galeria de la Escultura: La Torre de Agua." *SCA-Noticias*
(November 1997): 23.
Glusberg, J. "Ambasz y la Torre de Agua." *La Nacion*
(October 1, 1997): Section 5, 1-4.
— "Renovado exito de una muestra tematica." *El Cronista*
(November 26, 1997): Arquitectura y Diseño 5.
— "Como siempre, Ambasz." *La Nacion* (December 3,
1997): Section 5, 7.
— "Carta del Director." *Boletín especial, Museo Nacional de
Bellas Artes* (Buenos Aires, 1997): Premios Vitruvio 97: 1-2
"Mas Metros para el Arte." *Revista - La Nacion* 1482
(November 20, 1997): Personas, 20.
Ojeda, R. "The New American House". New York: Library of
Design, 1997: 132-139
Schempp, D. "Untererdische Architektur." *Glasforum* (June
1997): 3-6.
"Ser no ser de la Torre de Agua." *Pionero* (September 1997,
Issue 52): 1, 3.
"Spots." *La Nacion* (November 12, 1997): Section 5, 13.
"Vitruvio 97: un Panorama Brillante." *La Nacion* (December
1997): Section 5, 4.

1996

ACROS Fukuoka, Japan: Nikkei Architectural Books, 1996:
all.
Branzi, A. "Plastica e Libertà – Italy: The New Domestic
Landscape – L'allestimento con luogo di sperimentazione –
L'internazionalizzazione del design italiano." *Il Design
Italiano 1964/1990*. Milan, Italy: Triennale di Milano,
Electa, 1996: 50, 140, 247, and 380.
Cristina, M. and Michall, T. "Ruolo del Progetto, Il." *MODO*
171 (April 1996): 62.
"Emilio Ambasz: Anti-Maître et Meta-Architecture."
Dynamics 17/7 (1996): 59-64.
"Emilio Ambasz 'harika çocuk'." *Arredamento Dekorasyon*

83 (July-August 1996): cover, 74-86.

Grossman, L. "Ambasz, el coraje de la creación." *La Nacion* (February 29, 1996): Arquitectura, Section 5, 4.

Moiraghi, L. "Shin Sanda Mycal Cultural and Athletic Center." *L'ARCA Plus* 09 (1996): 146-153.

Montaner, J. "La Natura, meatro de l'arquitectura." *Homo Ecologicus*. Barcelona, Spain: Department of Culture, Generalita de Catalunya (1996): 152.

Neumann, C. "Soft Handkerchief Television." *Design Kalender 1997* Köln, Germany: DuMont Buchverlag GmbH, (1996): see the month of August, week 2 "Diseño Industrial en Estados Unidos." *Experimenta* 13/14 (December 1996): 30-42.

Righetti, P. "Green Over the Gray." *Modulo* 223 (July / August 1996): 584-591.

Sias, R. and Villani, L. "La banca sta cambiando: Tecnobanca è già cambiata." *Ufficiostile* 2 (March-April 1996): cover, 44-47.

"Storia Italiana, Una." *MODO* 171 (April 1996): 25-27, 91.

Ullmi, G. "Emilio Ambasz, Diseñada Hipernatural" *Clarin* (August 5, 1996): Arquitectura 1, 6-7.

Uluhogian, H. "Incontro con Emilio Ambasz." *Presenza Tecnica* 201 (February 1996): 8.

Villani, L. "Architettura e Natura." *MODO* 170 (March 1996): 18-21.

"Residenza Americana, Una." *La Casa Sui Campi* 4 (April 1996): 2-7.

1995

"ACROS Fukuoka." *Shinkenchiku* 70 (July 1995): 242-250.

"Ambasz alla Triennale." (exhibit review) *Domus* 767 (January 1995): I, XXIX.

"Ambasz o l'Arcadia Tecnologica." *Vetrospazio* 38 (September 1995): 8.

Arosio, E. "La Casa? È un paradiso artificiale." *L'Espresso* 43 (October 29, 1995): 129, 131.

Baba, S. "Fukuoka Becomes a Crossroads for Exciting Architecture." *Approach* (Autumn 1995): 14-21.

Blaich, R. "Consumer Electronics/Information/Work Tools/Good Goods." *New + Notable Product Design II* Rockport, MA USA: Rockport Publishers, 1995: 9-10, 117, 156, and 162.

Branch, M.A. "Paradise Missed." *PA (Progressive Architecture)* 6 (June 1995): 86-91.

Calazzo, M. "L'utopia dell'arte." *OLIS* 5 (February 1995): cover, 61-69.

Casciani, S. "Dreams of Power." *The Dream of Power*. Milan, Italy: BTicino SpA, 1995: 131-137.

Dagnino, T. "Los Paraísos terrenales de Emilio Ambasz." *El Cronista* (February 15, 1995): Arquitectura 1, 4-5.

de Brea, A. "Un modo diferente de existencia." *El Cronista* (December 6, 1995): Arquitectura, 12.

Downes, K. "Wallet-Sized Wonders." *SUN* (November 21, 1995): 36.

"Emilio Ambasz: Special Issue." *Korean Architects* 131 (July 1995): cover, 6-171.

"Espiritu del Diseño, El." *Arquitectura* (February 1995): 19.

"50 Años de arquitectura, diseño y construccion." *Clarin* (November 20, 1995): Architecture: 10.

Franceschini, P. "Il mattone 'firmato' dai grandi architetti." *Resto del Carlino* (February 12, 1995).

Fuchigami, M. "USA: Emilio Ambasz." *Crosscurrents: 51 World Architects*. Tokyo, Japan: Shokoku-sha Co., Ltd., 1995: 11-13, 130-133.

Glusberg, J. "VI Bienal de Arquitectura de Buenos Aires." *La Nacion* (October 5, 1995): Arquitectura, 6.

Goetz, J. "Wohnstile der Zukunft: Hausautomation Macht's Möglich." *Design Report* (September 1995): 116.

"Green Over the Gray: Emilio Ambasz, The." *Kenchiku Bunka* 585 (July 1995): cover, 57-90.

Hine, T. "The shape of rings to come." *The Philadelphia Inquirer* (August 20, 1995): 21.

"Call Waiting." *San Jose Mercury News* (October 15, 1995): West, 20-21.

Maki, F. "Emilio Ambasz: l'alchimista di natura e architettura." *Atmosphere* 32 (December 1994-January 1995): 22-29.

Michel, F. "Emilio Ambasz et le nouveau contrat naturel." *Cree (architecture interieure)* 268 (October-November 1995): 24.

Moiraghi, L. "La villa dissimulata – A Residence in Montana." *L'ARCA* 92 (April 1995): 48-55.

"USA Villa nel Montana." *L'ARCA Plus* 05 (Summer 1995): 162-169.

Morozzi, C. "Architectura: Ambasz in mostra, un omaggio." *MODO* 161 (January 1995): 26-27.

"Mycal Sanda." *TOTO (for the creative aqua scene)* 12 (November-December 1995): cover, inside cover.

"Mycal Sanda-Pororoca." *Shnikenchiku* 70 (April 1995): 129-142.

"News - Fukuoka." *Nikkei Architecture* 524 (June 19, 1995): cover, 5, 100-109.

Pröhl, U. "Architektur: Kunstgaleria under der Erde." *Hauser* (June 1995): 10.

Riotta, G. "Ambasz in casa fra prati, laghi e cascate." *Corriere della Sera* (February 13, 1995).

Sebastiano, U. "BTicino: Il nuovo Principe domestico." *Design Diffusion News (ddn)* 35 (September 1995): 52.

Strono, C. "Living and Light–Environmental Power." *L'ARCA* 96 (September 1995): 86-88.

"Venti anni di Ambasz." (book review) *L'ARCA* 89 (January 1995): 110.

Viganò, V. "Dentro e fuori Terra." *Abitare* 345 (November 1995): 136-139.

Vitta, M. "Natura e Architettura." *VIA - Valutazione Impatto Ambientale* 31 (November 1995): 5-16.

"Woran arbeiten Sie gerade, Emilio Ambasz?" *Design Report* (May 1995): 110.

1994

"Ambasz and Ambasz." (book review) *L'ARCA* (May 1994): 104.

"BA '93 Summary." *Revista* 32 (March-April 1994): 4-5.

Costa, P. "Emilio Ambasz." *Domus* (Argentina edition) CP67 (February 1994): 2-7.

"Emilio Ambasz." *La Prensa* (April 17, 1994): Talingo 1-3, 6-13.

Franke, C. "Handfreundliche Hüllen." *MACup* 100 (January 1994): 142.

Glusberg, J., "Ambasz y el diseño como hecho estético." *La Revista* 474 (August 1994): 62-63.

Hirst, A. "Democratic Design." *Metropolitan Home* 100 (March-April 1994): 40.

Imagawa, N. "Focus of Material and Shelter (Glass and Structure)." *Kenchiku Bunka* 570 (April 1994): 124-125.

Iribame, J. "Emilio Ambasz: el placer de inventar." *SCA Revista de Arquitectura* 172 (November-December 1994): cover, 41-63.

Lazo Margain, A. "Excelsior Industrial Emilio Ambasz en la Ciudad de México." *El Diseñador* (February 1, 2, and 3, 1994): Metropolitana 12-14.

— "Emilio Ambasz: Arquitectura y Diseño Industrial" *The 1994 Chicago International Biennale* Special Issue (June 1994): 3.

Rodriquez Sosa, G. "El Prototipo Arquiesencial." *Muebles y Decoración* 38 (April-May 1994): 66-68.

Schmidt-Lorenz, "Neue Entwürfe von Emilio Ambasz." *Design Report* 1 (January 1994): 18.

Sheridan, G. "Mi Credo: Fragmentos." *Vuelta* 207 (February 1994): I-VII.

"Trends." *AXIS* 50 (Winter 1994): 9.

Viganò, V. "Giardino d'inverno nell'isola di Hokkaido." *Abitare* 327 (March 1994): 143.

"What's Your Chair I.Q.?" *The New York Times* (September 29, 1994): Home, C3.

Wortmann, A. "Emilio Ambasz – Invention: The Reality of the Ideal" (book review). *Archis* (January 1994).

1993

"Ambasz per Rimini." *Domus* 747 (March 1993).

"Architecture and Design of Emilio Ambasz for Human Beings, The." *Serai* (June 3, 1993).

"Art Weekly – The Architectural Design of Emilio Ambasz from Toothbrushes to High Rise Building." *Pier* (May 1993).

Camerana, B. "Poetics or Pragmatics? Sei Progetti di Emilio Ambasz." *Eden* 1 (January 1993): 66-83.

"Consumer Product Awards." *ID* 4 (July-August 1993): 54 and 75.

Curutchet, C. "Mas Alla del Arcotris." *La Prensa* (December 1, 1993): Habitat, 5.

"Current Exhibition Tokyo." *The Chunichi Shimbun* (April 22, 1993).

"Emilio Ambasz." *ca (ciudad y arquitectura)* 73 (July-August-September 1993): 138-139.

"Emilio Ambasz." *Marco Polo* (January 1993): 135.

"Emilio Ambasz Architecture and Design." (book review) *Gekkan Gallery* 5 (May 1993).

"Emilio Ambasz Architecture and Design." (book review) *Apo* 37 (April 29 and May 6, 1993).

"Emilio Ambasz Architecture and Design." (book review) *Geijutsu Shincho* 5 (May 1993).

"Emilio Ambasz Architecture and Design." (book review) *Gekkan Tile* 371 (June 1993).

"Emilio Ambasz Architecture and Design." (book review) *Hanako* 244 (May 6 and 13, 1993).

"Emilio Ambasz Architecture and Design." (book review) *Interrian* 6 (June 1993).

"Emilio Ambasz Architecture and Design." (book review) *Journal of Architectural and Building Science* 1342 (May 1993).

"Emilio Ambasz Architecture and Design." (book review) *Kenchiku Bunka* 558 (April 1993).

"Emilio Ambasz Architecture and Design." (book review) *Kenchiku Chishiki* (May 1993).

"Emilio Ambasz Architecture and Design." (book review) *Kindaikenchiju* 4 (April 1993).

"Emilio Ambasz Architecture and Design." (book review) *Shitsunai* 461 (May 1993).

"Emilio Ambasz Architecture and Design." (book review) *Shukan Shincho* (June 10, 1993).

"Emilio Ambasz Architecture and Design." (book review) *The Shinbijutsu Shinbun* (April 21, 1993).

"Emilio Ambasz Architecture and Design." (book review) *Tokyo Walker* 17 and 18 (May 4 and 11, 1993).

"Emilio Ambasz Architecture and Design." (book review) *Shinkenchiju* 68 (June 1993): 254-256.

"Emilio Ambasz Architecture and Design from Pen to Botanical Garden." *Shitsunai* 462 (June 1993).

"Emilio Ambasz Exhibition at Tokyo Station Gallery." *Kokusai Geijutsu Shinbun* (June 15, 1993).

"Emilio Ambasz – Invention: The Reality of the Ideal" (book review) *Oculus* (December 1993): 9.

"Emilio Ambasz – Invention: The Reality of the Ideal" (book review) *Umbrella* (March 1993).

"Forma Poetica, Una." *Enlace* 4 (April 1993): 48-55.

"Future Architecture for Future Men of Culture." *Geijutsu Koron* 9 (September 1993).

"Global View." *Nikkei Architecture* 462 (June-July 1993): 35.

Glusberg, J. "Con su arquitectura, Ambasz intenta mejorar el futuro." *Ambito Financiero* (December 28, 1993): 2.

— "Emilio Ambasz y la realidad de lo ideal" *DyC (diseño y construccion)* (August 19-25, 1993): 4-5.

— "Emilio Ambasz y la realidad de lo ideal." *La Revista* 431 (October 4, 1993).

— "Profeta en su Tierra" *El Cronista* (April 21, 1993): Arquitectura y Diseño 1-2, 8.

— "Volver a lo Elemental" *El Cronista* (December 15, 1993): Arquitectura y Diseño 1-2, 8.

"Green Architects." *House Beautiful* 6 (June 1993): 86-87.

"In Short…" *Aera* 21 (May 25, 1993).

Irace. F. "Emilio Ambasz - Tokyo Station Gallery." *Abitare* 319 (June 1993): 175-176, 210.

Julier, Guy. *Encyclopaedia of 20 Century Design and Designers.* London UK, Thames and Hudson, 1993: 18.

LeBlanc, S. "Lucille Halsell Conservatory, 1988." *20 Century American Architecture.* New York, NY: Whitney Library of Design, 1993: 185.

Levinson, N. "The Monograph as Monument." (book review). *Architectural Record* (September 1993): 50.

Montaner, J. "Vapor de Aqua y Piramides di Cristal." *Europ Art* 14 (May-June 1993): 18-21.

Nakamura, T. (ed.) "Emilio Ambasz 1986-1992." *a+u* Special Issue (April 1993).

Nitschke, G. "The Japanese Garden in History." *Japanese Gardens.* Köln, Germany: Benedikt Taschen Verlag GmBH, 1993: 27.

"Person." *JA House* 86 (June 1993): 3.

"Person - Emilio Ambasz." *Shinkenchiku - Jutaku Tokushu* 6 (June 1993).

"Portable TV." *AXIS* 46 (Winter 1993): 26.

"Profile of Emilio Ambasz." *Nikkei Design* 6 (June 1993): 64-65.

"Reviews." *Interior Design* (June 1993): 62.

"Showcase: Exhibition at Tokyo Station Gallery " *AXIS* 48 (Summer 1993): 107.

Stern, M. "Is National Design Dead?" *Across the Board* 7 (September 1993): 32-37.

Stewart, D.B. "Etienne Lousi Boullée - Legacy of Le Corbusier" *AT* 7 (July 1993): 40-41.

"La tecnologia morbida di Emilio Ambasz." *L'Arca* 76 (November 1993): 86-87.

"Tokyo Station Gallery." *Tokyo Journal* (June 1993): 44.

"Tokyo Station Gallery - Emilio Ambasz Architecture and Design." *Train Vert* 5 (May 1993).

"Tokyo Station Gallery" *Tokyo Journal* (May 1993): 44.

"De Verzinselen van Ambasz." (book review) *Architectuur/Bouwen* (March 1993): 53.

1992

Aldersey-Williams H., "Double Agent." *Design Week*, 32 (August, 14 1992): 14-15.

"Architektur: Gärten Wachen in den Himmel." *Häuser* (February 1992): 10-11.

Barna, J.W. "Les Jardins du Futur." *L'Information Immobiliere* 47 (Spring 1992): cover, 87-99.

Bartolucci, M. "The Seeds of a Green Architecture." *Metropolis* 8 (April 1992): 41-43.

Buchanan, P. "Phoenix Phoenix." *The Architectural Review* 1139 (January 1992): 58-59.

"Concepts." *ID* 4 (July-August 1992): 178.

Dalce, J. "An Interview With Emilio Ambasz" *Product Design 5.* New York, NY: PBC International, Inc., 1992: 9-11.

Dibar, C., Barbero, H. "Arbales Entre el Hormicó." *Noticias de la Semana* (March 8, 1992): 144.

Doveil, F. "Il video nel portafoglio." *MODO* 145 (November 1992): 48-50.

"Emilio? It's Ambasz here… are you okay?" *Design Review* 5 (Summer 1992): 52-57.

"Euro Design NOW: Discussion." *AXIS* 42 (Winter 1992): 76.

Fuchigami, M. "Architect on the Scene: Emilio Ambasz." *Kenchiku Bunka* 550 (August 1992): 13-15.

Gazzaniga, L. "Prefectural Hall, Fukuoka." *Domus* 738 (May 1992): 38-41.

Hunt, S.H. "An Architect of America's New Generation - Emilio Ambasz." *Chinese Architects* 8 (August 1992): 99-104.

Jones, M. "Never Say Die." *Design* 524 (August 1992): 14-16.

McMurray, R. "The Town That Builds First Class." *ENR* 14 (April 6, 1992): C7-C9.

Neri, E. "E dagli USA solo gas." *Il Sabato* 11 (March 14, 1992): 74-75.

"Nuova spiaggia secondo Ambasz" *La Gazzetta di Rimini* (October 20, 1992): 14.

Nussbaum, B. "Winners: The Best Product Design of the Year." *International Business Week* (June 8, 1992): 60-74.

O'Reilly, E. "Twenty-five Stylish Hotels." *Conde Nast Traveler* (July 1992): 100-105, 133-137.

Premier Festival International des Jardins. France: 1992: 62-63.

"Products on Parade." *Allure* (August 1992): 32.

Putman, A. (ed.) "Furniture/Products". *International Design Yearbook.* New York, NY: Abbeville Press, 1992: 53, 174.

"Soft Sell." *Details* (December 1992).

"Sour Grapes: Why Emilio Left Home." *Blueprint* 88 (June 1992): 14.

"Trends." *AXIS* 43 (Spring 1992): 24.

1991

Buchanan, P. "Vertical Garden City." *The Architectural Review* 1137 (November 1991): 38-41.

Cabassi, C. "Attualità. Venezia Quarternario." *AU – Arredo Urbano* 40/41 (October-November 1991): 38-41.

"Collaborations." *Design Week* 25 (November 1991).

"Emilio Ambasz." *On Diseño* 128 (1991): 103-171.

"Emilio Ambasz: Garden Architecture Goes to Town." *Architectural Record* 7 (July 1991): 68-69.

"Emilio Ambasz: Poetry and Its Reasoning." *Techniques and Architecture* 394 (February-March 1991): 50-56.

Glusberg, J. "Un edificio jardin: El centro Internacional de Fukuoka." *El Cronista* 1991: 1, 8.

Hower, B.K. "Ambasz-Designed Bridge for Columbis, Indiana." *Inland Architect* 6 (November-December 1991): 25-26.

"Image Drawing." *FP (Fusion Planning)* 11 (November 1991): 1-3.

Kellogg, M.A. "The Greenhouse Effect." *Town and Country* 5133 (June 1991): 74-80.

Kenso, K. "Introduction to Architecture of the 1980s." *20th Century Architecture* 2250 (June 1991).

Lovati, C. "XVI Premio Compasso d'Oro." *Ufficiostile* 6 (July-August 1991): 76-77.

Okada, H. "Emilio Ambasz." *Shitsunai (Interiors)* 442 (October 1991): 138-141.

Parks, J., (ed.) *Contemporary Architectural Drawings*, Petaluma, CA: Pomegranate Artbooks, 1991: 8.

Philips, A. *The Best in Office Interior Design*. Switzerland: Notosusion SA, 1991.

Poniatowska, E. "Todo Mexico." *Luis Barragán*. Mexico City, Mexico: Editorial Diana, 1991: 8.

Rowe, P.G. "Poetic Operations." *Making a Middle Landscape*. Cambridge, Massachusetts: MIT Press, 1991: 285.

Sorkin, M. "Et in Arcadia Ego: Emilio Ambasz's States of Nature." *Exquisite Corpse – Writings on Buildings*. London, UK: VERSO – New Left Books: 312-320.

Sudjiic, D. "Emilio - It's Ambasz Here… Are You Okay?" *Design Review* 5 (Summer 1991): 52-57.

Von Radziewsky, E. "Mit Büchern Leben." *Architektur + Wohnen* 5 (October-November 1991): 120-124.

Zevi, B. "Emilio Ambasz: Works and Projects." *L'Architettura* 11 (November 1991): 889-905.

"Zu Diesem Heft 10 Büro-Systeme." *Moebel Interior Design* 10 (October 1991): 116.

1990

Albrecht, B., Amur, K.M. "80s Style Designs of the Decade." *Lighting*. New York, NY: Abbeville Press, 1990.

Bellini, M. "The International Design Yearbook 1990-91." *Textiles*. London, UK: Thames and Hudson, Ltd., 1990: 162-163.

Betsky, A. "Violated Perfection." *Revelatory Modernism*. New York, NY: Rizzoli International Publications, Inc., 1990: 92-93.

Blanca, O.T. *The International Design Yearbook*. London, U.K.: John Calmann and King, Ltd., 1990.

Buchanan, P. "Un Paraiso Enterrado." *Arquitectura Viva* 14 (September-October 1990): 16.

— "Metaphors, Narratives and Fables in New Design Thinking." *Design Issues* 1 (Fall 1990): 81.

"Collection Les Cahiers de Commarque (Le Patrimoine Troglodytique)." *Des Troglodytes à l'Archiecture-paysage*. Bertholon, France: Edition de l'Association Culturelle de Commarque, 1990.

Dana, A. "Revving Up to Quality." *Interiors* 10 (May 1990): 200.

"Das Büromöbel zwischen Renaissance und Sachlichkeit." *Form* 132 (1990): 29.

"Design Notebook." *Mirabella* (January 1990): 91.

"Emilio Ambasz and New Ajioka Project." *WWD – Womens Wear Daily* 412 (January 1990): 38.

Fisher, T. "Communicating Ideas Artfully." *Steelcase Design* 3 (1990).

"Fukuoka Competition Award Announcement." *The Japan Architect* 65 (October 1990): 157.

Glusberg, J. "Ambasz, Agrest-Gandelsonas, Pelli, Mochado y Silvetti, y Torre." *Arquitectura and Construccion* (July 4, 1990): 6-7.

Irace, F. "Emilio Ambasz: A Reasonable Realism". *Emerging Skylines*. New York, NY: Whitney Library of Design, 1990: 131-133.

Juresko, V. "Nova tehnologija stakla." *Covjek i prostor i* XXXVII (1990): 21.

Kulvik, B. "Aspen." *Form – Function* 1 (1990): 48.

Lemos, P. "Shutter Profile – Emilio Ambasz: The Architect as Philosopher." *Pan Am Clipper* 9 (September 1990): 87.

Maderuelo, J. "Artificios Ante la Falacia de la Naturaleza" *El Espacio Raptado*. Madrid, Spain: Mondadori España, 1990: 238, 243-244.

Miller, R.C. *Modern Design 1890-1990 in the Metropolitan Museum of Art*. New York, NY: Harry N. Abrams, Inc., 1990: 229.

Niesewand, N. *Textiles*. London, UK: Thames and Hudson Ltd., 1990: 162-163.

"Obihiro Project." *Brutus* 630 (1990): 171.

"Orgatec-Bilderbogen – 2. Stühl." *md* 1 (January 1990): 70.

"Pencil Points." *Progressive Architecture* 4 (April 1990): 30.

Pigeat, J. "Parcs et Jardins Contemporains." *Acclimatations*. Paris, France: La Maison Rustique, 1990: 56-57.

Salvadori, L. (ed.). 2Quaternario 90." *Casabella* 574 (December 1990): 2.

Semprini, R. "La città balneare." *Modo* 126 (October 1990): 52-53.

"Stationery of the Year." *BTOOL* 1 (January 1990): 7, 9-11, 21, 39.

"Stonework Deconstructed." *Stone World* 9 (September 1990): 28.

Zevi, B. "Architettura." *L'Espresso* 49 (December 9, 1990): 138.

"Zooabteilung Niederurseler Hang in Frankfurt." *aw* 141 (March 1990): 26-27.

1989

"3-D Package." *FP (Fusion Planning)* 25 (September 1989): 103.

"A Paintbox Every Artist Could Love." *Packaging Digest* 2 (February 1989): 52-53.

"American Scene." *Topic* 182 (1989): inside cover.

Buchanan, P. "Ambasz Urban Gardens." The *Architectural Review* 1111 (September 1989): 49-59.

"Büro Raume einer Versicherungsgesellschaft, New York, 1987." *Werk, Bauen + Wohnen* 11 (November 1989): 52-53.

Butor, M. "L'Architecture Demain." *Le Pouvoir Imaginatif du Monument*. Paris, France: Blassories sa, 1989: 40.

"Calendar of Events." *American Way* 23 (December 1, 1989): 96.

"Dallo spazzolino da denti al grattacielo." *Casa Vogue* 205 (February 1989): 122.

Davis, D. "Slaying the Neo-Modern Dragon." *Art in America* 1 (January 1989): 47.

Edelman, E. "Reclaiming Eden." *Art News* 2 (February 1989): 73-74.

"Emilio Ambasz and Giancarlo Piretti." *The Metropolitan Museum of Art Bulletin* 2 (Fall 1989): 73.

Filler, M. "Low Tech High Style. (Andy Warhol)" *Interview* 2 (February 1989): 64.

Fisher, T. "Ambasz & Holl at MoMA." *Progressive Architecture* 3 (March 1989): 33, 36.

Fisher, T. "Presenting Ideas." *Progressive Architecture* 6 (June 1989): 85.

Fritz-Hansen, D. and Kline, K., eds. *Clockwork* Cambridge, MA: MIT List Visual Arts Center, 1989: 24.

Gastil, R. "Briefing: Emilio Ambasz/Steven Holl." *Blueprint* 56 (April 1989): 61, 63.

Glasin, M. "Are You Sitting Comfortably?" *Design* 483 (March 1989): 36.

Goldberger, P. "Two Architects Who Tap into Our Deepest…" *New York Times* (February 12, 1989): 32.

Graff, V. "Arkadien in Texas." *Architektur & Wohnen* (March 1989): 84-89.

Green-Rutanen, L. "Emilio Ambasz: A New Age Architect." *Form and Function* 2 (February 1989): 28-33.

Heck, S. "Emilio Ambasz/Steven Holl: Architecture." *Architecture and Urbanism* 226 (July 1989): 5-14.

Krafft, A. "The Lucille Halsell Conservatory, USA." *Contemporary Architecture*. Paris, France and Lausanne, Switzerland: Bibliotheque des Arts, 1989: 244-247.

Lampugnani, V.M. "Emilio Ambasz: Il disegno del rito." *Domus* 705 (May 1989): 17-24.

Lazar, J. *Architecture for the Future.* Los Angeles, CA: The Museum of Contemporary Art, 1989: cassette.

Lester. "Art Facts – LJMCA Presents Major Retrospecta of Designs by Ambasz." *San Diego Daily Transcript* (January 9, 1989).

"Limitless Horizons." *New York Daily News* (October 15, 1989): 3.

Lipstadt, H., (ed.) *The Experimental Tradition.* New York, NY: Princeton Architectural Press, 1989: 147.

Matthew, L. "Subterranean Space." *Metropolis* 8 (April 1989): 46-51.

McDonough, M. "Emilio Ambasz and Steven Holl at MoMA." *ID Magazine* 2 (March-April 1989): 70-71.

Morozzi, C. "Poeta o tecnologo?" *Modo* 112 (March 1989): 36-39 (English 9-10).

Muschamp, H. "Myth Master." *Vogue* (March 1989): 340-344.

"Museum of American Folk Art Tower." *New York Architektur 1970-1990.* Munich, Germany: Prestel-Verlag, 1989: 94-95.

"New Faces of Modernish on Show." *Architectural Review* 3 (March 1989): 47.

Panizza, M. *Figure.* Rome, Italy: Edizioni Associate, 1989: 165.

Papadakis, A., Cooke, C., and Benjamin, A. *Deconstruction Omnibus Volume.* London, UK: Academy Editions, 1989: 260.

Pearlman, C. "Herlitz Aqua Color Box." *ID Magazine* 4 (July-August 1989): 40-41.

Pherson, C. "Enigmatic Emilio: A Fable." *Arcade* 3 (August-September 1989): 6.

Pursion, J. "Form & Function." *The Wall Street Journal* (June 21, 1989).

Robinson, D. "Just Add Water." *Innovation* 1 (February 1989): 36-38.

Russell, B. *Architecture and Design 1970-1990.* New York, NY: Harry N. Abrams, Inc., 1989.

Russell, J.S. "Emilio Ambasz: The Poetics of the Pragmatic." *Architectural Record* 1071 (October 1989).

Sesoki, T. "Special Report: Emilio Ambasz – The Poetics of the Pragmatic." *Approach* (September 1989): 1-23.

"Showroom for Mercedes Benz in Englewood, NJ, USA." *aw - architektur + wettbewerbe* 139 (September 1989): 17.

Sutherland, L. "Poetic Visions of a Landscape Dreamer." *Design Week* (June 16, 1989).

"World Exhibition 1992 Emilio Ambasz." *Architecture Intérieure* 1307 (June-July 1989): 134.

Wrede, S. "Emilio Ambasz Architecture." *MoMA Members Quarterly* (February 1989): 6.

Wrede, S. "Emilio Ambasz and Steven Holl." *Newsletter – The International Council of the MoMA* 16 (April 1989): 12.

Young, L. "Down with Industrial Design." *Design* 481 (March 1989): 59-51.

Young, M. "Crystal Pavilion." *Continental Airlines Profiles* 6 (June 1989): 16, 18.

1988

Appel, N.L. "Paradise Made: Two New Gardens in Texas." *Cite* (Spring-Summer 1988): 13-15.

Barret, J., Bertholon, M. *Terrasses Jardins.* 1988.

Capella, J., Larrea, Q. "Emilio Ambasz." *Designed by Architects in the 1980s,* New York, NY: Rizzoli International Publications, Inc., 1988: 14-15.

Casselti, A. "Oggetto Scultura di Emilio Ambasz." *Domina* 20 (October 1988): 44-45.

"Cubist Movement." *Architecture International* 2 (1988): 180-185.

Danto, A.C. "397 Chairs." *25 and 40.* New York, NY: Harry N. Abrams, Inc., 1988.

Dillon, D. "Drama of Nature and Form." *Architecture* (May 1988): 148-153.

"Emilio Ambasz San Antonio Botanical Conservatory, Texas." *Architectural Design* 3/4 (April 1988.): 46-47.

Filler, M. "Greenhouse Effects." *House & Garden* (September 1988): 58.

Irace, F. *La città che sale.* Milan, Italy: Arcadia Edizioni, 1988: 131-133.

"La nuove piazze di Emilio Ambasz." *L'Arca* 14 (Supplement, March 1988).

Links, C. "The New Expressionism." *Architecture Today.* New York, NY: Harry N. Abrams, 1988: 228-229.

Malone, M. "True Splendor in the Glass." *Newsweek* (September 12, 1988): 68-69.

Martellaro, J. "A Man and His Vision for Union Station." *The Kansas City Times* (January 23, 1988).

Mendini, A. "Celestial Gardens." *Ollo* 1 (October 1988).

"Milwaukee Art Museum." *The World of Art Today,* 1988: 149.

Muschamp, H. "Ground Up." *Artforum International* 2 (October 1988): 18-20.

— "Herbert Muschamp on Architecture – The Lie of the Land." *The New Republic* (December 19, 1988): 26-28.

"News and Events in the Botanical Community." *Garden* (September-October 1988): 27-28.

Peressut, L.B. "Emilio Ambasz: Lucille Halsell Conservtory." *Domus* 700 (December 1988): 36-43.

Pile, J.F. *Planning Interior Design.* New York, NY: Harry N. Abrams, Inc., 1988: 79.

Reginato, J. "On the Drawing Board." *Avenue* (November 1988): 129.

"Shimmering Strings." *Interior* (1988): 211.

"Soffio: Simplicity and Elegance Through Soft-Tech." *Innovation* (Winter 1988): 13.

Sparce, P. "Design in Italy." New York, NY: Abbeville Press, 1988: 192, 196-197.

Staebler, W.W. "Partition FGIC." *Architectural Detailing.* New York, NY: Whitney Library of Design, 1988: 168-171.

"The 1992 Seville Universal Exposition: Celebrating the 500th Anniversary of the New World." *Al-Handasah* 11

(January 1988): 16-25.

"The New Entrepreneurs." *Design* 476 (August 1988): 40-41.

Woods, M., Warren, A. "More Glass Than Wall." *Glass Houses.* New York, NY: Rizzoli International Publications, Inc., 1988: 186.

Wrede, S. "Geigy Graphics." *The Modern Poster.* New York, NY: The Museum of Modern Art, 1988: 198.

1987

Albertazzi, L. "Más allá de la Función." *Lapiz* 43 (January 1987): 8-11.

Aldersey-Williams, H. "Widening Horizons." *TWA Ambassador* (June 1987): 68.

Appel, N. "Glass Houses for People and Plants." *Cite at 5* (Fall 1987): 25.

Barna, J.W. "Light and Fog in San Antonio." *Texas Architect* 4 (July-August 1987): 28-31.

"Breaking Ground: Emilio Ambasz." *Connoisseur* 911 (December 1987): 48, 50.

Buchanan, P. "Curtains for Ambasz." *The Architectural Review* 1083 (May 1987): 73-77.

— "The Traps of Technology." *Artforum* 4, 1987: 139-145.

"Commentary – Furniture and Consumer Products." *ID – Industrial Design* (July-August 1987): 78, 102.

"Designer Profile: Giancarlo Piretti." *Interior Design* (March 1987): 246-249.

"Designing with a Lot of Bottle." *Design* 460 (April 1987): 46.

"Emilio Ambasz: Architecture Design Graphisme." *Techniques & Architecture* 371 (April-May 1987): 34-35.

"Emilio Ambasz: una mostra di progetti." *Domus* 683 (May 1987): 10-11.

"Escheimer Tor, Schillerstraße/Börsenplatz, Frankfurt." *aw - architektur + wettbewerbe* 132 (December 1987): 17-19.

"Fonti luminose: a comando dell'uomo." *Arredorama* 168 (March 1987): 57-60.

Glusberg, J. "Emilio Ambasz." *Bienal '87 de Arquitecture Cayc.* Catalogue, 1987: 19.

Goldberger, "A Spacious Sunken Garden will Bloom in San Antonio." *The New York Times* (June 11, 1987): C1 and C10.

Goodrich, K. "Profiles of the 1986 Industrial Design Excellence Award Winners." *Innovations* (Winter 1987): 7-9.

Imatake, M. "Brillant Talent: Emilio Ambasz." *IDEA* 202 (1987): 66-73.

Léon, H., Wohlhage, K. "Fragment, Leerraum, Geschwindigkeit und das Bild der klassischen Stadt." *Bauwelt* 36 Stadtbauwelt (September 1987): 1335.

"Listings for San Antonio Events." *Texas Monthly* 6 (June 1987): 70.

Matsui, K. (ed.) "Three Dimensional Graphics." *My Design Work, E. Ambasz.* Tokyo, Japan: Rikuyo-sha Publishing, Inc.,

1987: 8-9, 52-53, 123, 125-126, 138-139.

Matthews, T. "Emilio Ambasz: Technology and Myth, a Traveling Exhibition." *Architectural Record* 8 (August 1987): 161.

Murphy, J. "34th Annual P/A Awards: Mercedes Benz Showroom." *Progressive Architecture* 1 (January 1987): 104-105.

"New Products and Literature." *Progressive Architecture* 3 (March 1987): 169.

"News Briefs." *Architectural Record* 4 (April 1987): 47.

"Office Work Module: Privacy with Openness and Flexibility." *Innovation* (Winter 1987): 7-9.

"Report on New Design Trends in France." *FP (Fusion Planning)* 13 (July 1987): 80-81.

Ruiz, M.O. (ed.) *Exposicion Universal Expo '92 Sevilla: Ideas para una ordenacion del recinto.* Seville, Spain: Comisario General Exposicion Universal Sevilla, 1992 (1987): 9-24.

"San Antonio Botanical Conservatory." *Artforum* 4 (December 1987): 72, 74.

Sias, R. "Emilio Ambasz: I protagonisti del design." *Ufficiostile* 10 (October 1987): 40-47.

Smith, C.R. "1986 Architectural Projects Awards: What Might Be." *Oculus An Eye on New York Architecture* 6 (February 1987): 4 and 15.

— *Interior Design in 20th Century America: A History.* New York, NY: Harper & Row, 1987: 301-303 and 312.

Stephens, S. "The Architects vs. the Critics." *Avenue* 3 (November 1987): 143.

Tetlow, K. "Structures: Style and Substance." *Designers West* (August 1987).

— "Healthy Policies." *Interiors* 1 (1987): 116, 144.

Tickle, K. "IIDA International Interior Design Award 1987." *Interiors* (April 1987): 35-39.

Tironi, G. "La città del design: entre l'objet et la ville: entretien avec Emilio Ambasz." *Halle Sud* 13 (January-February-March 1987).

Truppin, A. "Inventive Genius." *Interiors* (April 1987): 171-187.

Vandeuvre, E. "Design/France." *FP (Fusion Planning)* 13 (July 1987): 78-81.

Waisman, M. "Emilio Ambasz." *Summarios* (January 1987): 8-15.

"Westweek 87 Program and Products." *Designers West* (Special edition, March 1987).

XIV Premio Compasso d'Oro. Milan, Italy: Silvana Editrice, 1987: 63, 118, and 123.

Zagari, F. "Ambasz e la Mimesi della Natura." *Arredo Urbano* 23 (October-December 1987): 72-76.

1986

"1976-1986 Orgatechnik." *MD* (October 1986): 44-46.

Allen, G., (ed.) "Introduction." *Emerging Voices.* New York, NY: The Architectural League of New York, 1986: 6.

Baserga, F. "Scultura di lastre: un capolavoro di Emilio Ambasz." *Marmo Macchine* 68 (Bimestre 2, 1986): 118-120.

Bayley, S., Garner, P., Sudjic, D. *Twentieth Century Style and Design.* New York, NY: Van Nostrand Reinhold Company: 260-261, 292, 298.

Boles, D. "Ambasz in Seville: 1992 Fair." *Progressive Architecture* 9 (September 1986): 43-46.

Brenner, D. "Magic Mountains." *Architectural Record* (June 1986): 132-135.

Buchanan, P. "Spanish Isles." *The Architects' Journal* (September 24, 1986): 32-33.

Burkhardt, F., Boiret, Y., (eds.) *Creer dans le Cree,* Paris, France: Electa France, May 28-September 7, 1986: 178-179.

Constantine, M., (ed.) *Word and Image: Posters from the Collection of the Museum of Modern Art.* New York, NY: The Museum of Modern Art, 1986: 136.

Dillon, D. "Moonscape in the Sun." *Spirit* (June 1986): 68-119.

Filler, M. "L System." *Surface and Ornament* (May 30-July 12, 1986).

Giovannini, P. "Offices Move Boldly Backward or Playfully Forward." *The New York Times* (January 19, 1986): F8.

Hanna, A. "'Equipment' Escargot Air Filter." *ID Magazine* 4 (July/August 1986): 79.

Jedamus, J. "Chairs that Ease the Spine." *Newsweek* 24 (June 16, 1986): 3.

La Société Generale des Eaux Minerales de Vittel, (ed.) *L'eau en Formes.* Paris, France: Centre Georges Pompidou, 1986.

Modern Redux. New York, NY: Grey Art Gallery and Study Center, 1986.

Modern Redux: Critical Alternatives for Architecture in the Next Decade. New York: Grey Art Gallery and Study Center, New York University (March 4 - April 19, 1986).

Morton, D. "Perspectives: Milan Furniture Fair." *Progressive Architecture* (December 1986): 38-40.

Palanco, R.L. "Siviglia 1992: Un concorso di idee per l'"Esposizione Universale." *Casabella* 528 (October 1986): 18-29.

Pearlman, C. "Environments: Financial Guaranty Insurance Company." *ID Magazine* (August 1986): 62.

"Plaza Mayor, Salamanca, Spain." *architektur +wettbewerbe* 127 (September 1986): 21.

Reif, R. "Rare Glimpse of the Furniture of a Modern Dutch Master." *The New York Times* (July 13, 1986): 30H.

Rinaldi, "A Lugano marmo e nuvole." *Casa Vogue* 172 (March 1986): 170-171.

"Spain: Columbus Expo." *TWA Ambassador* (December 1986): 9.

Stewart, D. "Modern Designers Still Can't Make the Perfect Chair." *Smithsonian* (April 1986): 102.

Tate, A., Smith, R.C. *International Design in the 20th Century.* New York, NY: Harper and Row, 1986: 519-521 and 530.

Tebaldi, M. "Siviglia: Concorso di idee per l'Esposizione Universale 1992." *Domus* 677 (November 1986): 80-88.

"The Technology of Horology." *Architectural Record* (January 1986): 57.

"Time Piece." *AXIS* (Winter 1986): 74-75.

Vider, E. "Light." *Almanac* (September-October 1986): 38-42.

Yerkes, S. "Design for the Times." *The Continental* (February 1986): 29-33.

1985

"21 Progettisti alla Ricerca delle Proprie Affinita." *Arredorama* 144 (March 1985): 30-32.

Abdulac, S. "Tokyo: Argentinian Designers' Show." *Mimar* 16 (April-June 1985): 16.

"Agamennone." *Ottagono* 76 (March 1985): 119.

"Architekt+Designer+Grafiker." *M-D Magazine* (June 1985): 38-41.

"Axis." *AXIS* (Summer 1985): 90.

"Axis Exhibit." *Interior Design News* (June 1985): 44.

Ban, S. "Emilio Ambasz Exhibition." *The Commercial Architecture* 6 (June 1985): 244-245.

"Banque Bruelles Lambert, Milano." *Process Architecture* 60 (July 1985): 48-53.

"Banque Bruxelles Lambert, New York." *Nikkei Architecture* (Special edition 1985): 185-189.

Barragán, L., Ferrera, R. *Ensayos y Apuntos para un Bosquejo Critico Luis Barragán.* Mexico City, Mexico: Museo Rufino Tamayo: 23-25.

Bayley, S., (ed.) *The Conran Directory of Design.* New York, NY: Villard Books: 73.

Bernard, A. "Fringe Benefits." *Manhattan, Inc.* (July 1985): 122-123.

"Biennale de Paris." *Architecture* (1985): 197.

Brown, T. "Landscape Strategies: The New Orleans Museum of Art Addition." *The Princeton Journal* (1985): 186-187.

Brozen, K. "Working it Out." *Interiors* (September 1985): 190-199 and 222.

Burgasser, J. "Furniture & Furnishings: Dorsal Seating Range." *Industrial Design Excellence USA 1980-1985.* McLean, VA: The Design Foundation, 1985: 44.

Compasso d'Oro 1954-1984. Milan, Italy: Electa: 85.

Conroy, S.B. "Toward the Grand Design." *The Washington Post* (August 24, 1985): 1-9.

Contemporary Landscape: From the Horizon of Postmodern Design. Kyoto, Japan: The National Museum of Modern Art, 1985: 38-39.

"Cordoba House." *AXIS* (September 1985): 90.

Corning, B. "Conservatory to be 'Unique in S.A.'." *Express-News* (August 28, 1985): 3B.

Diamonstein, B.L. "Emilio Ambasz." *American Architecture Now II*. New York, NY: Rizzoli International Publications, Inc., 1985: 19-27.

Dietsch, D.K. "Fringe Benefits." *Architectural Record* 11 (November 1985): 126-131.

"Elective Affinities." *Arredorama* (March 1985): 30-32.

"Elective Affinities." *AXIS* (September 1985): 65.

"Emilio Ambasz: Botanical Pleasures." *Domus* 667 (December 1985): 14-17.

"Emilio Ambasz: Plaza Mayor Salamanca." *Domus* 660 (April 1985): 12-13.

"Equipment ID. 1985 Annual Design Review." *Industrial Design* 4 (July-August 1985): 107.

Fawcett, S. "Lighting: Out of the Shadows." *Design* 439 (July 1985): 32-33.

Fiorentino, L. "Botanical Center Planting New Facility." *San Antonio Light* (August 28, 1985): C1.

Fonio, D.G. "The Elective Affinities." *La Mia Casa* 178 (1985): 68-71.

Giovannini, J. "Designer's Role, Here vs. Abroad." *The New York Times* (November 14, 1985): 23 and 25.

— "Made in America: ...U.S. ...Product Design." *The New York Times* (November 14, 1985): C1 & C8.

Greenberg, M. "Ambasz Designs Surreal Landscape for San Antonio." *Texas Architect* 2 (March-April 1985): 24-25.

Hanna, A. "Psychodrama in Milan." *Industrial Design* (May-June 1985): 16-21, 74 and 76.

Hendricks, D. "This Architect's Priority: Enhancing Creativity." *Express-News* (June 16, 1985): 1K and 9K.

Huidobro, M. "Les Bureaux d'une banque a New York." *Techniques et Architecture* 362 (October-November 1985): 179-180.

"ICISD '85 Interview with Emilio Ambasz." *AXIS* (Autumn 1985): 38-41.

Iliprandi, G. and Molinari, P., (eds.) *Omnibook 2: Italian Industrial Designers*. Udine, Italy: Magnus Edizioni, 1985: 20.

"Annual Design Review." *Industrial Design Magazine [ID]*. New York, NY: Gallery 91.

"Interior Design News." *Interior Design* (June 1985): 44.

Lazar, R. "Contract & Residential Furniture: Logotec Spotlight Range" *Industrial Design Excellence USA 1980-1985*. McLean, VA: The Design Foundation, 1985: 13.

"Le affinità elettive." *AXIS* (Spring 1985): 65.

"Le affinità elettive." *Domus* 660 (April 1985): 81-88.

"Le affinità elettive di ventuno progettisti." *L'Industria del mobile* 288 (May 1985): 49-58.

Marogna, G. "Voglia di Sicurezza." *Casa Vogue* 160 (February 1985): 140, 142.

Modo (January-February 1985): cover page.

"New & Notable." *Industrial Design* 76 (January-February 1985).

Pedretti, B. "Mostre alla triennale: Le affinità elettive." *Interni* 349 (April 1985): 44-53.

Shashaty, A. "Modern Industry – A Private Moveable Office Module." *Dun's Business Month* (June 1985): 85.

Shaw, E. "Argentine Architects Reshape Skylines and... U.S." *Argentine News* (August 7, 1985): 40-43.

Smetana, D. "Che cosa stanno facendo." *Casa Vogue* 164 (June 1985): 221.

Staebler, W. "Something About a Wall." *Interiors* (September 1985): 200-206.

Stadt Frankfurt am Main. Munich, Germany: Wettbewerbe Aktuell, 1985: 12-15.

Surface & Ornament. The Metropolitan Museum of Art with Formica Corporation and Architecture Club of Miami, May 1985.

Tapley, C. "Buildings & the Land: An Introduction." *Texas Architect* 2 (April 1985): 43.

"The Lucille Halsell Conservatory: Architectural Design Citation." *Progressive Architecture* (January 1985): 120-121.

"Things Seen." *Design* 439 (July 1985): 25.

"Vertebra." *AXIS* (September 1985): 90.

"Vintage Year for Design." Press release by *ID Magazine* (August 1985).

XIII Biennale de Paris. Paris, France: Grande Halle du Parc de la Villette, March 21, 1985.

Yoshida, Y. *A Style for the Year 2001. A joint effort of Shinkenchiku, ja and a+u*, 1985: 76-77.

1984

"Ambassador to the Interior." *Building Design Journal* (May 1984).

"Arquitectura y Diseño." *Guia del Ocio* (May 21-27, 1984).

Berg, P., (ed.) *Tit for Tat Lin*. New York, NY: The Alternative Museum, 1984: 6, 11-12, and 23.

"Biennial of Industrial Design." *BIO 10*. Yugoslavia: Yugoslavia Biennial, 1984: 31, 78, 81, 189, and 197.

Brenner, D. "Et in Arcadia Ambasz: Five Projects by Emilio Ambasz & Associates." *Architectural Record* 10 (September 1984): 120-133.

Brisebarre, J.J., (ed.) *Le Empire du Bureu 1900-2000*. February 1984: 80 and 210.

Buchanan, P. "The Poet's Garden." *The Architectural Review* (June 1984): 50-55.

Busch, A. "Product Design." *Industrial Design Magazine* (1984 85): 105 and 141.

— (ed.) *Product Design*. New York, NY: Robert Silver & Associates (US distrib.), 1984: 85, 89, 105, and 141.

Casciani, S. *Mobili come architetture: il disegno della produzione Zanotta*. Milan, Italy: Arcadia, 1984: 105, 110, and 126.

"Cultura y ocio: arquitectura y diseño. Exposicion Emilio Ambasz 1984." *Casa Viva* (May 1984): 64-68.

"Design en Colorcore." *Architecture Interieure Cree* (December 1983-January-February 1984): 117-124.

"Designing a Plaza for Houston." *Lotus International* 39 (1984): 62-69.

Dunlap, D.W. "Future Metropolis." *Omni* (October 1984): 116-123.

"Emilio Ambasz: Recent Project." *AMC* 6 (December 1984): 4-13.

"Emilio Ambasz: The Innovator for Aiming at Utopia." *IDEA* (November 1984): 88-95.

Emilio Ambasz 1984: Arquitectura, Diseño grafico e industrial. Madrid, Spain: MAD Centro de Diseño and Galería Ynguanzo, May 1984.

"Exposición: Emilio Ambasz 1984." *Casa & Jardin* 108 (1984).

"Exposiciones del arquitecto argentino Emilio Ambasz." *Cultura* (May 14, 1984): 21.

"Exposión en Madrid: Emilio Ambasz, creador de objetos." *Diario* 16 (May 14, 1984).

"Floating Architecture in New Orleans." *Design* 426 (June 1984): 21.

Gaibis, C. "Cultura: exposiciones del arquitecto argentino Emilio Ambasz: considerado uno de los mejores del mundo." *ABC* (May 14, 1984).

Gandee, C. "Offices for Banque Bruxelles Lambert, New York City." *Record Interiors 1984* (Mid-September 1984): 92-97.

Giovanni, O. "L'arcipelago delle arti." *Casa Vogue* 152 (May 1984): 226.

Glancey, J. "The Gordon Russell Furniture Award." *The Architectural Review* 1053 (November 1984): 25-41.

Glueck, G. "Tit for Tat Lin." *The New York Times* (November 16, 1984).

Glusberg, J., (ed.) "Emilio Ambasz." *Architecture in Latin America Horizonte '82 – IBA '84*. Berlin, Germany: Internationale Bauausstellung, 1984: 37.

Gosling, D. "Definitions of Urban Design." *AD - Architectural Design (Urbanism)* 12 (1984): 16-25.

— and Maitland, B. *Concepts of Urban Design*. New York, NY: St. Martin's Press, 1984: 121-123, 131.

Graff, V. "Monumente der Verschwendung." *Du, Die Zeitschrift für Kunst und Kultur* (April 1984): 30-35.

Greer, N.R. "Light as a Tool of Design." *Architecture* (October 1984): 55.

Irace, F. "Piazza A Houston: un progetto di Emilio Ambasz." *Diagonalle* (March 1984): 42-43.

Ito, K. "New Orleans Museum of Art." *Space Design* 237 (June 1984): 49-54.

"Japanese Architecture." *Nikkei Architecture* (December 31, 1984): 34-39.

Kassler, E.B. "Cordoba House." *Modern Gardens and the Landscape*. New York, NY: The Museum of Modern Art, 1984: 130.

Kleihues, J. and Glusberg, J., (eds.) "Buenos Aires a través de sus escritore, artistas y arquitectos." Buenos Aires, Argentina: 1984.

Lucan, J. "Emilio Ambasz: Projets Récents." *AMC: Revue D'Architecture* (December 1984): 4-15.

"MAD." *D.M.A. Hogares* 196 (June 1984).

Maitland, B. "The Uses of History." *AD – Architectural Design (Urbanism)* 12 (1984): 4-14.

Millán, L. "E Makes Architecture, A Designs Architecture." *La Nación* (July 1, 1984): 2-3.

— "Emilio más Ambasz." *La Nación* (1984).

Onetti, J. "El Diseño como una de las Bellas Artes." *Diario 16* (May 11, 1984): 4-5.

Perales, M. "Ambasz en Madrid." *Arquitectos 77* (April 1984): 38-48.

Samaniego, F. "Los Diseños de Emilio Ambasz." *El País* (May 5, 1984).

Santobeña, A. "Un genial creador de 'objetos': Emilio Ambasz: da forma poetica a lo pragmatico." *El Europeo* (May 31, 1984): 73-74.

"Servicio de Novedades." *Summa* 203 (August 1984): 81.

"Sintesis de la Memoria." *Exposicion Universal Expo '92, Sevilla* Spain: 1984: 9-24.

"Su Diseño." *Mercado* (May 25, 1984).

Sun, M., Hart, C. "Color as Substance: Plastic Laminates." *ID – Industrial Design Magazine* (January-February 1984): 54-57.

Szenasey, S.S., (ed.) "Merchant Bankers / At Home Study." *The Office Book Design Series Private and Executive Office. Mobile and Resilient Chairs / Vertebra Seating System / Dorsal.* New York, NY: Facts on File: 24-25, 32-33, 36-37.

"Tendenze & Novità." *Capital Casa* 10 (October 1984): 16-17.

"The Arts Community: Squaring Art with History: Cubism & Constructs." *New York Daily News* (November 8, 1984).

"The Island: The Project of Emilio Ambasz for the New Orleans Museum of Art." *Gran Bazar* (June-July 1984): 64-66.

1983

Archer, B.J. *Follies: Architecture for the Late-Twentieth Century Landscape.* New York, NY: Rizzoli International Publications, Inc., 1983: 34-37.

"Automatisch-Dynamisches Sitzen." *Moebel Interior Design* (October 10, 1983): 56-57.

Becarra, B. "Dialogo con el arquitecto Emilio Ambasz." *Trama* (May 1983): 20-27.

Boissiére, O. "Di faccia e di taglio." *La Mia Casa* (December 1983): 100.

Boles, D.D. "Financial Institution Winner." *Interiors* 6 (January 1983): 100-103.

Botta, M. "Houston Commentary." *Domus* (May 1983): 2-5.

Brion, G.C. "Architettura da protagonisti con case e oggetti in piacevole misura d'uomo." *La Republica* (October 8, 1983).

Buchanan, P. "An Awe-Filled Arcadia: The Architectural Quest of Emilio Ambasz." *Architecture and Urbanism* 155 (August 1983): 30-35.

— "High Tech: Another British Thoroughbred." *The Architectural Review* (July 1983): 19.

Burgasser, J. "1982 Awards Program Profiles: The Dorsal Seating Range – Emilio Ambasz, IDSA and Giancarlo Piretti." *Innovation* 1 (Winter 1983): 23-25.

Busch, A. "Annual Design Review – Contract and Residential." *Industrial Design Magazine* (September-October 1983): 42-44, 49.

— "Contract and Residential Furniture." *Product Design* (1982-1983): 105 and 141.

— "Home Electronics and Entertainment." *Product Design* (1982-1983): 85.

— "Who's Who: Award Winning Designers." *Interiors* (January 1983): 120-121.

"Correspondencias: escultura y arquitectura en el Museo de Bellas Artes de Bilbao." *El Correo Español* (March 15, 1983): 9.

Davis, D. "Arquitectos de vanguardia reviven las construcciones extravagantes para jardines." *La Nación* (November 27, 1983).

— "Bringing Back the Follies." *Newsweek* (November 14, 1983): 104.

de Gorbea, X.S. "Correspondencias: 5 Arquitectos – 5 Escultores." *DEIA* (March 15, 1983).

Dinelli, F. "Nuova Sede della Banca Bruxelles Lambert a Losanna/Renovation of a Bank in Lausanne." *L'Industria delle Construzioni* 140 (June 1983): 54-57.

Filler, M. "Ambasz and the Poetics of Architectural Space." *Architecture and Urbanism* 155 (August 1983): 62-66.

— "Folk Art Museum's Striking New Tower." *House and Garden* (January 1983): 186.

— "Journal: In Praise of Follies." *House and Garden* (December 1983): 216.

Fitch, J.M. "Neither Reason nor Follies." *Metropolis* (November 1983): 15.

Frateili, E. *Il disegno industriale italiano 1928-1981.* Torino, Italy: C.E.L.I.D., 1983: 117.

Glancy, J. "Design Review: Milan Furniture Fair." *The Architectural Review* 1042 (December 1983): 74/12.

Halliday, S. "Tour d'objets: Ambasz at Krueger." *Skyline* (April 1983): 23.

Herdeg, W., (ed.) *Graphis Annual: The International Annual of Advertising and Editorial Graphics.* Zurich, Switzerland: Graphis Press Corporation, 1983: 73.

Irace, F. "Follies." *Domus* 644 (November 1983): 24-29.

— "L'usine verte." *Domus* 636 (February 1983): 22-25.

— "Paradise Lost. Garden Regained." *Emilio Ambasz: 10 anni di architettura, grafica e design,* Milan, Italy: Centrodomus. Exhibition, 1983.

Krug, K. "Mehr Licht als Leuchte." *Form* (January 1983): 10-13.

"L'Analisi economica del design: Ambasz-Piretti." *È Design* (October 10-November 7, 1983).

"Las 'correspondencias' entre arquitectura y escultura en la obra de diez grandes artistas contemporáneos." *Diario SUR* (February 3, 1983).

Melissa, L. "Letter from New York: Italian 'New Design'." *Interni Annual '83* (1983): 23.

Mendini, A. "Colloquio con Emilio Ambasz." *Domus* 639 (May 1983): 1.

— Irace, F., Gravagnuolo, B. "Emilio Ambasz." *Domus – Il Design oggi in Italia tra produzione consumo e qualcos'altro* (1983): 27.

"Mostre: Emilio Ambasz." *Casa Vogue* 145 (October 1983): inset between 289-190.

Nakamura, T. "Banque Bruxelles Lambert, Lausanne." *Architecture and Urbanism* 155 (August 1983): 67-73.

— "House for a Couple – North-East USA." *Architecture and Urbanism* 155 (August 1983): 52-55.

— "Houston Center Plaza." *Architecture and Urbanism* 155 (August 1983): 46-51.

— "Museum of American Folk Art, New York City." *Architecture and Urbanism* 155 (August 1983): 36-39.

— "Schlumberger Engineering Research Laboratory." *Architecture and Urbanism* 155 (August 1983): 40-45.

— "The Four Gates to Columbus." *Architecture and Urbanism* 155 (August 1983): 58-61.

— "To AMBASZ from a+u." *Architecture and Urbanism* 155 (August 1983): 79-82.

— "Wood House – New Canaan." *Architecture and Urbanism* 155 (August 1983): 56-57.

"Orgatechnik – A Really Big Show." *Progressive Architecture* (January 1983): 27.

Ovsejevich, D.L., (ed.) "Diseño: Emilio Ambasz." *Libro de oro de las artes visuales argentinas.* Buenos Aires, Argentina: Fundacion Konex, 1983: 86.

Pansera, A., (ed.) "Emilio Ambasz's Design: nuove frontiere e strategie del design italiano degli anni ottanta." *It's Design: New Frontiers and Strategies of Italian Design in the Eighties.* Milan, Italy: Alinari, 1983: 21-36.

Portoghesi, P. "Alle soglie del nuovo design." *Europeo* 43 (October 22, 1983): 109.

Schultz, G. "Büroleuchten." *Moebel + Decoration* (April 1983): 75.

Sedofsky, L. "New York New." *Paris Vogue* 640 (April 1983): 302.

Slavin, M. "15 Honored at Big I Champagne Breakfast Gala." *Interiors* 9 (April 1983): 110-113.

— "Interiors Awards: Quartet of Designers Chooses the Big I's." *Interiors* (January 1983): 94-118.

— "People and Events: Honoring Ambasz." *Interiors* (November 1983): 20.

"Things Seen (Pool of Light)." *Design* (January 1983): 21.

Tomoiku, A. "Materialidea." *SD* 8303 (1983):13-14.

Txomin, B. "5 arquitectos, 5 escultores en el Museo de Bellas Artes de Bilbao." *Fula del Oeio* (March 18, 1983).

Venosta, C., (ed.) *From the Spoon to the City: Through the Work of 100 Designers*. Milan, Italy: Padiglione della Triennale. 1983: 26-27.

"'Vertebra.' Design Furniture from Italy: Production, Techniquess and Modernity, 92-93." Stuttgart, Germany: Stuttgart Design Center, May 1983.

Zannini, G. "Libro de oro de las artes visuales argentinos." *Biografia de los Nominales*. Argentina: Fundación Konex, 1983.

1982

"Architectura Latinoamericana Mostrada en Europa." *La Prensa* (July 6, 1982): 7.

"Arquitectura Latinoamericana Actual, esa Desconocida." *La Nación* (June 2, 1982): 1.3a.

Bill, M. "Design: In Weiss Farbiges Licht." *Form* 98 (February 1982): 48.

— "Personalien aus der Design Szene: Emilio Ambasz." *Form* 98 (February 1982): 54.

Brosterman, N. "Folk Architecture." *Express* (Spring 1982): 21.

Buchanan, P. "Bank, Lausanne, Switzerland." *The Architectural Review* (August 1982): 53-55.

— "Contemporary de Chirico: Precursor to Post-Modernism." *The Architectural Review* 1025 (July 1982): 46-7.

Castelli, L., Ruina, E., (eds.) *Materialidea*, Milan, Italy: Padiglione D'Arte Contemporanea, 1982

Da Silva Ramos, P. "Portraits D'Amerique." *Vogue Paris* 625 (April 1982): 218.

Dardi, C. "Fink and Steiner House, Southampton/NY, Longarini House, Southampton/NY, Woods House, New Canaan, Connecticut." *Domus* 628 (May 1982): 16-21.

Daulte, F. "L'Art Vaudios dans une Banque Internationale." *L'Oeil* (May 1982): 40-45.

Doubilet, S. "Cummins Appoints Ambasz." *Progressive Architecture* (July 1982): 40.

Emery, M. "Banque Bruxelles Lambert, Lausanne, Suisse." *L'Architecture d'aujord'hui* 222 (September 1982): 88-89.

Fernandes, J.C. "USA: La Valijita y el Courtain-Wall." *Vivienda* 235 (February 1982): 8.

Fernandez, R. "Encuentros: Emilio Ambasz." *Dos Puntos* 4 (March-April 1982): 36-43.

Filler, M. "Gran Rifiuto on 53rd Street." *New York Arts Journal* 14 (1982): 32-34.

— "Portraits D'Amerique." *Paris Vogue* (April 1982): 214-228.

Gimenez, C., Munoz, J., (eds.) *Correspondencias: 5 Arquitectos / 5 Escultores*. Madrid, Spain: Palacio de las Alhajas, 1982.

Giovanni, O. "A Losanna, la nuova sede di una banca. I preziosi segreti." *Casa Vogue* 134 (1982): 208-211.

Glusberg, J. "Latinoamerica y su Arquitectura en Berlin." *Espacio* (September-October-November 1982): 14-19.

— "Una constante búsqueda de la poesia y los auténticos origenes de la arquitectura." *Clarin Arquitectura, Ingenieria, Planeamiento y Diseño* (February 19, 1982): 24-25.

Gregotti, V. *Il disegno del prodotto industriale: Italia 1860-1980*. Milano: Gruppo Editroiale Electa, 1982: 392.

Guerra, R. "5 Arquitectos, 5 Escultores." *Q62, Consejo Superior de los Colegios de Arquitectos* (December 1982): 33-37.

Guisasa, F. "Correspondencias: 5 Arquitectos + 5 Escultores." *Q* (December 1982): 30-62.

Harvie, A.E. "Ambasz to Consult at Cummins Engine." *ID Magazine* (July-August 1982): 13.

Klickowski, H. "a/actualidad." *Ambiente* 33 (August 1982): 7-8.

"Latinoamérica en Berlín." *Clarin* (June 11, 1982): 2.

Marin-Medina, J. "Una Propuesta de Cultura Arquitectónica." *Informaciones* (November 4, 1982): 26-27.

Mazzocchi, G. "Bank Landscape." *Domus* 629 (June 1982): 56-57.

Morozzi, C. "La finta pelle del progetto." *Modo* 55 (December 1982): 60-62.

Pallasmaa, J. "University of Houston College of Architecture Honors Studio." *Explorations – Löytöretkiä: Houston Arkkitehtskoulun Opilastöitä* (December 1982): 13, 16-17.

Penney, R. "Diversity and Human Factors Emerge in Furnishings Design." *ID Magazine* (September-October 1982): 24-29.

Petrina, A. "Reportaje: Emilio Ambasz." *Summa* 174 (May 1982): 21-22.

Portoghesi, P. *Postmodern – L'architettura nella società post-industriale*. Milan, Italy: Electra, 1982: 106-107.

Pragnell, P. "Points of Interest: Up." *Skyline* (June 1982): 8.

Rawson, D. "Future Scenarios." *Gentlemen's Quarterly* (October 1982): 240-243.

Searing, H. *New American Art Museums*. New York, NY: Whitney Museum of American Art, 1982: 12.

Sisto, M. "Il cubo assente." *Casa Vogue* (March 1982): 208-211.

— "Mostre: Sei grandi firme per Alcantara: dai divanetti rigidi ai corridoi molli." *Casa Vogue* 133 (September 1982): 384-395.

Slavin, M. "Cummins Taps Ambasz." *Interiors* (July 1982): 18.

Smith, J.M. "Maker of Myths and Machines: An Interview with Emilio Ambasz." *Crit* 11 (Spring 1982): 21-24.

Viladas, P. "Mainly on the Plain – Banque Bruxelles Lambert, Lausanne, Switzerland." *Progressive Architecture* (April 1982): 72.

Wagner, W. "New York's Museum of Folk Art Introduces a Well Mannered Tower." *Architectural Record* (July 1982): 53.

Zevi, B. "Dal Barocco alle Ande." *L'Expresso* (August 29, 1982): 75.

1981

"ADI (Associazione per il Disegno Industriale)". *Comune di Milano*. Milan, Italy: Electa: 33.

An Exhibition of Architectural Drawings and Models by Emilio Ambasz, Michael Graves, Leon Krier, Aldo Rossi. Boston, MA: Vesti Corporation, Fine Arts Management, 1981.

Belloni, A. "Prëmiertes Design aus Italien Österreich Japan." *Moebel + Decoration* (December 1981): 65.

Blau, D. "Emilio Ambasz." *Flash Art* 101 (January-February 1981): 51.

Brown, T. "An Architect's Dream: Ancient Simplicity Meets Modern Art." *Home Energy Digest* (Spring 1981): 32-34.

Buchanan, P. "Reconaissance: Houses for Sale." *The Architectural Review* 1007 (January 1981): 5-8.

Carlsen, P. "Designing the Post-Industrial World." *Art News* (February 1981): 80-86.

Casati, C. "Columbus II Mito." *La Mia Casa* 141 (October 1981): 106-107.

Davidson, S. "Cover Story: Land of Miracles." *Time* (August 17, 1981): 15.

Della Corte, E. "Product Review: Back to Economics." *Interiors* 12 (July 1981): 60-61.

Diffrient, N. "Top Award: Logotec Spotlight Range." *Industrial Design Magazine, Designers Choice* (1981): 27.

Elquezabal, E. "Compasso d'Oro 1981." *Summa* (December 1981): 19.

Filler, M. "Harbinger: Ten Architects." *Art in America* (Summer 1981): 114-123.

Furniture by Architects: Contemporary Chairs, Tables, and Lamps. Cambridge, MA: Hayden Gallery, Massachusetts Institute of Technology, 1981.

Glusberg, J. "Emilio Ambasz en Buenos Aires." *Clarin Arquitectura, Ingenieria, Planeamiento y Diseño* (December 18, 1981): 1.

Goldberger, P. "A Meeting of Artistic Minds." *The New York Times Magazine* (March 1, 1981): 70-73.

Grossman, L.J. "Emilio Ambasz o la Inefable Presencia de la Arquitectura." *La Nación* (December 20, 1981): 1.3a.

Irace, F. "Museum as Work of Art." *Domus* 615 (March 1981): 13-16.

Lewin, S.G. "Art and Antiques: Drawing Towards a New Architecture." *Town and Country* 5010 (February 1981): 172-174.

Maerker, C. "Wohnhäuser Wie Skulpturen-Wer Will Sie? Erdloch Vom Wunderkind." *Art* (February 1981): 90-91.

Morton, D.A. "Innovative Furniture in America." *Progressive Architecture* 5 (May 1981): 36.

Portoghesi, P. "L'architettura: ma la casa è finita

sottoterra." *Europeo* 43 (October 26, 1981): 103.
Querci, A. "Il momento e le opinioni: dieci anni dopo, il design italiano negli USA." *Architectural Digest* (September 1981): 40.
Russell, B. "The Editor's Word: Winners." *Interiors* (December 1981): 61.
Schultz, G. "Preiswert und Trotzdem Beweglich." *Moebel + Decoration* (February 1981): 36-37.
Smith, P. "A Millenarian Hope: The Architecture of Emilio Ambasz." *ARTS* 6 (February 1981): 110-113.
— "Books." *Manhattan Catalogue* 14 (April 1981): 41.
— "Viewpoints Architects and Architecture: The Underground Activity of Emilio Ambasz." *Gentlemen's Quarterly* 4 (April 1981): 30.
Sorkin M., *L'isola: il progetto di Emilio Ambasz per il New Orleans Museum of Art*, in "Gran Bazaar", (May-June 1981): 64-66
— "The Odd Couples." *The Village Voice* (March 18-24, 1981): 78.
Terra-2: The International Exposition of International Architecture. Wroclaw, Poland: Museum of Architecture, 1981.
"The Underground Activity of Emilio Ambasz." *GQ* 4 (April 1981): 30.

1980

Archer, B.J. , (ed.) *Houses for Sale*. New York, NY: Rizzoli International Publications Inc., 1980: 3-16.
— "Houses for Sale." *Architecture and Urbanism* (December 1980): 81-112.
Arditi, F. "Che bella casa! L'appendo al chiodo." *Europeo* 44 (October 27, 1980): 117-118.
Barre, F. "Aménagement de Banque, Milan." *L'Architecture d'aujourd'hui* 210 (September 1980): 70-73.
Blake, J.E. "Look Who's Lighting Up Britain." *Design* 379 (July 1980): 40-43.
Blumenthal, M. "Projet d'une maison pour un couple, a Cordoue, Espangne." *Techniques et Architecture* 331 (June-July 1980): 118-119.
"Castelli's Vertebra Chairs." *Form* 111 (1980): 54.
Crossley, M. "Review: 'City Segments'" *The Houston Post* (November 30, 1980): 16AA.
Davis, D. "Selling Houses as Art." *Newsweek* (October 27, 1980): 111.
— "The Solar Revolution." *Newsweek* (April 7, 1980): 79-80.
Dean, A.O. "Luis Barragán, Austere Architect of Silent Spaces." *Smithsonian* 8 (November 1980): 152-156, 158 and 160.
Dixon, J.M. "Milan Bank: Correction." *Progressive Architecture* 4 (April 1980): 4.
Doubilet, S. "Castelli: It Ain't Necessary So." *Progressive Architecture* 12 (December 1980): 32.

"Emilio Ambasz: House for a Couple, Cordoba, Spain, Award." *Progressive Architecture* 1 (January 1980): 94-95.
Esterow, M. "The Utopian and the Pragmatic." *Art News* 9 (November 1980): 14-15, 161.
Filler, M. "Eight Houses in Search of Their Owners." *House and Garden* 12 (December 1980): 104-105.
Foster, D. "Images and Ideas: 'City Segments' Exhibition." *Architecture Minnesota* (November 1980): 68-70.
Garner, P. *Twentieth-Century Furniture*. New York, NY: Van Nostrand Reinhold Company, 1980: 219.
Gehig, F. "The 27th P/A Awards, Architectural Design: Emilio Ambasz." *Progressive Architecture* (January 1980): 94-95.
Goldberger, P. "Exhibition Dream Houses that Can Really be Built." *The New York Times Magazine* (October 12, 1980): 117, 129-130.
Horsley, C.B. "N.Y. Show Turns Spotlight on Custom Single-Family Dwellings." *International Herald Tribune* (November 24, 1980): 165.
— "Shop for a Custom House in an Art Gallery." *The New York Times* (August 24, 1980): C-8.
Houses for Sale. New York, NY: Leo Castelli Gallery, October 1980.
Huxtable, A.L. "Focus on the Museum Tower." *The New York Times* (August 24, 1980): C27-C28.
Irace, F. "Poetics of the Pragmatic: The Architecture of Emilio Ambasz." *Architectural Design* (December 1980): 154-157.
— "The Poetics of the Pragmatic." *Architecture and Urbanism* 116 (May 1980): 55-60.
Johnson, M.J. "Architecture for Sale at New York's Leo Castelli Gallery." *Architectural Record* (October 1980): 33.
Kosstrin, J. "Bad Press is Better than No Press at All, or So Speak the Wise Men of the Media." *Fetish* (Fall 1980): 4.
Larson, K. "Art: Architecture Invitational." *The Village Voice* (July 2-8, 1980): 48.
Maack, K.J. "'High Tech' – eine Chance für das Design?" *Form* 89 (January 1980): 7-8.
— "Logotec-Design: Emilio Ambasz and Giancarlo Piretti." *ERCO Lichtbericht* (April 1980): 12-13.
Mendini, A. "Elliptical Section Spot." *Domus* 605 (April 1980): 40.
— "Houses for Sale." *Domus* 611 (November 1980): 30-32.
— "Museo in Torre." *Domus* 612 (December 1980): 33.
Miller, N. "Black Ribbons and Lace." *Progressive Architecture* 3 (March 1980): 98-101.
Minardi, B. "The Myth of the Cave." *Domus* 608 (August 1980): 20-23.
Mosquera, L.M. "Diseño de Interiores, Línea Vértebra." *Summa* 157 (December 1980): 93-95.
Nakamura, T. "Special Issue: Emilio Ambasz." *Architecture and Urbanism* (May 1980): 33-60.
Papademetriou, C. "Inside 'Inside Outside'." *Texas Architect* 4 (July-August 1980): 79-81.

Pasta, A. "Ristrutturazione della Banca Bruxelles Lambert a Milano / Interior Alterations for a Bank in Milan." *L'Industria della Costruzione* 108 (October 1980): 5-8.
Pietrantoni, M. "Fairy-Tale and Ritual." *Domus* 603 (February 1980): 33-36.
Post, H. "Good Housekeeping, or Gimme Shelter." *New York* 1 (December 29, 1980): 28.
Rense, P. "Emilio Ambasz: House for a Couple in Cordoba, Spain." *Architectural Design* (December 1980): 152-153.
Schultz, G. "Ein Stuhl der 'Lebt'." *Moebel + Decoration* (August 1980): 44-45.
Smith, C.R. "Underground Buildings." *House and Garden, Building and Remodeling Guide* 6 (November-December 1980): 106-107.
Sorkin, M. "Drawings for Sale." *The Village Voice* (November 12-18, 1980): 85-86.
— "The Architecture of Emilio Ambasz." *Architecture and Urbanism* 116 (May 1980): 36-39.
Sutphen, M. "High Finance in a Stage Set." *Interiors* (June 1980): 62-65.
Wiseman, C. "Having Fun with Classics." *New York* 39 (October 6, 1980): 35-43.

1979

Blumenthal, M. "Deux propositions alternatives." *Techniques et Architecture* 325 (June-July 1979): 101-104.
Carlsen, P. and Friedman, D. "The First 50 Years." *Gentlemen's Quarterly* 9 (November 1979): 146-151.
Casati, C. "Concorso pro Memoria in Germania." *Domus* 598 (September 1979): 40-41.
— "Per una Piccola Cooperativa." *Domus* 594 (May 1979): 38-40.
Constantine, E. "Artistic Alternates to Modernism Architectural Projects by Roger Ferri and Allan Greenberg Museum of Modern Art, New York, June 2-July 25." *Progressive Architecture* 5 (May 1979): 30.
Dixon, J.M. "Working the Land." *Progressive Architecture* 4 (April 1979): 142-143.
Filler, M. "Interior Design: On the Threshold." *Progressive Architecture* 9 (September 1979): 129.
— "Rooms Without People: Notes on the Development of the Model Room." *Design Quarterly* 109 (1979): 4-15.
Gregotti, V. "Le grandi matite sono spuntate." *L'Espresso* (March 4, 1979): 176-177.
Irace, F. "C'era una volta un luogo un cliente e un architetto." *Modo* 22 (September 1979): 31-36.
Laine, C.K., (ed.), "McDonalds' Competition." *Metamorphosis*. The Association of Student Chapters, American Institute of Architects, 1979.
McQuade, W. "Pursuing the Poetic Artifact." *Portfolio – The Magazine of the Visual Arts* 4 (October-November 1979): 76-80.

Permar, M.E. "The Most Innovative McDonald's of the Future." *Crit* 5 (Spring 1979): 26-27.
Stephens, S. "Book of Lists." *Progressive Architecture* 12 (December 1979): 56, 59.

1978

Ashton, D. "The Art of Architectural Drawings: A Review of a Show of Architectural Drawings and Models." *Artscanada* 218/219 (February/March 1978): 34-37.
Casati, C. "Architettura: come disegnano gli architetti." *Domus* 578 (January 1978): 4.
Davis, D. "Paper Buildings." *Newsweek* (February 6, 1978): 76-77.
"Design Directions: Other Voices." *The AIA Journal* 6 (Mid-May 1978): 160.
Fitzgibbons, R.M. "Body Furniture in the News." *House and Garden* 8 (August 1978): 108-109.
Gropp, L.O. "Color Abets Form for Mexican Architect." *Decorating: A House and Garden Guide* (Summer 1978): 68-69.
Kubát, B. "Suet Nábytku." *Umenní a Remesla* (March 1978): 56-58.
Locker, F.C., (ed.) *1978 Contemporary Authors,* Detroit, MI: Gale Research Company, 1978: 19-20.
Masaru, K. "Emilio Ambasz and His Surrealist Obsession." *Graphic Design* 69: 13-28.
Morton, D. "Emilio Ambasz: Poetic Pragmatics." *Progressive Architecture* (September 1978): 98-101.
Raggi, F. "Emilio Ambasz: una relazione sul mio lavoro." *Europa / America Architecture Urbane / Alternative Suburbane.* Venice, Italy: La Biennale di Venezia, 1978: 106-111.
Rose, B. "The Fine Italian Hand." *Vogue* 4 (April 1978): 247-248, 320 and 322-323.
Scäfer, S."Forum Unberührt." *Bauen + Wohen* (Janaury 1978): 3.
Vergottini, B. and Iliprandi, G. *New York, Inclusive Tour. Naples,* Italy: Alberto Marotta Editore S.P.A., 1978.

1977

Alexandroff, G. "Centre d'Informatique, Park 'Las Promesas,' Mexico City." *L'architecture d'aujourd'hui* (September 1977): 18-21.
Apraxine, P., (ed.) "Emilio Ambasz." *Architecture I.* New York, NY: Leo Castelli Gallery, 1977: 6-7.
Bauman, H.H. "Bürostühle aus einer Initiative." *Form* 79 (March 1977): 34-35.
Bonta, J.P. *Sistemas de Significación en Arquitectura* 69. Barcelona, Spain: Gustavo Gili, 1977: 279.
Casati, C. "Underground Farm." *Domus* 576 (November 1977): 41-43.
Dixon, J.M. "Elusive Outcome." *Progressive Architecture* 8 (May 1977): 90.
"Emilio Ambasz: Le designer comme réalisateur." *L'architecture d'aujourd'hui* 193 (October 1977): 64-66.
"For Sale: Advanced Design, Tested and Ready to Run." *Design* (October 1977).
Fox, M. *Print Casebooks 2: The Best in Exhibition Design.* Washington, D.C.: RC Publications, Inc. 1977: 14-16.
Goldberger, P. "Architectural Drawings Raised to an Art." *The New York Times* (December 12, 1977).
Hess, T. B. "Drawn and Quartered." *New York* 41 (October 10, 1977): 70-72.
Huxtable, A.L."Architectural Drawings as Art Gallery." *The New York Times* (October 23, 1977): D-27.
McGrath, N. "Emilio Ambasz Conjures a Calmness." *Decorating: A House and Garden Guide* (Winter 1977-1978).
Nakamura, T. "Emilio Ambasz." *Shinkenchiku* (December 1977): 186-187.
Nydele, A., (ed.) *Design Review: Industrial Design 23rd Annual.* New York, NY: Whitney Library of Design (December 1977): 160.
Ponti, G. "'Vertebra' Seating System." *Domus* 572 (July 1977): 38-39.
Reif, R. "Swivel, Whirl, Rock and Roll – In Comfort." *The New York Times* (June 30, 1977): 6.
Russell, B. "How to Beat Backaches and Pains in a New Hot Seat." *House and Garden* 3 (March 1977): 130.
Stern, R.A.M. "Architects of the New '40 under 40'." *Architecture and Urbanism* 77 (January 1977): 72-73.
"Vertebralement Bien Assis." *Vogue Hommes* (1977).
"Emilio Ambasz" *A View of Contemporary World Architects.* Tokyo, Japan: Shinkenchiku-sha, 1977: 186.
Waisman, M. "La arquitectura alternativa de Emilio Ambasz." *Summarios* 11 (September 1977): 29-32.

1976

"A Cooperative of Mexican-American Grape Growers." *Space Design* 146 (October 1976): 8-12.
Bendixson, T. "Taxi: The Taxi Project: Realistic Solutions for Today." *RIBA Journal* (December 1976).
Casati, C. "In Peru: Floating Units." *Domus* 555 (February 1976): 30-31.
"Community Arts Center." *Space Design* 146 (October 1976): 13-19.
"Crate Containers Italy: The New Domestic Landscape." *Space Design* 146 (October 1976): 28-29.
Donovan, H. "Call Me a Taxi, You Yellow Cab." *Time* 26 (June 21, 1976): 60-61.
"Ecco il taxi Alfa Romeo." *Corriere della* Sera (October 1976).
"Educational and Agrarian Community Centers." *Space Design* 146 (October 1976): 20-27.
"Emilio Ambasz A Beaux-Arts Courthouse in Grand Rapids, Mich." *Progressive Architecture* 1 (January 1976): 60-61.
"Europa-America: architetture urbane / alternative suburbane". Venice: The Venice Biennale, *Magazzini del Sale alle Zattere* (June 20, 1976).
"Giugaro: Proposta di un taxi per gli anni ottanta!" *Il Fiorino* (1976).
Hasegawa, A. "Special Feature: Up-and-Coming Light: Emilio Ambasz – His Works and Thoughts." *Space Design* 7610: 4-44.
Huxtable, A.L. *Kicked a Building Lately?* New York, NY: Quadrangle/The New York Times Book Company, 1976: 51, 205, and 207.
"Invisible Storage." *House and Garden* 8 (1976): 64-67.
Kron, J. "The Tip off on Taxi Interactions." *New York* 25 (1976): 50.
Moore, A.C. "23rd Annual Awards – Emilio Ambasz." *Progressive Architecture* (1976): 60-61.
Mosquera, L.M. "Distinciones a Arquitectos Argentinos: Emilio Ambasz." *Summa* 103 (August 1976): 14.
Négréanu, G. "Projet d'Équipments de Secours pour Zones Inondées." *CREE* (December 1975-January 1976): 61-63.
"Oporta Giugiaro." *Autosprint* (July 6, 1976).
Ponti, G. "Taxi a New York." *Domus* 560 (July 1976): 40-44.
Princeton's Beaux Arts and Its New Academicism from Labatut to the Program of Geddes. New York, NY: The Institute for Architecture and Urban Studies, 1976.
Reiss, B. "I'll be Down to Get You in a Steam Taxi, Honey." *New York Magazine* 25 (January 27-February 18, 1976): 44-47.
"Seating System'Vertebra'." *Space Design* 146 (October 1976): 30-33.
Tafuri, M. "Emilio Ambasz: Village des Chicanos." *L'architecture d'aujourd'hui* 186 (August/September 1976): 70-72.
— "Les Cendres de Jefferson." *L'architecture d'aujord'hui* 186 (August-September 1976): 53-58.
Tallmer, J. "Taxi, Mister?" *New York Post* (July 10, 1976): 32.
"The Taxi Project: Realistic Solutions for Today." *Space Design* 146 (October 1976.): 34-44.
"Un taxi per gli USA progettato a Torino." *La Stampa.* (June 19, 1976).
"Uno studio internazionale: taxi per New York." *Stampa Sera* (June 24, 1976): 3.
Zevi, B. "Architettura: piazza Italia è uno stivale." *L'Espresso* (April 25, 1976): 100-101.

1975

Casati, C., (ed.) "Edifici mobili galleggianti: A Centre for Applied Computer Research." *Domus* 546 (March 1975): 1-4.
— "Recycling and Restoration." *Domus* 551 (October

1975): 8-10.

Fox, M. *The Print Casebooks: The Best in Posters.* First annual edition. Washington D.C.: RC Publications, Inc., 1975: 6.

Hasegawa, A., ed. "Center for Applied Computer Research and Programming Park 'Las Promesas,' Outskirts of Mexico City, Mexico." *Space Design* 132 (August 1975): 56-61.

Négréanu, G. "Projet pour un Centre de Calcul à Mexico." *CREE* 36 (August-September 1975): 66-67.

Ryder, S.L. "The Art of High Art." *Progressive Architecture* 3 (March 1975): 62-67.

1974

Noblet, J. *Design.* Chêne, France: Editions Stock, 1974: 371.

1971

Portas, N. *Arquitectura: Forma de Conocimiento forma de Comunicacion.* Barcelona, Spain: Escuela Tecnica Superior de Arquitectura de Barcelona, 1971: 1 and 6.

1970

McQuade, W. "Pursuing the Poetic Artifact." *Porfolio* (October-November 1970): 76-80.

1967

Kurtz, S.A. *Wasteland: Building the American Dream.* New York, NY: Praeger Publishers, 1967.

Page Number		Project Name	Photo Credits
08/09		Casa de Retiro Espiritual	Fernando Alda
10		Center for Applied Computer Research	Louis Checkman
16		Schlumberger Research Laboratories	Louis Checkman
19	top	San Antonio Botanical Center Lucille Halsell Conservatory	Louis Checkman
19	bottom	Private Estate	N/A, Photographer
40	top	Commercial & Residential Development, The Hague	Bradley Whitermore
41		Commercial & Residential Development, The Hague	Bradley Whitermore
44/47		ENI Headquarters	Courtesy of EA&A
50/51		Mamba	Michael Moran
52	top, bottom	Mamba	Michael Moran
54/55		New Town Center, Chiba	Louis Checkman
56/57		New Town Center, Chiba	Louis Checkman
58	bottom	New Town Center, Chiba	Louis Checkman
59		New Town Center, Chiba	Louis Checkman
60/61		New Town Center, Chiba	Louis Checkman
64/65		Nichii Obihiro Department Store	Courtesy of Nichii
67	top, bottom	Nichii Obihiro Department Store	Courtesy of Nichii
68		Nichii Obihiro Department Store	Peter Norris
69		Nichii Obihiro Department Store	Peter Norris
70/71		Worldbridge Trade and Investment Center	Ryuzo Masunaga
78/79		Fukuoka Prefectural Hall	Hiromi Watanabe
81		Fukuoka Prefectural Hall	Hiromi Watanabe
83		Fukuoka Prefectural Hall	Hiromi Watanabe
85		Fukuoka Prefectural Hall	Hiromi Watanabe
86/87		Fukuoka Prefectural Hall	Hiromi Watanabe
88/89		National Diet Library	Peter Norris
91		National Diet Library	Peter Norris
92/93		Mycal Cultural and Athletic Center	Shinwa Studio
96	top, bottom	Mycal Cultural and Athletic Center	Shinwa Studio
97		Mycal Cultural and Athletic Center	Shinwa Studio
98	top, bottom	Mycal Cultural and Athletic Center	Shinwa Studio
99		Mycal Cultural and Athletic Center	Shinwa Studio
102/103		Shopping Center, Amersfoort	Bradley Whitermore
104/105	top	Shopping Center, Amersfoort	Bradley Whitermore
105	bottom	Shopping Center, Amersfoort	Bradley Whitermore
111		Office Complex and Park, La Venta	Ryuzo Masunaga
113		Office Complex and Park, La Venta	Ryuzo Masunaga
114/115		Nuova Concordia	Richard Scanlan
116		Nuova Concordia	Courtesy Gruppo Putignano
117		Nuova Concordia	Courtesy Gruppo Putignano
119	top	Nuova Concordia	Richard Scanlan
119	top	Nuova Concordia	Courtesy Gruppo Putignano
120/121		Winnisook Lodge	Bradley Whitermore
122/123	bottom	Winnisook Lodge	Bradley Whitermore
125		Winnisook Lodge	Bradley Whitermore
126		Eye Bank	Bradley Whitermore
128	bottom	Eye Bank	Bradley Whitermore
129	bottom	Eye Bank	Bradley Whitermore
130	bottom	Eye Bank	Bradley Whitermore
131	bottom	Eye Bank	Bradley Whitermore
134/135		Lucille Halsell Conservatory	Louis Checkman
136/137		Lucille Halsell Conservatory	Greg Hursley
140		Lucille Halsell Conservatory	Greg Hursley
141		Lucille Halsell Conservatory	Greg Hursley
142	top	Lucille Halsell Conservatory	Greg Hursley
142	bottom	Lucille Halsell Conservatory	Greg Hursley
143	top	Lucille Halsell Conservatory	Greg Hursley
143	bottom	Lucille Halsell Conservatory	Richard Payne
144/145		Thermal Gardens, Sirmione	Michael Moran
147		Thermal Gardens, Sirmione	Michael Moran
148/149		Thermal Gardens, Sirmione	Michael Moran
150/151		Baron Edmund de Rothschild Memorial Museum	Richard Scanlan
154		Baron Edmund de Rothschild Memorial Museum	Richard Scanlan
155		Baron Edmund de Rothschild Memorial Museum	Richard Scanlan
160		Plaza Mayor	Unknown
162/163		Marina Bellaria	Courtesy of EA&A
164		Marina Bellaria	Courtesy of EA&A

Page Number		Project Name	Photo Credits
165		Marina Bellaria	Courtesy of EA&A
166/167		Houston Center Plaza	Louis Checkman
170/171		Rimini Seaside Development Center	Richard Scanlan
175	all	Rimini Seaside Development Center	Richard Scanlan
184/185		Office Complex, Hilversum	Courtesy of EA&A
192/193		Private Estate	Richard Barnes
194	top	Private Estate	Richard Barnes
194	bottom	Private Estate	Ryuzo Masunaga
195	top	Private Estate	Richard Barnes
195	bottom	Private Estate	Ryuzo Masunaga
196		Private Estate	Daniel Brown
197		Private Estate	Nicolas Guagnini
189/199		Private Estate	Richard Barnes
200/201		House for Leo Castelli	Louis Checkman
203		House for Leo Castelli	Louis Checkman
204		House for Leo Castelli	Louis Checkman
205		House for Leo Castelli	Louis Checkman
206/207		Casa de Retiro Espiritual	Fernando Alda
208/209	top	Casa de Retiro Espiritual	Fernando Alda
208	lower left	Casa de Retiro Espiritual	Louis Checkman
208	lower center	Casa de Retiro Espiritual	Louis Checkman
208	lower right	Casa de Retiro Espiritual	Louis Checkman
209	lower left	Casa de Retiro Espiritual	Louis Checkman
209	center	Casa de Retiro Espiritual	Louis Checkman
209	lower right	Casa de Retiro Espiritual	Louis Checkman
211		Casa de Retiro Espiritual	Fernando Alda
212/213		Casa de Retiro Espiritual	Fernando Alda
214		Casa de Retiro Espiritual	Fernando Alda
215		Casa de Retiro Espiritual	Fernando Alda
216/217		Casa de Retiro Espiritual	Fernando Alda
218		Casa de Retiro Espiritual	Fernando Alda
219		Casa de Retiro Espiritual	Fernando Alda
220/221		Casa de Retiro Espiritual	Fernando Alda
223		Casa de Retiro Espiritual	Fernando Alda
226/227		Glory Art Museum	Peter Norris
229	top, bottom	Glory Art Museum	Peter Norris
230		Glory Art Museum	Peter Norris
231		Glory Art Museum	Peter Norris
236/237		Barbie Knoll	Jeremy Edmiston
238		Barbie Knoll	Jeremy Edmiston
239		Barbie Knoll	Jeremy Edmiston
240/241		Barbie Knoll	Jeremy Edmiston
244/245		Emilio's Folly	Louis Checkman
249		Emilio's Folly	Louis Checkman
Cover Front/Back		Casa de Retiro Espiritual	Fernando Alda

Associate Architects :

Project Name	Associate Architects
Private Estate, pp 19, 191/199	Jay Kirby, James Hoffmann, James Decker
Lucille Halsell Conservatory, pp 19, 134/143	Jones & Kell, Inc.
Commercial & Residential Development, The Hague, pp 38/43	Fabio Mariani
ENI Headquarters, pp 44/48	Fabio Mariani
Fukuoka Prefectural Hall, pp 78/87	Nihon Sekkei
Nuova Concordia Resort Housing Development, pp 114/119	Angelo Rocco Dongiovani, Raffaelo Roberto
Baron Edmund de Rothschild Memorial Museum, pp 150/155	Arthur Spector
Office Complex, Hilversum, pp182/185	Fabio Mariani, Paolo de Vescovi & T. Kiumurgis
Casa de Retiro Espiritual, pp Cover, 8/9, 206/223	Felipe Palomino González
Mamba, pp 50/53	Alvaro Arrese
Marina di Bellaria, pp162/165	Paolo de Vescovi & T. Kiumurgis